Progress, Change and Developm
Early Childhood Education and Care

In 2000, the Millennium Development Goals set out targets aimed at creating a safer, more prosperous, and more equitable world. If these goals were to be achieved, children's lives would indeed be transformed. In this collection, achievements against these targets are identified, with each contributor examining the progress made in early years provision in Australia, China, England, Greece, the Netherlands, Portugal, South Africa, and Sweden. They highlight the priorities and agendas of their respective governments, and focus on the trends and issues which are particularly relevant to each situation, thereby revealing the social and educational inequalities that persist across countries.

A common theme running through this volume concerns the political tensions that arise when governments and educators hold fundamentally different views about the nature and purpose of early years education and the needs of children and families. It is clear that although the past two decades have seen many changes in attitude towards the importance of the early years of life; politically, economically, and environmentally, much still remains to be done if the Millennium Development Goals for young children and their families are to be fully met. Despite this, this volume demonstrates that those who work in this area continue to experience a deep concern for the well-being of young children, which transcends cultures, frontiers, and political and sectarian divides.

This book was originally published as a special issue of the *International Journal of Early Years Education*.

Elizabeth A. Coates was sometime Associate Professor and Director of the Early Childhood Studies undergraduate programme at the University of Warwick, UK. Her present part-time teaching includes child development, education, and early years' policy and practice. During her time at Warwick she organized and directed five triennial international early years conferences and was founding Editor of the *International Journal of Early Years Education*. Her background as an early years teacher has been a strong influence and, with Andrew Coates, she is involved in a longitudinal action research project which focuses on young children (3–7 years) talking and drawing together. This has resulted in a number of conference papers and publications including "The Subjects and Meanings of Young Children's Drawings" in *Exploring Children's Creative Narratives* (edited by Faulkner and Coates, 2011), and "Recognising 'The Sacred Spark of Wonder' – Scribbling and Related Talk as Evidence of how Young Children's Thinking May be Identified" in *The Routledge International Handbook of Young Children's Thinking and Understanding* (edited by Robson and Quinn, 2015).

Dorothy Faulkner is a member of the Childhood and Youth Studies Research Group in the Centre for Education and Educational Technology at the Open University, UK. She is a developmental psychologist with research expertise in sociocognitive development during the early years, psychological approaches to the development of creative thinking and problem solving, and the psychology of education. In 2009, she chaired the production of the Open University Masters course, Understanding Children's Learning and Development, and has contributed to a number of edited collections over the past 20 years including *Cultural Worlds of Early Childhood, Learning Relationships in the Classroom*, and *Making Sense of Social Development* (1998), *Rethinking Collaborative Learning* (2000), and *Exploring Children's Creative Narratives* (2011). Her recent research projects include the design and evaluation of computer and web-based environments to support social communication between children with poorly developed pragmatic skills (Murphy, Faulkner and Farley, 2013, 2015), and an in-depth evaluation of the impact of a curriculum initiative designed to foster narrative development, literacy understanding, and communication skills in early years settings in the UK, (Cremin, Swann, Flewitt, Faulkner and Kucirkova, 2013; Faulkner 2014).

Progress, Change and Development in Early Childhood Education and Care

International perspectives

Edited by

Elizabeth A. Coates and Dorothy Faulkner

LONDON AND NEW YORK

First published 2016 by Routledge

2 Park Square, Milton Park, Abingdon, Oxfordshire OX14 4RN
711 Third Avenue, New York, NY 10017

Routledge is an imprint of the Taylor & Francis Group, an informa business

First issued in paperback 2018

British Library Cataloguing in Publication Data
A catalogue record for this book is available from the British Library

ISBN 13: 978-1-138-64250-8 (hbk)
ISBN 13: 978-1-138-39167-3 (pbk)

Typeset in Times New Roman
by RefineCatch Limited, Bungay, Suffolk

Publisher's Note
The publisher accepts responsibility for any inconsistencies that may have arisen during the conversion of this book from journal articles to book chapters, namely the possible inclusion of journal terminology.

Disclaimer
Every effort has been made to contact copyright holders for their permission to reprint material in this book. The publishers would be grateful to hear from any copyright holder who is not here acknowledged and will undertake to rectify any errors or omissions in future editions of this book.

MIX
Paper from
responsible sources
FSC
www.fsc.org
FSC™ C013985

Printed in the United Kingdom
by Henry Ling Limited

Contents

Citation Information

The chapters in this book were originally published in the *International Journal of Early Years Education*, volume 21, issues 2–3 (June–September 2013). When citing this material, please use the original page numbering for each article, as follows:

Editorial

International Perspectives on Progress, Change and Development in Early Childhood Education and Care, 1993 to 2013
Elizabeth A. Coates and Dorothy Faulkner
International Journal of Early Years Education, volume 21, issues 2–3
(June–September 2013) pp. 121–124

Chapter 1

A participatory process of developing a recommendation for the government about the education of children from birth to three years: the case of Portugal
Teresa Vasconcelos
International Journal of Early Years Education, volume 21, issues 2–3
(June–September 2013) pp. 125–140

Chapter 2

A review and analysis of the current policy on early childhood education in mainland China
Yan Liu and Yue-Juan Pan
International Journal of Early Years Education, volume 21, issues 2–3
(June–September 2013) pp. 141–151

Chapter 3

Early childhood development in South Africa – progress since the end of apartheid
Eric Atmore
International Journal of Early Years Education, volume 21, issues 2–3
(June–September 2013) pp. 152–162

Chapter 4

Trends and tensions: Australian and international research about starting school
Sue Dockett and Bob Perry
International Journal of Early Years Education, volume 21, issues 2–3
(June–September 2013) pp. 163–177

CITATION INFORMATION

Chapter 5
Educational innovation between freedom and fixation: the cultural-political construction of innovations in early childhood education in the Netherlands
Bert van Oers
International Journal of Early Years Education, volume 21, issues 2–3
(June–September 2013) pp. 178–191

Chapter 6
Promoting critical awareness in the initial training of preschool teachers in Greece: resistance and perspectives
Evangelia Kourti and Alexandra Androussou
International Journal of Early Years Education, volume 21, issues 2–3
(June–September 2013) pp. 192–206

Chapter 7
Preschool a source for young children's learning and well-being
Sonja Sheridan and Ingrid Pramling Samuelsson
International Journal of Early Years Education, volume 21, issues 2–3
(June–September 2013) pp. 207–222

Chapter 8
Mothers' experiences with a mother–child education programme in five countries
Sevda Bekman and Aylin Atmaca Koçak
International Journal of Early Years Education, volume 21, issues 2–3
(June–September 2013) pp. 223–243

Chapter 9
Early childhood policy and practice in England: twenty years of change
Dorothy Faulkner and Elizabeth A. Coates
International Journal of Early Years Education, volume 21, issues 2–3
(June–September 2013) pp. 244–263

For any permission-related enquiries please visit:
http://www.tandfonline.com/page/help/permissions

Notes on Contributors

Alexandra Androussou is Assistant Professor in the Department of Early Childhood Education at the University of Athens, Greece.

Aylin Atmaca Koçak is based in the Student Counselling and Guidance Centre at Boğaziçi University, Istanbul, Turkey.

Eric Atmore is Adjunct Associate Professor in the Department of Social Development at the University of Cape Town, South Africa.

Sevda Bekman is Professor in the Department of Primary Education at Boğaziçi University, Istanbul, Turkey.

Elizabeth A. Coates was sometime Associate Professor and Director of the Early Childhood Studies undergraduate programme at the University of Warwick, UK.

Sue Dockett is Professor in Early Childhood Studies in the School of Education at Charles Sturt University, Albury, Australia.

Dorothy Faulkner is a member of the Childhood and Youth Studies Research Group in the Centre for Education and Educational Technology at the Open University, UK.

Evangelia Kourti is Associate Professor in the Department of Early Childhood Education at the University of Athens, Greece.

Yan Liu is Professor of Early Childhood Education in the Faculty of Education at Beijing Normal University, Beijing, China.

Yue-Juan Pan is Associate Professor of Early Childhood Education in the Faculty of Education at Beijing Normal University, Beijing, China.

Bob Perry is Professor in Mathematics and Transition to School in the School of Education at Charles Sturt University, Albury, Australia.

Ingrid Pramling Samuelsson is Professor and Coordinator for Early Childhood Education in the Department of Education, University of Gothenburg, Sweden.

Sonja Sheridan is an Associate Professor in the Department of Education, Communication and Learning at the University of Gothenburg, Sweden.

Bert van Oers is Professor in the Department of Theory and Research in Education at the Vrije Universiteit Amsterdam, The Netherlands.

Teresa Vasconcelos is coordinating Professor in the Lisbon School of Education at the Polytechnic Institute of Lisbon, Portugal.

INTRODUCTION

International Perspectives on Progress, Change and Development in Early Childhood Education and Care, 1993 to 2013

It is a privilege to have been asked to put together this special double issue to mark the journal's twentieth anniversary. As founding editor and reviews editor we were members of a team that, recognising the increasing global interest in early years' education, launched the *International Journal of Early Years Education* at the *First Warwick International Early Years Conference* in March 1993. At the time, this interest was inspired by international efforts to redress the material and social inequalities, economic exploitation and violation of children's rights that persisted (and continue to persist) across the world. The year 1989 marked the 30th anniversary of the Declaration of the Rights of the Child and the 10th anniversary of the *International Year of the Child*, and in 1990, the *United Nations Convention on the Rights of the Child* (UNCRC) came into force. The 42 articles of the UNCRC commit governments to provide a legislative framework and service for children that protects, for example, their right to education, their right to develop their personalities, talents and abilities to the full and their right to proper care and protection, (UNCRC Articles 28, 29, 30 and 20).

Thus, in the editorial of the first issue, Elizabeth wrote: 'The care and education of all young children must be seen as an area of paramount importance both now and in the future, and it seems appropriate, therefore, that the last decade of the twentieth century should see the birth of a new journal devoted to the promotion of effective early years education world wide. This decade has been and promises to continue to be a period of change, as boundaries, cultural and national, are redefined'.

Reflecting these concerns, the first issue of the journal contained articles on children's rights in South Africa; the reform of early childhood education in Poland; German and British research on the importance of family and friendships to young children; arguments for the need to raise the status of early childhood professionals in Australia and elsewhere and, from New Zealand, a theoretical rational for abandoning the distinction between care and education in favour of a system of early childhood *educare* for all young children including indigenous minorities.

As we move into the second decade of the twenty-first century, once again, we are in the grip of political, economic and environmental changes that are redefining cultural and national boundaries and that have profound implications for the distribution or redistribution of global resources. The impact of these changes on children's development and their right to protection, care and education is an ongoing and serious international concern. Against this backdrop, UN member states set an ambitious target of meeting eight, measurable *Millennium Development Goals* by 2015 as outlined in the Millennium Declaration. This was signed on 2 September 2000 by the leaders of 189 member states and details their commitment to building a safer, more prosperous and equitable world. The eradication of social and material inequalities that directly affect children (such poor access to primary education and health care) is articulated in several of these goals and remains of paramount importance.

As in the first issue, the international contributors to this special issue are researchers and educators who have been and still are closely involved with the journal. Over the years, they have contributed to and informed debate in their own countries and further afield. Their articles review and reflect upon national and international research and development activities that have led to significant initiatives and innovations in policy and practice in early years education and care over the past 20 years. Readers will note several common trends and issues raised by these contributors that relate to relevant articles of the UNCRC and the Millennium Development Goals, although their contributions inevitably reflect differences in national agendas, priorities and approaches. Many authors focus on the impact of early intervention programmes on children's development and outline the need for policy change to address social and educational inequality. Other authors discuss the development of innovative early years pedagogy and approaches to training preschool teachers. A common theme running through many of the contributions relates to the political tensions that arise when governments and educators hold fundamentally different views about the nature and purpose of early years education and the needs of children and families.

Seeking changes in provision for children under the age of three forms the basis of Vasconcelos's article where she interrogates the way Portugal has responded to the 2001 OECD evaluation of its early childhood education programme. As a strong advocate for young children's right to education, Vasconcelos has been heavily involved in the drive for coherent guidelines for the education and care of children from birth to three years. Her main focus, however, is on the processes involved in drawing up the *Public Statement on Early Childhood Education in Portugal*, which was approved by the Portuguese National Council of Education, but which has yet to be put into practice. The eleven recommendations contained within this statement will be familiar to anyone working with young children, as these stress the importance of the quality of the services and of the environments provided for children, as well as the status, qualifications and pay of early years educators.

Similar concerns are raised by Lui and Pan who examine the dramatic rise in the number of kindergartens in China over the past three decades. High fees, lack of qualified teachers and large classes have caused major social concerns resulting in the recognition by the Chinese Central Government of the status of early childhood education as an integral part of education and social public welfare. Lui and Pan question the ability of local governments to interpret and implement the latest policies, particularly, in relation to the difficulties in providing accessible kindergartens in many rural areas. They recommend that central government should identify developmental goals, which relate to actual regional conditions, that that they should reform the public revenue and tax system and the early childhood education funding system. In addition, they examine the existing public services for early childhood and suggest that new models of service delivery are required.

The situation of young black children under Apartheid is the starting point for Atmore's discussion of children's right to education in South Africa. His description of their life of hunger and malnutrition, with little access to health care and education is powerful. This is a salutary reminder of why the UNRC and Millennium Development Goals are needed, although there have been many positive moves to alleviate the situation in South Africa, from the introduction of a preschool year to an increase in social development budgets, with more children in good-quality provision than before. However, Atmore highlights that even in 2012, when the South African Constitution laid down the right of all children to a basic education, many young children still suffer the consequences of social and economic inequalities. Finally, he outlines how the audit of early childhood provision he undertook in 2000 provided the foundation for a series of recommendations aimed at improving the opportunities and educational experience of all young children.

Dockett and Perry take a more global approach and focus on the trends observed when reviewing recent 'starting school' literature, which encompasses readiness for school, the transition to compulsory schooling and support for families. In their article, they first discuss the situation in Australia, which has seen the introduction of a national curriculum framework for early childhood education and an early years reform agenda. These aim to improve educational provision for all, including the indigenous population. Next, in a move away from national issues, Dockett and Perry provide an informative survey of research from numerous countries that has examined problems relating to starting school. A key focus here is on marginalised groups who do not enjoy the same access to early childhood services as other groups. The evidence suggests that children belonging to these groups are 'less school ready' than their peers. Dockett and Perry highlight the importance of a positive transition into school for all children and call for more research to establish how this can be achieved.

Unlike Australia, the Netherlands has no National Curriculum, and schools and early childhood settings have a legal right to choose their own pedagogical approach. Van Oers points out, however, that this is not as liberal as it might seem. Centrally imposed standards and formal assessment regimes create tensions between schools and the government. According to van Oers, successive governments have taken a particularly narrow view of early childhood education and see it largely as a way of solving social problems related to disadvantage. Providers are expected to privilege language development and the development of literacy and numeracy skills over and above other aspects of young children's development, such as their social, personal and emotional development. In his article, Van Oers outlines several alternative approaches to early years education and care and discusses one of these, Developmental Education, in-depth. This high-quality, evidence-based preschool initiative is based on holistic principles and formative assessment practices designed to safeguard young children's well-being and allow them achieve their full potential, as is their right.

Although mainly concerned with education provision for young children, other articles raise questions about the nature of the training offered to student teachers. Kourti and Androussou discuss two new areas: intercultural education and media education, recently introduced into early years of initial teacher-training programmes. The need for inter-cultural education was prompted by recent waves of immigration, and the recognition that immigrant children were in danger of educational marginalisation, and the recognition that Greek society needed to embrace a more multi-cultural ethos. The inclusion of media education was prompted by government educational initiatives to introduce information and communication technologies into pre- and primary schools. Kourti and Androussou argue that as the current school system in Greece is highly centralised and traditional, many teachers have only a limited understanding of the educational needs of young children growing up in a world increasingly dominated by new media. They describe a pedagogic approach to these new courses that encourages critical reflection and challenges students to question their cultural biases and assumptions about education and role of the media. The dominance of traditional educational practice in Greece, however, results in student resistance and unwillingness to embrace innovative pedagogies.

Sheridan and Pramling Samuelsson examine debates related to children's learning and well-being in Swedish preschools and discuss how their own research has informed these debates. Their theoretical framework is based on interactionist perspectives, which bring together theories of learning in which individuals and the environment influence and are influenced by one another in continuous interaction and communication. They discuss pedagogical quality as an educational phenomenon and stress its importance in relation to the conditions for children's learning. Their studies show how changes in policy and views on children's learning have affected pedagogy, which they see as moving from a Froebelian tradition to one based on new theories and empirical research. The introduction of a revised curriculum with integrated goals is designed to emphasise the importance of keeping precise records of children's development including more searching evaluations.

A research programme of a different kind is reported by Turkish academics Bekman and Koçak who discuss a long-standing intervention programme involving five countries. The Mother–Child Education Programme (MOCEP) emphasises the interrelationships between the child, the family and social support systems. Bekman and Koçak first outline the original aims of MOCEP and discuss previous evaluations of the programme. This long-standing intervention programme originated in Turkey in 1993, the same year that this journal was founded. The intervening years have seen several large-scale evaluations of MOCEP. The current article, however, reports new, research that focuses on mothers' perceptions of the programme and the changes they have noticed in their children and in themselves. This research replicates the findings of earlier MOCEP evaluations: more importantly, it offers new insights on how early intervention programmes empower mothers by encouraging them to envisage different possibilities for their children and mother–child relationships.

In the final article in this collection, Faulkner and Coates offer a critical review of 20 years of government initiatives and interventions that have brought about significant changes in early years education and other services for children and families in England. They discusses how and why the 'children's workforce' has become increasingly professionalised over the years and outline how major research programmes such as the Effective Provision of Pre-School Education project (EPPE) and the Millennium Cohort Study have informed our understanding of the effects of social disadvantage and the characteristics of 'high-quality' preschool provision that can alleviate this. There is now persuasive evidence that investment in state-maintained early education is highly cost effective, particularly for disadvantaged children. The current government, however, is shifting the burden of funding training and high-quality integrated services for children and families in England from the state to the private and voluntary sector. It remains to be seen whether this is a backward step or move in the right direction.

The articles in this special issue demonstrate that despite differences in culture, governmental support and access to education, it would seem that the work and concerns of early years educators transcends frontiers. The commonalities highlighted in these articles show a universal solicitude for the disadvantaged and recognition of the need for high-quality provision and a highly qualified work force. The concern for the rights of the child expressed in the very first issue are still evident today, and although there has been much progress, it seems unlikely that universal acknowledgement of these rights and the Millennium Developmental Goals can be achieved by 2015.

Elizabeth A. Coates and Dorothy Faulkner

A participatory process of developing a recommendation for the government about the education of children from birth to three years: the case of Portugal

Teresa Vasconcelos

Lisbon School of Education, Polytechnic Institute of Lisbon, Lisbon

This article describes how the Portuguese National Council for Education initiated a participatory process that gave rise to the development of a 'public statement', 'The Education for Children from Zero to Six Years'. This statement and its 11 recommendations were directed towards the Ministry of Education and called for a shift in support for children from zero to three years (traditionally the responsibility of the Ministry of Solidarity and Social Affairs), from being primarily care-based to being primarily rights-based with an educational focus. This participatory process is described and analysed. It involved broad participation by civil society with representation from a range of stakeholders, including family representatives, professional associations, unions, experts and researchers – all of whom brought their experience, insights and knowledge. This article also describes how, in spite of a change of government, the statement has continued to influence early year educators and policy-makers. Finally, the rationale underlying the statement's 11 recommendations, and the recommendations themselves, are outlined and discussed.

Introduction

In 2011, the Portuguese Conselho Nacional de Educação (CNE, National Council of Education) presented a public statement containing a 'historical' set of recommendations to the Government (specifically to the Ministries of Education and Social Affairs) concerning 'The Education of Children from Zero to Three Years' (see Vasconcelos 2012). The CNE is a consultative council, under the responsibility of the Assembleia da República (National Parliament), and is comprised of representatives and stakeholders from Portuguese civil society. The CNE's public statement was approved unanimously on 29 March 2011, and consisted of a set of 11 recommendations, which will be outlined in this paper. The author of this paper (herself a Council member for three years) was the Rapporteur.

This was the first time that the provision for the education of children aged zero to three (traditionally the responsibility of the Ministry of Solidarity and Social Affairs) had been discussed seriously by the Educational Council and assumed to be the responsibility of *both* the Ministry of Education and the Ministry of Social Affairs. The statement was developed in response to the 2001 Organisation for Economic Cooperation and Development (OECD) evaluation of early childhood education (ECE) and care in

Portugal (Starting Strong I). This evaluation recommended that Portugal should pay greater attention to the provision of education for children under three years, rather than persist in its view that service provision for children and families should be limited to childcare and support for working families.

The statutes of the CNE identifies its role and responsibilities as follows:

> The National Council of Education (CNE) is an organization, with advisory functions, whose President is elected by the National Parliament.

> The National Council of Education (CNE) is responsible for issuing opinions, statements and recommendations about all educational issues, either by its own initiative or by responding to solicitations that may be proposed by the Government or the Assembly of the Republic.

> The National Council of Education (CNE) promotes the participation of various social forces, cultural and economic, aiming at a social dialogue and consensus-building in Education. (Law n° 31/87)

The first of the 11 recommendations from the 2011 public statement approved by the CNE declared that education from zero to three years should be assumed as a child's right and not just a social need. This point of departure influenced all subsequent recommendations in the document.[1]

This article describes and evaluates the participatory process that led to the development of this public statement. Initially, however, background information is presented that describes the current situation in Portugal in relation to the education of babies and children under three. This is followed by an account of initiatives that took place during the late 1990s, which brought the situation of three- to six-year-old children to political attention and led to the consequent expansion and development of new educational settings for this age range.

Background information

In order to understand the wider context in which the 2011 public statement was developed, it is important to understand its background. In 2005, a report on the Application of the Convention of Children's Rights in Portugal declared that:

> (...) There is a need to develop strategies based on children's rights which must be coordinated at a multi-sectorial level so as to affirm the superior interest of the child. This superior interest of the child should become a departure point to plan the organisation of education and care services. Those services need to be coherent with present international legislation guidelines about children from birth to eight years old. It is vital to support children under three years old, by means of pedagogical supervision and not only being guided by issues of care and support to working families. (CNDC, 25)

This statement from the 2005 report clearly highlights the situation existing in Portugal and the need to pay further attention to supporting children under three years of age. As Portugal has been one of the European countries where most women work outside their homes while they have very young children, there is a pressing need for improvement in this area. Women have four months of maternal leave, after which parents have to find their own support for the care of their young children. Fathers are entitled by law to have a paternal leave of one month, but most of them do not use it, either because of work pressure or because they think it is unnecessary.

In 2008, the CNE produced a report entitled 'Education from Zero to Twelve Years – A Continuum', coordinated by I. Alarcão (CNE 2008).[2] This included a review of available research evidence, including my paper 'Early Education and the Promotion of Social Cohesion' (Vasconcelos 2009a). Following this report, a Statement ('Parecer') to the government was produced. This highlighted the need to consider the continuum of education from birth to age 12, and called for a specific focus on the continuum from birth to age six.

It is also important to note that in 2010 for the first time, again at the instigation of the CNE, the Annual Report on the State of Education introduced a section on the educational situation of children under three. Until that time, this had been totally absent from the Council's educational guidelines. The 2010 Annual Report stated that:

> Between 2000 and 2009 the coverage rates of care structures for children from zero to three years – crèches and child-minders – had an increase of 76.3%, having registered in the present year a coverage rate of 34.9%. This situation allowed Portugal to achieve the European goal of 33% of children attending services for zero to three by 2010. (CNE 2010)

This increased rate of coverage, however, has not led to an improvement in the educational quality of crèches or other types of provision (childminders, etc.) despite the fact that the Ministry of Social Affairs has a strategic plan for this age level, and the Ministry of Education has one for children from three to six years.

The main problem is that working with under-threes is not considered educational; therefore, early childhood teachers (in Portugal we call them 'early childhood educators') who work with babies and small children do not have these working years counted towards their 'teaching career'. This has profound consequences for their wages, benefits and retirement allowances and leads to a situation of rapid staff 'turn-over'. As soon as they can, early childhood educators move into teaching posts where they are working with three- to six-year-olds, so that they can enjoy those benefits. For early childhood educators who work with zero- to three-year-olds, this situation is socially unjust as they have the same years of training as those who work in kindergartens or primary schools, though with different training curricula. It is also extremely problematic in terms of continuity of care; in any one school year, children under three may have one, two or three early educators in a row.

According to the Ministry of Social Affairs, since 2001, the support for 'social action' (my inverted commas) relating to children below the age of three years has increased through conventions, cooperation programmes and agreements with private social institutions ('charities') or through direct support to families. During the last five years, a special programme called PAPI (Programa de Apoio à Primeira Infância, a support programme for children from zero to three years) was introduced to develop service provision for this age group by increasing the financing of private, non-profit social service structures. To date, however, there is no direct initiative by the state to create public services for children under three.

Immediately following the presentation of the 2011 public statement to parliament and the government, general elections took place and a new government came into power. Immediately, this government worsened the situation of babies and children under three by introducing new legislation (Ministry of Solidarity and Social Affairs, Portaria n° 262, 31 August 2011), outlining the criteria for the installation and operation of crèches. This new legislation signalled a clear step back from the recommendations contained in the CNE's 2011 statement. According to this new legislation, it is no longer a requirement to have a licenced educator for babies and children under 18 months of age, the number of children per educator has been increased from 10 to 15 and special child-to-educator ratios are not considered necessary for the integration of children with special needs.

This legislation also ignored previous OECD recommendations, as the following brief history of educational reform in Portugal illustrates. In 1994, a 'parecer' (statement) was developed at the CNE, by then-councillor João Formosinho. Between 1995 and 2005, this statement prompted the government to produce a significant strategy supporting the expansion of public, pre-school education for three- to six-year-olds and the creation of a national network of kindergartens (public, private and non-profit) under the responsibility of the Ministry of Education. This increased the coverage to 75% (89% for five-year-olds), from a starting point of less than 30%. This was a very significant effort and has been described in detail by Vasconcelos (1997). The OECD (2001) considered it highly innovative due to its provision for the appointment of a professional early educator to every classroom (instead of teacher-assistants) and the creation of a set of curriculum guidelines in 1997 for children from three to six years. These curriculum guidelines were negotiated and discussed throughout one school year by professionals in the field, together with researchers and other stakeholders, prior to the publication of the final version (Vasconcelos 2003). Again, the OECD (2001) regarded this process of negotiation as exemplary (OECD 2001: 'Providing Curricular Guidance in Portugal', 111). Nevertheless, the insights of OECD external examiners outlined in the 'Country Report' (DEB/OCDE 2000) recommended that new educational policies still needed to be developed for babies and children under three years.

At the same time, researchers and professionals in Portugal were calling for policies for three- to six-year-olds to be expanded to cover the education of children from zero to six years. Financial restrictions, however, did not permit the Ministry of Education to take this further step, and this has had the long-term consequences for children under three that have already been outlined above. A further study by the present author for the CNE (2003), evaluated the government's expansion and implementation plan (1995–1999) for children aged three to six years, and again affirmed the need to pay attention to educational intentionality in settings for children from birth to age three. This study took the view that it was political error that the new Law for Early Education did not take this age group into account.

The importance of investing in the early years (0–3)

The set of 11 recommendations is based on research that has investigated the importance of investing in the early stages of development. Shonkoff and Philips (2000, 311) present evidence from recent brain research, neuroscience data and early intervention studies that has established that high-quality interventions between zero and three years have a measurable influence on children's developmental trajectories, particularly those whose lives may be threatened by socio-economic disadvantage, family instability and diagnosed incapacities. Neuroscience studies emphasise the central role of positive early experiences in the lives of young children as a condition for their support and adaptation to life. If early experiences are toxic or negative, children are at risk of developing dysfunctional patterns of behaviour. The Portuguese researcher Gabriela Portugal has concluded that if three quarters of the brain develops after birth, in close relationship with the external environment, this suggests that evolution has equipped human beings with an 'ecological brain' (2009, 46) that throughout life is dependent on the development context. She proposes, therefore, that the child has an ecological brain. She argues that, from a neurological standpoint, there is no one right way to promote positive development, since warm and responsive care may take different forms, depending on the social, cultural and emotional contexts of individual children's development. By contrast, since the late 1990s, Shore claims that careful, attentive, affectionate and responsive early interactions are vital to the health and well-being of all young children (Shore 1997) regardless of the particular developmental context. Similarly, Shonkoff and Philips (2000) maintain that, from an early age, a child's powerful capacities, complex emotions and social competencies should primarily be developed through interaction.

Brain research, therefore, has highlighted the importance of environmental conditions for all developmental processes that take place in the brain. Each time the child interacts with the environment and is stimulated to collect and process information, a series of complex environmental and physical signals travel through and activate the neuronal circuits (Portugal 2011). During early childhood, in any interaction with an adult, thousands of brain cells are activated, connections are made and strengthened, and new synapses and cellular connections are established – all of which give specificity to the intricate cerebral circuit, which persists throughout the life span (Shore 1997).

Thus, early experiences are crucial for a child's brain development. Interaction with the environment, including social interaction with others, is a central requisite. These early experiences have a key impact on the cerebral architecture and influence the nature and extent of children's future adult capacities (Portugal 2009).

For the seminar that contributed to the preparation of the 2011 public statement (the process leading up to drafting this statement outlined in the next section), Portuguese researcher Oliveira-Formosinho (2011) carried out a significant review. In this review, she cites the studies and reports by Melhuish (2004) and others who have investigated the effects of early attendance in crèches on children's later development. For example, she cites the National Institute of Child Health and Human Development (NICHD) study in 2003 that reported that low-quality childcare at home and in institutionalised day care increased the risk of insecure parent–child attachment. By contrast, Maccoby and Lewis (2003) present evidence from both ethnographic and experimental studies offering convincing evidence that services outside the home environment can make a positive contribution to the social development of young children, provided they promote: (1) attachment to the care service and to a group of peers, (2) constructivist and non-didactic learning, (3) an intrinsic motivation and (4) group structures that support social development. According to this review, there are correlations between the quality of services, cognitive development and the social young children's competence (Oliveira-Formosinho 2011). Oliveira-Formosinho also reports that several studies (e.g. Vandell 2004; Vandell et al. 2010) have identified key differences in family background that are likely to influence children's development. For example, in the USA, the Office of Planning, Research and Evaluation (OPRE 2010) and Vandell et al. (2010) have reported that the positive effects of high-quality early childhood services experienced during the pre-school years persist throughout the primary school years, and sometimes even into adolescence. Studies such as those by Vandell et al. (2010), Halle et al. (2009), Melhuish (2004) and Burchinal et al. (2000) demonstrate that these effects may be differentiated for children from disadvantaged social backgrounds, and that high-quality services may have more of a positive impact on these children's cognitive, social and linguistic development.

Even more recently, a report from the French International Labour Organization (Organisation Internationale du Travail, OIT) concerning 'Éducation et Éducateurs pour la Petite Enfance' (Education and Educators for the Early Years) emphasises the need for quality for ECE from the standpoint of working families and children's rights (OIT 2012).

This report argues for 'logique d'apprentissage centré sur l'enfant' (43) (child-centred learning) and more pedagogical autonomy for professionals and paraprofessionals working in the field.

A participatory process of developing the public statement
Public consultation

During the preparation of the 2011 public statement, a first consultation was held on 8 November 2010 at the CNE. The president of the CNE, Ana Bettencourt, presided over this session. It involved the presence and participation of parent associations, practising early childhood teachers (from crèches and day-care centres), stakeholders, private and non-profit organisations, teacher associations, childminders and family day-care workers, specialists and researchers, representatives from the Ministry of Education and Ministry of Social Affairs, specialists in Early Intervention, representatives from the Commission on the Status of Women, the Commission for Protection of Minors at Risk, the Institute of the Child, worker's unions and, of course, members of the CNE. By way of preparation for this consultation, a set of guiding questions were developed by the present author. These were sent to participants beforehand so that they could prepare a five-minute presentation based (whenever possible) on a written one-to-two page paper (which was later to be handed to the National Council team). During the course of the seminar, these presentations were followed by a further discussion of the policies for very young children that participants would like represented in the statement under preparation. Most participants were of the opinion that the education of children from birth to age three should become the responsibility of the Ministry of Education, in terms of the pedagogical guidelines, staff issues and supervision and training of professionals and paraprofessionals. It was also asserted that the care and education of children from birth to age three should be the responsibility of both parents and not just the mother. Childminders had a strong voice in this discussion because of their 'invisible' and non-recognised work; these early childhood workers lack social benefits and the right to retirement allowance, etc., as they care for children under the age of three in their own homes.

Research seminar

A research seminar was conducted a few weeks later, also under the sponsorship of the CNE and hosted by its president, Ana Bettencourt, together with the Secretary of State for Social Affairs. At the opening conference, a Spanish High Officer of the Ministry of Education described how since 2008, the Ministry of Education in Spain had been sponsoring all educational settings for children under three (in connection with autonomous governments and municipalities) through a programme called 'Educa3' (Caravaca 2011). This Spanish programme provided financial sponsorship; clear guidelines about the quality of settings, supervision and in-service formation; and certified staff.

Two expert panels were also presented at this seminar: one on Research and Practices (with three of the main researchers from Portugal who are specialists in the development of birth to age three) and a second panel on Children's Rights, Early Intervention and Community Needs (with different experts in the area of children's rights, early intervention and community development).

As a starting point, seminar participants were reminded that that since Portugal is a country with an ageing population, during the last 24 years around one million children should have been born in order for the age pyramid to be well balanced; as this had not happened, children were considered by one of the presenters as a 'scarce good'. But children were also identified as social actors, human beings and young citizens. It was pointed out that there was a need for coherent, integrated and multidimensional policies for children from birth to the age of 12 (or further), that guaranteed their well-being and respected their rights. It was also pointed out that research on the impact of placing babies and very young children in settings for zero- to three-year-olds had produced somewhat inconsistent and ambiguous findings concerning the quality of early attachment. At the same time, other research revealed a need for quality supervision of these settings. Seminar participants reflected on the need for appropriate early intervention, for settings to be inclusive and the need for family involvement – not as 'consumers of services', but as partners. The concept of 'family' was expanded to encompass a community of affection, care and education. The seminar's conclusions identified the need for multi-sector social responsibility for the care, protection and education of young children, the need to increase the number of childcare settings on offer and the need to provide high-quality education in these settings. The connection between early education and adult and family education was also discussed (Vasconcelos 2009b). Finally, the role of the state in promoting and regulating these services, and being accountable for them, was also emphasised.

Dissemination

The public statement was unanimously approved by the CNE, with some important feedback and suggestions from the different councillors. It was then sent to the Parliament, the Minister of Education and the Minister of Social Affairs. As previously stated, there followed a change in government (to a more conservative one), that had consequences for policy and decision-making. The newly elected government did not follow through on the dissemination of this public statement.

Notwithstanding this change in government, the National Association of Early Childhood Professionals (APEI) continues to carry out important work at the governmental level in Portugal. For many years, APEI has insisted on the need for the state to take political measures for children from birth to age three, as well as recommending that all contexts for children of this age level should become the responsibility of the Ministry of Education and not of the Ministry of Solidarity and Social Affairs. As well as publishing CNE's public statement in its journal (Vasconcelos 2012), which is read by thousands of professionals, APEI has conducted a set of seminars throughout the country about the education of children under three. These have been led by the author of the 2011 CNE statement, and have been accompanied by presentations and discussions of examples of excellent practice developed by 'zero to three' professionals local to the geographical area where each seminar was held. Hundreds of early childhood educators have attended these seminars, and have accepted the public statement's set of recommendations as their own vision for educating children from birth to age three.

Recommendations

Globally, the 2011 public statement presents education and care of children from zero to three years as a multi- and interdisciplinary area of activity, the complexities of which need to be considered as a whole. It acknowledges interfaces with the plurality of social and political systems, and affirms the diversity of ways of looking at young children. It argues that some of the concepts emerging from the Activity Theory such as relational agency (Edwards 2005), co-configuration (Daniels et al. 2007) and knot-working (Engeström, Engeström, and Vähähä 1999) are key to understanding how the statement's set of 11 recommendations should combine input from all political and administrative authorities, stakeholders and professionals. These concepts imply inter-agency working by employing mutual resources; a capacity to recognise and assess competences distributed in the local systems; the need to negotiate the frontiers for responsible social action; and the capacity for connecting previously unconnected 'activity systems' (Edwards 2005) that, after the development of the project and assessment of its results, may disappear and be formed elsewhere.

The investment in services of care and education for children from birth to age three represents a significant and urgent potential, namely 'to provide young children with the best possible start in life, aiming at reducing early inequalities, accelerating progresses towards equality of women, stimulating school success and investing in citizenship' (UNICEF 2008, 31).

Starting Strong II (OECD 2006) insists that the issue of transitions in young children's lives is in need of attention as is the need for 'building bridges across administrative departments, staff-training, regulations and curricula' (57), and promoting a 'strong and equal partnership with the educational system' (OECD 2006).

To help with understanding how the issue of children's rights was developed throughout the public statement, I next outline each of the set of 11 recommendations made in the statement in turn, and discuss how these are connected with children's *right* to education from birth until age three.

- First Recommendation: Education from zero to three years must be assumed as a right of young children and not just as a social need for working families.

High quality of education for children from birth to age three is a factor that influences equality of opportunities, social inclusion and cohesion, and is a condition *sine qua non* for implementing the United Nations Convention on the Rights of the Child (UNICEF 1989). There is an intrinsic value in creating quality settings for children from birth to age three, not just because of the needs of working families; independently of that factor, there is now scientific evidence demonstrating that experience of group life may be key to the development of 18- to 36-month-old children.

- Second Recommendation: First responsibility belongs to the families, but families need the support of the state and civil society to fulfil their role.

Portuguese legislation considers that preschool education should be complementary to families' responsibilities, and that this should establish close cooperation with families. For this reason, it is important that family perspectives are heard and taken into account when developing policies for this age group. It is also argued that there should be universal education during the early years, so that all children under the age of six can have access to this. Families – any kind of family, in the broadest sense of the word – should become competent partners in the setting they have chosen for their children: they should be part of the institutional dynamics, and should be encouraged to develop a cooperative relationship with staff. In turn, professionals need to ensure that families are fully involved in the setting's educational programme, especially those families who are hard to reach due to difficult socio-economic circumstances. These families need to be able to experience (under the guidance of professionals) new ways of teaching and learning and thus to gain a sense of empowerment that enables them to demonstrate that they are competent and capable of educating their own children.

- Third Recommendation: Pedagogical 'tutelage' (responsibility for pedagogical quality) will become the responsibility of Ministry of Education (in connection with Ministry of Solidarity and Social Affairs, who should oversee the situation of care and general coverage of services in the whole country and deal with issues of health, safety and security).

First of all, the government needs to take the education of zero- to three-year-olds into consideration in the Framework Law for the Educational System (which, with brief revisions, is dated from 1986), as well as the Framework Law for Pre-school Education (which dates from 1997). As soon as this legislation is renewed, the Ministry of Education should, step by step, call for itself to be given total responsibility for the education of children from birth to age three. Until then, several ministries–particularly the Education, Social Affairs and Health ministries–need to undertake a joint work programme. In addition, the Ministry of Education needs to assume pedagogical tutelage (responsibility for the pedagogical quality) of services for children of this age level. This means assuming responsibility for guaranteeing and supervising the educational quality of the settings. Private, non-profit settings ('charities') financially supported by the state are not only accountable to the Ministry of Education for the quality of their pedagogical work, they also have responsibility for receiving those children most at need, either socio-economically or in terms of their special learning needs, or because they come from minority or deprived backgrounds.

- Fourth Recommendation: A new role for local authorities should be introduced in relation to services from zero to three years.

Municipalities and local communities, which are the structures most connected to their local population, should be the front-line service providers prepared to create and supervise services responsive to local needs and expectations of families. According to the OIT Report (2012), 'social dialogue within early childhood settings has difficulties because of inter-sectorial and inter-governmental coordination' (66). This means that the central government will need to work in cooperation with municipalities and local communities by transferring responsibilities and allocating funds. Local communities appear to be the most prepared to provide integrated policies for the early years and also to connect those policies with compulsory school, institutions for the elderly, libraries, community-cultural centres, etc. There is a need to create local structures within municipalities, integrating social partners that could follow, supervise and support the work being developed by local communities and the settings under their responsibility.

- Fifth Recommendation: Increase the diversity of services to be sure that they meet the wide-ranging needs of children and families.

Despite the fact that in Portugal the crèche is the main institution for children from zero to three years, there are a variety of other settings which cater for this age group: for example, family day-care centres, childminders, playgroups and family support groups. This diversity of provision has led some authors to encourage researchers and service providers to adopt an 'anthropological perspective on early childhood that is able to respond to the complexities and paradoxes of our times with flexibility and awareness' (Bove 2012, 13).

Usually, private non-profit organisations offer services both for children from zero to three years and for children from three to six years. It is possible, therefore, that these settings could act as a central hub employing specially trained early childhood professionals to radiate a system of pedagogical support, supervision of family day-care and support for isolated childminders in the area. The risk of isolation and stress is very high for childminders and family day-care workers (Leavitt 1994). They should feel part of a network of services and professionals with whom they could interact and be pedagogically stimulated by each other's work, thus avoiding being permanently confined to their own homes. Any kind of service, though, also has a very important role to play in early intervention and in detecting specific needs of children and their families.

- Sixth Recommendation: The Ministry of Education should invest in service quality and set pedagogical guidelines for services working with children aged zero to three years.

The Ministry of Education is responsible for ensuring that this specific recommendation is put into action. As previously mentioned, 'pedagogical tutelage' is under its responsibility. The crèche (or other similar services) needs to be 'a sensitive context, stimulating and promoting autonomy; a context where levels of well-being and implication/involvement of children are high; where child's experiences are taken into account' (Portugal 2011, 45–57). The Ministry of Education needs to create and ensure the implementation of a very smooth and flexible set of pedagogical guidelines for this age level. These pedagogical guidelines, according to international standards (OECD 2012), should ensure that:

- There is a smooth transition between home to early childhood services, preventing feelings of anxiety in young children and families;
- There is family participation in services, with a warm and sensitive attitude from the adults, both staff and parents;
- That children's right to play is guaranteed with diverse learning opportunities that encourage exploration, experimentation and challenge, in order to support children's growth and development;
- That children's overall emotional development and stability are promoted by prioritising relationship building (child to adult; child to child; children to children) and independence.

Attention needs to be paid to adult–child ratios in order to guarantee security and intimate, responsive relationships that promote development. The quality of an educational context is not only characterised by rich interactions between educator and child, but also by similar interactions with the child's family and amongst professionals themselves. The quality of the environment needs to be peaceful, relaxing, stimulating, aesthetically relevant but not overexciting for young children. Children are natural explorers and researchers at their own level. Outside spaces are very important, so they should be stimulating, bringing children to the direct exploration of nature – sand, water, plants and animals. Attention needs to be paid to issues of inter- and multiculturalism, gender, race, etc., with respect to the kind of adult–child and child–child interactions, and the choice of materials, games, toys, stories, songs and nursery rhymes. It is important not to forget that, due to the extended working hours of families, there should also be close supervision of the quality of these transition hours.

- Seventh Recommendation: Improve the overall quality of the workforce associated with this age group, focusing on initial training, qualifications, professional development and work terms and conditions.

In the course of the seminar discussion, one of the participants characterised the profile of the professional for very young children as calling for 'an ethical, cultural and technical qualification'.

Because we are talking about our most vulnerable citizens – children under the age of three – there is clearly a need for highly qualified professionals. Yet, in almost every part of the world, we see a common pattern: there is no need for high qualifications for the care of the youngest children. This is a cause for considerable concern, as recent research on brain development (presented above) tells us exactly the contrary. It is clear, therefore, that there is a need for early childhood educators who are specialised in working with children from birth to age three.

There is also a concern on the part of the government and civil society that there should be an equal gender balance in the workforce. Incentives need to be found in order to attract men into working with younger children.

The OECD (2006) study stresses that frequently there is a disparity in salaries among childcare workers and teachers and, in most countries, caretakers for children under three have a very limited, mainly informal, training with low salaries and benefits; consequently, there is a significant turnover. As mentioned previously, this happens in Portugal, and policies need to be put in place to ensure that early years educators trained to work with children under three remain with this age group rather than moving to work with older children. Their work needs to be recognised as teaching ('educare') since they have responsibility for the educational quality of basic routines.

Working with very young children is stressful and exhausting (Leavitt 1994), but it can simultaneously be a very rewarding and meaningful experience. Attention needs to be paid to the initial and in-service training and also to the profile of those working with the younger ones, whether they are educators, auxiliary staff or childminders. Training programmes need to relate to the previous recommendation, which advocates the need for early years professionals to demonstrate a professional profile that is sensitive not only to young children's emotional needs and non-verbal signs, but also to the quality of pedagogical work and related ethics. Also, attention needs to be paid to preparing professionals to work with children from minority backgrounds.

Specific attention needs to be paid to childminders and the 'professionalisation' of their work, with corresponding specific training, pedagogical support and supervision. In Portugal at the moment, the work situation of childminders represents a serious social injustice, not only because they are paid minimum salaries and have no social benefits, but also because they are not allowed to join a union that may safeguard and fight for their employment rights. We suggest that local administrative communities could have a key role in training, qualifying and become a binding entity upon which childminders could depend and with whom they could have a professional relationship.

- Eighth Recommendation: Revise Decree-Law number 43/2007, concerning Teacher Education.

The revision of this decree-law will make training for working in crèches part of teacher education at the level of a master's degree, under the responsibility of the Ministry of Education. These professionals may work directly with children from zero to three years or supervise the activities developed by childminders or family day-care centres.

We consider that there needs to be specific training at the initial level for educators/ teachers preparing to work with children under three. We argue that this must be extended to in-service, graduate and postgraduate specialisations, so that these educators/teachers can contribute to our knowledge and understanding of the educational needs of children under three by developing research in this field 'on their own terms'.

Specific attention needs to be paid to the training of these educators in children's rights and how those rights can be incorporated and reflected in their work contexts; at this very early age, children have less 'voice' or autonomy, as they are still learning the basic skills of communication. For these various reasons, we strongly recommend that 'an ethical, cultural and technical qualification' for professionals should be designed that encompasses these requirements.

- Ninth Recommendation: Provide early intervention for vulnerable families and their young children.

This is a key recommendation. We have children with 'diversified learning needs' (OECD 2006), as well as those who, due to the vulnerability of their families, need to have services of higher quality in order to maintain the principles of equity clearly enshrined in Portuguese legislation. Each setting needs to have an early-intervention plan for children who require it, connecting with specialised teams located in central schools. Also, the network of family day-care centres and childminders must not be forgotten. In any decision-making process, however, the superior interest of the child and related ethical principles also need to be taken into account, so as to avoid early 'labelling' of the child and unnecessary intrusions into families' privacy. 'Quality of inclusion' should to be a priority (CNE 2003). Attention must be given to the problems faced by immigrant families who are very vulnerable. Here it is even more important for the approach to be multi- and interdisciplinary in order to prevent the 'fragmentation' of the child between services and tutelages.

- Tenth Recommendation: Increase investment in research into the learning and development of children aged zero to three years, their families and the educational services that support them.

The researchers who were consulted throughout the preparation of this recommendation clearly identified a lack of research in Portugal that investigates the needs of these very young children. They also pointed out that even the international research is sometimes contradictory and inconclusive. They argued that the government (along with private entities) needs to support research so that political decision-making can be based on sound evidence. The International Labour Organisation's report (OIT 2012) asserts that there is a need for more research in this area across all countries. There is a continuing need to evaluate the impact that early institutionalisation of young children may have on their further development – for example, a crèche can have a positive or negative impact depending on its quality. Research needs to be undertaken into the quality of all settings for children under three, and guidelines or frameworks developed to help in their evaluation. It is also important to evaluate the impact that political measures and decisions may have when these are put into practice. As suggested by one of our seminar participants, we recommend the creation of a 'Child's Observatory', designed to collect and disseminate up-to-date, evidence-based information about the quality of all existing settings for young children in our country.

- Eleventh Recommendation: Give a 'voice' to our youngest citizens.

This last recommendation is key to a *rights-based* approach to the education of our youngest children. Recognising their enormous power to explore, to discover, to communicate, to create and to construct meaning, it is essential that we listen to these children, and that we pay serious attention to all their diverse forms of expression. In order to comply with the UN Convention on the Rights of the Child, we must recognise their right to speak (in their own terms and ways), to be listened to and to have effective autonomy and participation. We have to find new and more creative ways to ensure this right to speak, interpreting their attempts to express themselves and respecting their will, their need for autonomy and for independent exploration. In formulating this recommendation we are insistent that in order to realise the principles of fairness and positive discrimination enshrined in the Portuguese National Framework Law for Pre-school Education (see Vasconcelos 1997), we cannot forget children with diverse learning rights (OECD 2006) or those who, due to the vulnerability of their families, have the right to educational experiences of high quality.

Final considerations

It was an historical moment in Portugal when, in April 2011, the CNE approved unanimously the above set of recommendations to the government, concerning the education of children from zero to three years. Yet, traditionally in Portugal, we are rather 'good' at producing legislation and guidelines and 'weak' in providing the means to put them into practice in the field.

After the publication of these recommendations, as discussed earlier, a contradictory ruling from the Ministry of Solidarity and Social Affairs (Ruling n° 262/2011 of August 2011) concerning the criteria used to organise services for children under three created a strong concern – almost 'indignation' – among those working in the field, who felt that we needed to take steps forwards rather than backwards. This ruling, mentioned at the beginning of this paper, clearly contradicts the recommendations outlined above and is a significant backwards step. It represents an economic, neoliberal view of the care for the youngest members of society.

However, two interesting sets of guidance by the Confederation of Solidarity Institutions (CNIS 2012a, 2012b) – Aims and Educational Practices in Crèches (G. Portugal) and Observing and Listening in Crèches (C. Parente) – were produced after the publication of the 2011 recommendations. This fact gives hope that, despite contradictory political measures, this guidance will enable those who work in the field to improve the quality of educational settings for our youngest children despite the new ruling.

The present government's educational plan also states its intention to prepare a set of pedagogical guidelines for guaranteeing quality educational work in crèches. The previous government had affirmed the same intention, although this was never accomplished. We hope to see action on the plan this time.

We believe that a new right should be inscribed in our concerns and actions: the right of access to crèches and childcare services of high quality, especially for children from disadvantaged socio-economic backgrounds and with diverse learning rights. As Van Oudenhoven and Wazir (2006) affirm, there is a need for a rights-based approach to protecting the needs and powers of our youngest citizens. In all matters concerning the provision of education and care for children younger than three, the children and their families should have a voice in matters that concern them. Van Oudenhoven and Wazir conclude:

> It is a profound statement that requires dramatic changes in perceptions, values, legislation and intervention. [...] We believe that the application of a rights-based approach creates new needs and challenges for children and, indeed, for their families and society at large. (2006, 89)

In Portugal, education and care for children from zero to three years needs to be a national citizenship project, as it was in 1996 for children from three to six years, so that young children, especially the most vulnerable ones, are regarded as a collective social responsibility and not just a responsibility of the state or of their families.

Despite current economic hardship and the serious increase in the level of child poverty, the strength of public support for these recommendations lends hope for change: we remain quite sceptical, however, about how existing and future governments will put them into action. It is our conviction that professionals, families, researchers, local communities and the larger population will take the recommendations into their own hands to develop a transformative and empowering educational process (Freire 1997), that ensures a future for the youngest of our citizens.

Notes

1. European Council of Barcelona, March 2002.
2. The author of this paper was then the National Director for Basic Education.

References

Bove, C. M. 2012. "Leaving home for nursery: Italy's approach to supporting transition into formal ECEC services." *Children in Europe*, May 2012: 12–13.

Burchinal, M. R., J. E. Roberts, R. Riggins Jr., S. A. Zeisel, E. Neebe, and D. Bryant. 2000. "Relating Quality of Centre-based Childcare to Early Cognitive and Language Development Longitudinally." *Child Development* 71 (2): 339–357. doi:10.1111/1467-8624.00149

Caravaca, M. G. 2011. "Plan Impulso de la Educación Infantil EDUCA3. [Plan to promote childhood education 0–3 "Educa3"]" In *Conselho Nacional de Educação. Educação das Crianças dos 0 aos 3 anos* [Educating Children from Zero to Three Years], edited by T. Vasconcelos, 23–31. Lisboa: CNE (Estudos e Seminários).

CNDC (Comissão Nacional dos Direitos da Criança). 2005. *Relatório sobre a Aplicação da Convenção dos Direitos da Criança em Portugal* [Report about the Application of the Convention of Children's Rights in Portugal]. Lisboa: CNDC.

CNE (Conselho Nacional de Educação). 1994. *A Educação Pré-escolar em Portugal* [Preschool Education in Portugal]- Parecer no1/94. Edited by J. Formosinho, Pareceres e Recomendações 1994-Vol 1, Lisboa: Conselho Nacional de Educação

CNE (Conselho Nacional de Educação). 2003. *Educação de Infância em Portugal: Situação e contextos numa perspectiva de promoção de equidade e combate à exlusão* [Early Childhood

Education in Portugal: Situation and Contexts under a Perspective of Promoting Equity and Preventing Social Exclusion]. Edited by T. Vasconcelos. Lisboa: CNE (Estudos e Relatórios).

CNE (Conselho Nacional de _Educação). 2008. *A Educação das Crianças dos 0 aos 12 anos* [Education from 0 to 12 years], Relatório do Estudo. Lisboa: Conselho Nacional de Educação.

CNE (Conselho Nacional de Educação). 2010. *Estado da Educação 2010: Percursos Escolares* [The State of Education 2010: Educational Paths]. Lisboa: CNE.

CNIS (Confederação Nacional das Instituições de Solidariedade [National Confederation of Solidarity Institutions]). 2012a. *Finalidades e Práticas Educativas em Creche* [Aims and Educational Practices in Creches]. Edited by G. Portugal. Porto: Confederação Nacional das Instituições de Solidariedade.

CNIS. 2012b. *Observar e Escutar em Creche* [Observing and Listening to Children in Creches]. Edited by C. Parente. Porto: Confederação Nacional das Instituições de Solidariedade.

Daniels, H., J. Leadbetter, P. Warmington, A. Edwards, D. Martin, A. Popova, A. Apostolov, D. Middleton, and S. Brown. 2007. "Learning in and for Multiagency Working." *Oxford Review of Education* 33 (4): 521–538. doi:10.1080/03054980701450811

DEB/OCDE. 2000. *A Educação Pré-Escolar e os Cuidados para a Primeira Infância em Portugal* [Education and Care for Early Childhood in Portugal]. Edited by T. Vasconcelos. Lisboa: Ministério da Educação/Departamento da Educação Básica.

Edwards, A. 2005. "Relational Agency: Learning to be a Resourceful Practitioner." *International Journal of Educational Research* 43 (3): 168–182. doi:10.1016/j.ijer.2006.06.010

Engeström, Y., R. Engeström, and T. Vähähä. 1999. "When the Centre Does Not Hold: The Importance of Knotworking." In *Activity Theory and Social Practice: Cultural–Historical Approaches*, edited by S. Chaiklin, M. Hedegaard and U. J. Jensens, 345–374. Aarhus, Denmark: Aarhus University Press.

Freire, P. 1997. *Pedagogia da Autonomia: Saberes necessários à prática educativa* [Pedagogy for Autonomy: Knowledge Necessary for Educational Practice]. São Paulo: Paz e Terra.

Halle, T., N. Forry, E. Hair, K. Perper, L. Wandner, J. Wessel, and J. Vick. 2009. *Disparities in Early Learning and Development: Lesson from the Early Childhood Longitudinal Study – Birth Cohort (ECLS-B)*. Washington, DC: Child Trends.

Law n° 31/87. 9 July 1987. Creation of *Conselho Nacional de Educação* [National Council of Education]. Lisboa.

Leavitt, R. 1994. *Power and Emotion in Infant-Toddler Day Care*. Albany, NY: State University of New York Press.

Maccoby, E. E., and C. C. Lewis. 2003. "Less Day Care or Different Day Care? [Comment]." *Child Development* 74 (4): 1069–1075. http://www.ncbi.nlm.nih.gov/pubmed/12938704

Melhuish, E. C. 2004. *A Literature Review of the Impact of Early Years Provision upon Young Children, with Emphasis Given to Children from Disadvantaged Backgrounds: Report to the Comptroller and Auditor General*. London: National Audit Office.

Ministério da Educação. 2007. Project-Law number 43/200: Teacher Education in Portugal, Lisbon.

Ministério da Solidariedade e da Segurança Social. 2011. Portaria [Ruling] n° 262/2011, 31 de Agosto [New Criteria for Creation and Expanding of Crèches], Lisbon.

NICHD (National Institute of Child Health and Human Development). 2003. NICHD Study of Early Child Care and Youth Development (SECCYD). http://www.nichd.nih.gov/research/supported/seccyd/overview.cfm

OECD. 2001. *Starting Strong I: Early education and care – Education and skills*. Paris: OECD.

OECD. 2006. *Starting Strong II: Early Education and Care*. Paris: OECD.

OECD. 2012. *Starting Strong III: A Quality Toolbox for Early Childhood Education and Care*. Paris: OECD.

OIT (Work International Organization). 2012. *Un Bon Départ: Education et éducateurs de la petite enfance* [A Good Start: Education and Educators for Young Children]. Genève: Bureau International du Travail.

Oliveira-Formosinho, J. 2011. "Educação das Crianças até aos 3 anos: Algumas lições da investigação [Education for Children under Three: Some Lessons from Research]." In *Educação das Crianças dos 0 aos 3 anos* [Educating Children from 0 to 3], edited by T. Vasconcelos, 59–87. Lisboa: CNE (Estudos e Seminários).

OPRE (Office of Planning). 2010. *Differentiating among Measures of Quality: Key Characteristics and Their Coverage in Existing Measures*. Washington, DC: Office of Planning, Research and

Evaluation – Administration for Children and Families; US Department of Health and Human Services.

Portugal, G. 2009. "Desenvolvimento e aprendizagem na Infância [Development and Early Learning]." In *Conselho Nacional de Educação (2008): A Educação dos 0 aos 12 anos* [Education from Zero to Twelve Years], edited by I. Alarcão, 33–67. Lisboa: CNE (Estudos e Relatórios).

Portugal, G. 2011. "Do âmago da intervenção em creche – O primado das relações e a importância dos espaços [The Core of Intervention in Crèches – Primacy to Relationships and the Importance of Spaces]." In *Educação das Crianças dos 0 aos 3 anos* [Educating Children from Zero to Three Years], edited by T. Vasconcelos, 45–57. Lisboa: CNE (Estudos e Seminários).

Shonkoff, J. P., and D. A. Phillips, eds. 2000. *From Neurons to Neighbourhood: The Science of Early Childhood Development*. Washington, DC: National Academy Press.

Shore, R. 1997. *Rethinking the Brain*. New York: Families and Work Institute.

UNICEF. 1989. *UN Convention on the Rights of the Child*. UNICEF UK. http://www.unicef.org.uk/UNICEFs-Work/Our-mission/UN-Convention/

UNICEF. 2008. *Transitions in Care in the First Years: Innocenti Report Card n° 8*. Florence: UNICEF (Innocenti Research Centre).

Vandell, D. 2004. "Early Child Care: The Known and the Unknown." *Merrill-Palmer Quartely* 50 (3): 387–414. doi:10.1353/mpq.2004.0027

Vandell, D. L., J. Belsky, M. Burchinal, L. Steinberg, N. Vandergrift, and NICHD (Early Child Care Research Network). 2010. "Do Effects of Early Child Care Extend to Age 15 Years? Results from NICHD Study of Child Care and Young Development." *Child Development* 81 (3): 737–756. doi:10.1111/j.1467-8624.2010.01431.x

Van Oudenhoven, N., and R. Wazir. 2006. *Newly Emerging Needs of Children: An Exploration*. Antwerpen: Garant.

Vasconcelos, T. 1997. "Planting the Field of Portuguese Preschool in Portugal: Old Roots and New Policies." *European Early Childhood Research Journal* 5 (1): 5–15. doi:10.1080/13502939785207971

Vasconcelos, T. 2003. "Co-constructing Curriculum Guidelines for Early Childhood in Portugal: A Bottom-up Perspective." In *Researching Early Childhood – Vol. 5: Care, Play and Learning: Curricula for Early Childhood Education*, edited by M. Lohmander, 193–210. Goteberg, Sweden: Goteborg University.

Vasconcelos, T. 2009a. "Educação de Infância e Promoção da Coesão Social [Early Education and the Promotion of Social Cohesion]." In *Conselho Nacional de Educação (2008): A Educação dos 0 aos 12 anos* [Education from Zero to Twelve], edited by I. Alarcão, 141–175. Lisboa: CNE (Estudos e Relatórios).

Vasconcelos, T. 2009b. *A Educação de Infância no Cruzamento de Fronteiras* [Early Childhood Education and Border Crossing]. Lisboa: Texto Editores.

Vasconcelos, T. 2012. "Recomendação do Conselho Nacional de Educação para a Criança dos zero aos três anos – propostas da/para a 'criança futura' [National Council of Education's Recommendation for Children from Zero to Three: A Proposal for the Future of Young Children]." *Cadernos de Educação de Infância* 95 (January/April): 7–13.

A review and analysis of the current policy on early childhood education in mainland China

Yan Liu and Yue-Juan Pan

Faculty of Education, Beijing Normal University, Beijing, China

Compared with the former policies on early childhood education, the policies recently issued in mainland China clearly defined early childhood education as an integral part of education and social public welfare and stipulated the responsibilities of the government in its development, shifting the developmental orientation to promoting social equity. In implementing the new policies, the developmental goals that the local governments set appear divorced from reality, and the developmental paths collide with the current macro social and economic system. This means that the development mode that many local governments exploited is not sustainable. It is suggested that the government should design developmental goals according to actual conditions, reform the public revenue and tax system, and the ECE funding system and introduce a new way to provide public ECE service.

Introduction

Recently the Chinese government introduced a series of policies and measures for early childhood education (ECE). These provided an unprecedented platform and opportunity for the development of early childhood education, and were referred to as the coming spring for ECE in China. Meanwhile, questions arose including as to how to interpret these new policies, how to guarantee that the policies were implemented and what new problems might arise after their implementation. China is so large and complex that the resources possessed and the real situations faced vary greatly across different regions. The texts of the policies issued by central government generally proposed abstract and guiding ideology and principles, whilst their interpretation and implementation was seen as solely the responsibility of local governments. This paper is stimulated by and concerned with these questions, and aims to review and analyse the current policies, to provide information and suggestions to make the policies' implementation more rational and effective.

Background

The policy texts were produced in reaction to social concerns at a particular moment and in a particular context. It is necessary, therefore, to go back to the context to understand and interpret them.

The Reform and Open Door policy announced by Deng Xiaoping in December 1978 set in motion the transformation of every area of Chinese society and communication with foreign countries. After more than three decades of efforts since then, China has made great achievements in each aspect of economic and social construction. The economic growth has brought enormous advances in the development of the ECE in mainland China. Compared with the situation three decades ago, the number of kindergartens and teachers and the ratio of eligible children enrolled in kindergartens have risen dramatically. The statistics showed that the total number of children in kindergartens across the country had risen from 11.5 million in 1980 to 23.49 million in 2007 (Pang 2009, 29). The level of educational degrees and the qualifications gained by teachers also showed great improvement. At the same time, the governments from central to local levels gradually increased the investment in ECE. The total quantity of the funding in 2000 was 10 times that of 1991, and in 2005 it was twice that of 2000 (Pang 2009, 29).

Although great achievements have been made, there are still many problems. These problems have become more and more prominent since the economic transformation from planning mode to market mode in the 1990s. Firstly, the public resources for ECE are scarce. On the one hand, the percentage of public funding for ECE only amounts to about 0.06% gross domestic product (Wang 2011). On the other hand, kindergartens face a severe lack of qualified and committed teachers. This lack of resources has severely affected the provision and quality of kindergartens. It is still common in kindergartens today for one teacher to organise more than 35 children in one class. Many teachers do not have a teaching qualification certificate and the general level of education is relatively low, with the majority having a secondary specialised school diploma or postsecondary college diploma. Liu et al. (2012) investigated 108 kindergartens in three provinces in 2009 and found that average class size of the 108 classes was 39, with 18 classes having more than 50 children and one class having as many as 90 children. Her research also evaluated the overall quality of kindergarten education; looking at the care offered, the curriculum, the daily routine and the physical environment; and found the quality of the sampled kindergartens was generally low, with 45 classrooms only reaching the minimum level below which the level of education was considered inadequate and 43 classrooms reaching a satisfactory level.

Numerous data sets have revealed that the development of ECE remains uneven in different regions, and between urban and rural areas. For example, the statistics of the Ministry of Education in 2009 showed that the enrolment rates of eligible children in rural areas lagged about 30% behind urban areas (Ministry of Education 2009). Liu (2011) found that the percentage of teachers with a qualification certificate in urban areas was significantly higher than that in rural areas (82.5% versus 61.5%). Cai (2007) found the budgeted funding correlated significantly with a kindergarten's fixed asset, spatial area and quantity of books per child, but the Gini Coefficient of the budget funding among different provinces remained at 0.6 from 1998 to 2004. As a whole, the developmental indicators in urban areas – including the enrolment ratio, the number and qualifications of teachers and the government funding – are better than those in rural areas.

The problem for ordinary people who found it difficult to enrol in and afford quality kindergartens became more and more serious after the reform of public enterprise and institutes. These enterprise and institutes were government owned.

Before the reform, they ran hospitals, schools and kindergartens, and dining rooms, which were provided for their employees as welfare. After the reform, many kindergartens that were affiliated to public enterprise and institutes were transferred to the local educational authority, or even closed or sold to the market, and thus the number of private kindergartens grew dramatically. However the management institutions were not adapted to govern and monitor the private sector and many private kindergartens charged very high tuition fees, beyond ordinary people's means. Public kindergartens were cheaper and believed by people to guarantee quality, but provided few enrolment slots, which could hardly satisfy the enormous social needs. These were worsened by pressure from the baby boom as the birth rate has increased since the turn of the century after a steady decline since the middle of the 1980s. As a result, access to affordable and quality programmes remained uneven among families with different social economic status (SES), while the government gradually increased the funding for early childhood education.

The critical deficiencies lying behind the above-mentioned problems are the shortage and unfair distribution of quality public resource and the government not fulfilling its responsibility. As a result of social and economic development, people's awareness of their rights and concerns with early childhood education are growing. Meanwhile many proposals made by members of the NCCPPCC (the National Committee of the Chinese People's Political Consultative Conference) and media reports in recent years centre on issues of early childhood education. The lack of accessible and affordable quality kindergartens and the deficiency of early childhood education have become a major social problem. Public attention has urged the government to take some measures to solve the problems.

New development of early childhood education policy

The governments at each level in China from central to the local level of province, city, county and town, generally, issue files or hold meetings to take one affair seriously. As a reaction to the demanding needs of and the wide-range concerns about ECE, the central government issued a series of files and subsequently held several meetings in a very short period.

1. In January 2009, the draft of the Outline of China's National Plan for Medium and Long-term Education Reform and Development (2010–2020) (abbreviated as the Outline) was open for comments. The Outline marked ECE as one of eight important development missions in the future decade. Out of the eight, ECE received the largest quantity of public comments and suggestions (Feng et al. 2009).
2. On 8 June 2010, President Hu Jintao wrote an official comment on the article 'Few public kindergartens' published in *Press Proof on Domestic Development* of the Xinhua News Agency, which said that it needed to study the problem of ECE as a special mission and solve the problem of accessibility first.
3. On 30 June 2010, Liu Yandong (member of the Political Bureau of the CPC Central Committee and State Councilor), held the first special-issue seminar in Zhongnanhai in Beijing, and emphasised that it should see solving the problems of the accessibility and affordability of kindergarten as a breakthrough in the implementation of the Outline. He stated that the local government is the main body responsible for basically universalising preschool education and solving the problem of accessibility.

4. On 29 July 2010, the Outline of China's National Plan for Medium and Long-term Education Reform and Development (2010–2020) (State Council 2010a) was officially announced.
5. On 3 November 2010, Premier Wen Jiabao held an executive meeting of the State Council, and specifically discussed the affair of early childhood education.
6. On 21 November 2010, the State Council issued the Proposals on the Development of Early Childhood Education (State Council 2010b, abbreviated as State Ten Proposals).
7. On 1 December 2010, Yuan Guiren (the Minister from the Ministry of Education) held a National Meeting via TV and Tel on Early Childhood Education, which was the first meeting on ECE held on the behalf of the State Council.
8. On 24–25 January 2011, the National Meeting on Education was held and ECE was one focus. The meeting decided to launch the implementation of a three-year action plan on ECE, to fully implement a Promotion Programme on ECE in Rural Areas and to speed up the construction of rural kindergartens in central and western China.

Policy adjustment is a rearrangement of power and duties and a reallocation of resources and benefits among stakeholders. The ECE policies issued recently obviously showed the government's will to change the existing pattern of distribution of rights and responsibility according to the equity principle.

The ECE service is reaffirmed again as an attribute of the facilities of education and public welfare

The scholars maintain that it is important to clarify the attribution of the ECE service in deciding what role the government should play in its development and how it should be developed (Lui 2009; Sha and Pang 2010). Chinese literature discusses whether ECE should be regarded as public or quasi-public goods. If the place of ECE is seen as educational and public welfare, then it is quasi-public goods, and the government should invest public funding, and the ECE should not be marketised. The existing long-term problems, in reality, result from the government leaving the attribution of ECE unresolved (Hong and Pang 2009).

Before the 1990s, policy suggested that the place of ECE was as part of the socialist education system and the social public welfare, but essentially the kindergarten education at that time was in the position of welfare provided by work units. In the State Council's stipulation on Company and Enterprise, autonomously running Primary and Middle Schools, and Kindergartens (State Council 1955), the government required that work units like companies, enterprises, institutes and government branches should set up their own kindergartens to let parents work contentedly. Therefore, work units (most of them were public before the 1990s) usually saw kindergartens as welfare for their employees. These constituted the majority of kindergartens. This kind of kindergarten was owned and regulated by the government or work units, and was either not-for-profit and totally free of charge, or charged parents, only low fees for meals and care. Most of the costs were paid by the government or work units.

Under these circumstances the government began to launch the system reform of public enterprise in the 1980s. Their policy on ECE proposed to transfer the schools and kindergartens sponsored by public enterprises to the local educational authority, and began the socialisation of the kindergarten. The Ministry of Education proposed to 'support individual personnel to set up kindergarten' in Proposals on Development of Early Childhood Education in Rural Areas (Ministry of Education 1983), and in the following year relayed the Beijing Trial Regulations on Social Sectors Running Schools, which encouraged social sectors to run schools of each level and type (Ministry of Education 1984). From then on, the process of socialisation of kindergarten education has progressed steadily. The majority of kindergartens sponsored by the public work units were sold to the market and separated from the units they had been affiliated to. As the number of such kind of kindergartens reduced, the number of private kindergartens rose dramatically. The position of kindergarten education as welfare for the employees of work units gradually weakened and ceased.

The policies did not clearly define the socialisation of kindergarten education, and private kindergartens were allowed to keep some of the money left after they had covered their costs as rational repay, in order to encourage the development of the private sector (Ministry of Education 1983, 1984; National People's Congress Standing Committee 2002). Some private kindergartens, therefore, charged very high fees to maximise profit, and these were beyond affordability for ordinary people. The public were confused about whether the ECE service should be private goods provided by the market, operating according to the rule that those who benefit from it should pay for it and those who have money could buy it, or whether the ECE service should be public goods provided by the government on the grounds of need rather than ability to pay.

Support for the view that early childhood education and care should be seen as a public good is growing (Organization for Economic Co-operation and Development [OECD] 2006). This opinion was supported by the recent policy texts. The State Ten Principles asserted that 'early childhood education is the beginning of life-long learning, and an important part of civil education system, and is the important social public welfare', which will help to clarify the ambiguous understanding and reverse the tendency of the over-marketisation of ECE. Based on the view of ECE as public welfare and shared benefits, the Outline clearly set the goals as 'basically universalising preschool education', and the State Ten Proposals emphasised the need to 'build the public ECE service system widely covering urban and rural areas and with rational distribution' and 'guarantee eligible children receiving preschool education with basic quality' (State Council 2010a, 2010b).

The government takes more responsibilities and responsibilities are defined more clearly than before

Since the system reform of public work units, the market was introduced into the ECE field, and the relationship between government and market changed accordingly. Before the reform the government participated more than the market in ECE, and gradually gave way to it. The policy texts consistently emphasised that the government had the responsibility for developing ECE, but did not clearly define the role of the governments and the branches at different levels. Therefore, the stipulation just stayed on paper; governments at different levels passed the buck to each other and different branches compartmentalised with each other in practice. After 1998, 29 of 31 provinces, autonomous regions and municipalities cancelled branches responsible for managing ECE, with the exception of Beijing and Tianjin (Pang 2009). Some local governments scarcely invested in ECE; therefore, the majority of kindergartens were private. One investigation pointed out that in about half the counties in mainland China, 80% of the kindergartens were private (China Early Childhood Education Development Strategies

Research Team 2010). According to the policies, private kindergartens were required to charge tuition fees according to their costs and only received the quality evaluation by local educational authorities on a voluntary basis. Whilst the local educational authorities had the power to register, examine and approve, they were unable to ban or provide funding and personnel. As a result, the price and quality of private kindergartens were totally regulated by the market. What the market pursues is profit and efficiency, instead of quality and equality. Recently, with the increasing demand for more accessible, affordable quality kindergartens, the issue of the government's responsibility in ECE has been thrown into sharp focus.

The ECE is an integral part of education and social public welfare, and thus it has the attribute of public goods; therefore, the government should take responsibility when the market does not work. Compared with policy texts before, the latest policy concretely defined the government's responsibility, and designed accountability mechanisms. On the one hand, it explicitly required the government to fulfil its responsibility in investment, indicating that the funding should be allocated in the educational budget and the increment of funding that should be directed to ECE. The budgeted allocation is a compulsory indicator to show whether the government has fulfilled its financial responsibilities, and provides a powerful guarantee for funding for ECE. On the other hand, it required that the government should put the development of ECE on to the local development agenda, and build monitoring, appraisal and accountability mechanisms. These include establishing professional standards for kindergarten teachers and clarifying the minimum qualification required; providing training programmes for kindergarten principals and teachers at national and provincial level; deciding the cost per child in public kindergartens and the funding standard per child; implementing the kindergarten licencing system and developing programme standards based on types of kindergartens, and monitoring and supervising kindergartens according to these types; regulating the tuition fees of kindergartens; issuing guidelines for learning and development in early childhood; and improving the working mechanisms to let governments at each level and different branches coordinate with each other.

The orientation of the development of ECE is directed to promoting social equity

In accordance with the need to support the construction of industrialisation and urbanisation, the government, after the establishment of the People's Republic of China (PRC), exploited strategies that developed cities and industry first, and then countries and agriculture. The urban-rural structure has been established since then; it is pervasive across different sectors of Chinese society and continues till the present day. The State Council's Decision about Reforming Schooling System in 1951 (State Council 1951) proposed that kindergartens should be set up first in cities in adequate conditions and then gradually generalised. Influenced by this urban-rural dual structure, the limited funding was given to public kindergartens in cities to develop backbone or model kindergartens. Kindergartens sponsored by the private sector or communities could gain hardly any public funding. This skewed funding policy was the result of the government's weak financial capacity at the beginning stage of the process of industrialisation and urbanisation. The government had to concentrate their limited resources on the development of industry in the cities, resulting in an increased need for public kindergartens. However, this funding policy led to institutional inequality: children in rural areas, in private kindergartens and those from families not working in public work units could not gain public funding support. Such institutional deficiency became more and more obvious as the economy and society in China developed further.

The development priority and the thinking mode of the central government were changed dramatically in the policy texts issued recently. The Outline definitely stipulated 'basically universalising preschool education' and 'strengthening preschool education in rural areas' as the goals to be pursued in future decades, and stressed that the government has responsibilities to support non-governmental kindergartens and families who cannot afford kindergarten education. The State Ten Principles required that government should support private kindergartens, providing affordable quality services by buying service, reducing tax, awarding and sending teachers with public teacher identity registration, developing the subsidy system to provide support for disadvantaged families and children receiving ECE, and allocating special funding to develop kindergartens in rural areas and in central and western China. All these prescriptions showed the government's will to universalise an accessible, affordable and quality ECE service, and to reflect the changes in the orientation of the government's development strategies from efficiency to equity.

Challenges and problems in implementing the current policies

There is great diversity of social customs and variety in economic development among different regions in China. Therefore, the policy texts issued by central government generally propose guiding goals and principles, and then leave space for local government to implement them according to their own real conditions. The enactment of policy texts is subject to local government's interpretation, understanding and emphasis. In such a context, the implementation of current policies encountered several challenges and problems.

The developmental goals go far beyond the real conditions

The State Ten Principles required local governments to design three-year action plans. In China, the whole country is administratively divided into provinces and autonomous regions. The provinces are divided into cities, and cities into counties.

The three-year action plan was expected to be based on the unit of county, and not on city or province. Every county designed their own three-year action plan, setting the goals of development, breaking down the development task and ascertaining the funding required. However, the local governments used the upper limits of the development goals proposed by the Outline as their own developmental goals, which went far beyond their capability. Guizhou province, for example, set the goal that the ratio of enrolment in three years of kindergarten education should raise to 59% by 2013, and to 70% by 2020. Now the ratio of enrolment in Guizhou has so far only reached 55.4%. To be able to fulfil these goals, several difficulties have to be overcome. First is the lack of kindergarten teachers. There were 14,623 teachers in 2010 and the teacher–children ratio was 1:31 (the average at national level is 1:27). The number of enrolled three to six-year-olds in 2012 reached 1,400,000, and the number of eligible children enrolled in kindergartens should be 826,000 if the ratio of 59% is to be achieved. Even if the ratio of teacher-children is kept at the national average 1:27, there is still a shortage of about 30,592 teachers. Second there is the lack of funding. Guizhou province planned to build 1,000 new public kindergartens by 2020. The cost to build one township central kindergarten is estimated to be 2,090,000 RMB; therefore, the province needs an extra 2.4 billion RMB of revenue. Third is the geographical layout of kindergartens. Guizhou province planned to build 500 township and community kindergartens, and residential kindergartens in regions with scattered populations, by 2013 (Liu, Shi, and Qiu 2011). Guizhou province is located in a mountainous area, and the geographical parameter that one kindergarten can cover is very limited. In the towns, it is not possible for one kindergarten to cater for all eligible children. Likewise, it is neither feasible nor rational to build residential kindergartens for very young children.

The need to increase funding collides with the existent funding system

The State Council's Suggestions to Strengthen Early Childhood Education in 1988 stipulated that local government is responsible for funding for ECE (State Council 1988). The Guidance on Reform and Development of Early Childhood Education in 2003 (State Council) adhered to this basic principle and proposed that the county government should be responsible for establishing public kindergartens, whilst the town government should be responsible for developing ECE in rural areas and establishing township central kindergartens. Though the Outline and the State Ten Principles required the government to increase funding for ECE, they did not change the main body responsible for funding. The three-year action plan was required to be developed within the county range, and the main body of funding still remained at the level of county and town. After the implementation of the Tax Sharing System, and the Rural Tax and Fee Reform in the mid-1990s, the revenue capability of local government, especially at the level of county and town, reduced dramatically. However, the local government has heavy responsibilities for public expenditure. Nowadays some local governments have made loans to universalise the nine-year compulsory education, and have no capability to increase funding to universalise kindergarten education.

Meanwhile, many local governments did not change their governing thinking mode, which was shaped in the era of economic planning. Providing financial support to private kindergartens was still thought to be letting the private sector use state-owned property to make a profit. While the State Ten Principles emphasised that the government should take a leading role, it was not to be seen as the body which was responsible for taking charge of everything, and the social agents were to be encouraged and supported in developing ECE. However many regions used the funding mainly to build new public kindergartens, and rebuild or expand old public kindergartens. In Beijing, for instance, the public funding was mainly invested in kindergartens set up by the local educational authority, but the amount of children enrolled in these kindergartens was only 20% of those eligible. The other kinds of kindergartens enrolled about 80% of the eligible children, but rarely received public funding support (Liu, Shi, and Qiu 2011). Because the government shared most of the costs of public kindergartens, they could charge a low price and provide relatively higher quality, and compete unfairly with private kindergartens. Therefore, the developmental move to universalise kindergarten education through establishing more public kindergartens has worsened the environment for the development of private kindergartens. Since the number of children admitted to public kindergartens is very limited, and the government does not have enough capability to provide ECE service for all eligible children, the developmental mode to only fund public kindergartens is not sustainable and does not help to solve the problem of access to affordable quality kindergarten.

In short, the developmental goals are divorced from reality, and the developmental paths collide with the current macro social and economic system and squeeze the space for private kindergartens. Therefore, the development mode exploited by many local governments is not sustainable.

Suggestions to guarantee the implementation of the policies

Design developmental goals according to actual conditions

Local governments should implement the Outline and the State Ten Principles with positive measures and steady steps based on actual local conditions and avoid making any hasty, unfounded advances. Factors including economic developmental level, distribution of eligible children, change of birth rate, flow of population and potential provision of kindergarten teachers should be taken into consideration. ECE resources should not be abandoned after those eligible children born at the height of the baby boom have enrolled in kindergarten.

Three concrete measures are recommended to support the implementation of recent policies. First, the rate of enrolment should be differentiated from the rate of provision. Many local governments use the enrolment rate as an indicator for universalising kindergarten education. However it is difficult for eligible children in rural, remote and mountain areas, which have a scattered population, to go to kindergarten. Early childhood education should be provided in a variety of ways to allow access in these areas. Second, a half-day programme is an alternative choice in disadvantaged regions, especially for families with grandparents helping to care for children in rural areas. Kindergartens in China generally provide full-day programmes, but a half-day programme could serve twice as many children, and the cost therefore, would be reduced. Third, the kindergartens in rural areas could consider renting an appropriate house or rebuilding redundant or idle classrooms in schools, instead of building new campuses and classrooms, and then use the funding to enrich children's books and play materials and teachers' salaries and working conditions.

Reform the public revenue and tax system and the ECE funding system

The current revenue and tax system resulted in the imbalance between the financial capability of government at central and local levels and their responsibilities for public expenditure. The policy texts did not explicitly define the percentage that the government at each level should contribute in funding for ECE; therefore, the governments at the higher level and those at the lower level pass the buck to each other. The governments at the lower level shoulder many responsibilities, but without the financial capabilities to guarantee fulfilling them. To completely change the situation, the public revenue and tax system should be reformed, and balance the financial capability and expenditure responsibility of the government at each level.

The higher-level government should also be made to take responsibility for the majority of the ECE funding, and the percentage of funding that government at each level should take should be clearly and rationally defined. Meanwhile, the local government should distribute funding and public resources fairly among kindergartens with different sponsoring bodies, and thus create a fair environment for the different types of kindergarten to compete and survive.

Innovate ways to provide public ECE service

The recent policies affirmed the leading role of government in the development of ECE, but the leading role does not mean the governments themselves should directly set up kindergartens, and also does not mean that governments should provide all the funding. That the government should set up kindergartens to cover all the eligible children goes

29

beyond its financial capability under the current economic development level, and such a move is not helpful for the sustainable development of ECE. The government could provide public ECE and encourage private sector involvement in ECE provision through buying their services. Take Anhui province as an example. In order to provide more accessible and affordable kindergarten education, the Anhui government builds and rebuilds public kindergartens. On the other hand, it also provides funding support to private kindergartens, whose fees and quality level are in accordance with the standard the government set.

References

Cai, Y. Q. 2007. *Financial Investment in Early Childhood Education and Policy*. Beijing: Educational Science Publishing House, 113–119. [In Chinese.]

China Early Childhood Education Development Strategies Research Team. 2010. *Research on Development Strategies of Early Childhood Education in China*. Beijing: Educational Science Publishing House, 23. [In Chinese.]

Feng, X. X., L. Y. Wang, S. J. Xiao, X. M. Tang, and R. H. Zhang. 2009. "Focusing on the Outline of China's National Plan for Medium- and Long-term Education Reform and Development: Analysis on Comments and Suggestions." *Studies in Preschool Education* 6: 3–9. [In Chinese.]

"Few Public Kindergartens, Expensive Private Kindergartens, Disordered Kindergartens without Registration, Arduous Kindergartens in Rural Areas." In *Press Proof on Domestic Development*. Beijing: Xinhua News Agency.

Hong, X. M., and L. J. Pang. 2009. "Institutional Guaranteeing and Responsibility of Government in Development of Early Childhood Education." *Studies in Preschool Education* 1: 5. [In Chinese.]

Liu, Y., J. Shi, and Z. H. Qiu. 2011. "The Status and Issues of the Preschool Education Development after State Ten Principles." *Research in Educational Development* 24: 1–6. [In Chinese.]

Liu, Y., X. P. Yang, Y. Tu, and Y. J. Pan. 2012. "The Comparative Study on One-year Preschool Education Quality in Urban and Rural Areas in Mainland China." *Journal of Educational Studies* 8 (3): 74–83. [In Chinese.]

Lui, Z. L. 2009. "Kindergarten Education Must Maintain the Attribute of Education and Social Welfare." *Educational Research* 5: 31–36.[In Chinese.]

Liu, Z. L. 2011. *Evaluation of Kindergarten Education Quality in Mainland China: Investigation in Eleven Cities*. Beijing: Educational Science Publishing House.

Ministry of Education. 1983. *Proposals on Development of Early Childhood Education in Rural Areas (Guan Yu Fa Zhan Nong Cun You Er Jiao Yu de Ji Dian Yi Jian)*. People's Republic of China: Ministry of Education. [In Chinese.]

Ministry of Education. 1984. *Notice to Relay the 'Beijing Trial Regulations on Social Sectors Running Schools' (Jiao Yu Bu Zhuan Fa 'Beijing Shi She Hui Li Liang Ban Xue Shi Xing Ban Fa' de Tong Zhi)*. People's Republic of China: Ministry of Education. [In Chinese.]

Ministry of Education. 2009. *Educational Statistics Data: Early Childhood Education*. [In Chinese.] http://www.moe.edu.cn/publicfiles/business/htmlfiles/moe/s4965/index.html

National People's Congress Standing Committee. 2002. *People's Republic of China Acts on Promoting Private Education (Zhong Hua Ren Min Gong He Guo Min Ban Jiao Yu Cu Jin Fa)*. People's Republic of China: National People's Congress Standing Committee. [In Chinese.]

OECD. 2006. *Starting Strong II: Early Childhood Education and Care*. Paris: OECD, 12.

Pang, L. J., ed. 2009. *Three Decades of Reform in Education in China: Early Childhood Education*. Beijing: Beijing Normal University Press, 47. [In Chinese.]

Sha, L., and L. J. Pang. 2010. "Analysis on ECE Legislation of France and its Inspirations." *Studies in Preschool Education* 9: 3–8. [In Chinese.]

State Council. 1951. *State Council's Decision about Reforming Schooling System (Zheng Wu Yuan Guan Yu Gai Ge Xue Zhi de Jue Ding)*. People's Republic of China: State Council. [In Chinese.]

State Council. 1955. *State Council's Stipulation on Company and Enterprise Autonomously Running Primary and Middle Schools and Kindergartens (Guo Wu Yuan Guan Yu Gong*

Kuang, Qi Ye Zi Ban Zhong, Xiao Xue He You Er Yuan de Gui Ding). People's Republic of China: State Council. [In Chinese]

State Council. 1988. *Suggestions to Strengthen Early Childhood Education (Guan Yu Jia Qiang You Er Jiao Yu Gong Zuo de Yi Jian)*. People's Republic of China: State Council. [In Chinese.]

State Council. 2003. *Guidance on Reform and Development of Early Childhood Education (Guan Yu You Er Jiao Yu Gai Ge yu Fa Zhan de Zhi Dao Yi Jian)*. People's Republic of China: State Council. [In Chinese.]

State Council. 2010a. *Outline of China's National Plan for Medium- and Long-term Education Reform and Development (2010–2020) (Guo Jia Zhong Chang Qi Jiao Yu Gai Ge he Fa Zhan Gui Hua Gang Yao)*. People's Republic of China: State Council. [In Chinese.]

State Council. 2010b. *Proposals on Development of Early Childhood Education (Guo Wu Yuan Guan Yu Dang Qian Fa Zhan Xue Qian Jiao Yu de Ruo Gan Yi Jian)*. People's Republic of China: State Council. [In Chinese.]

Wang, H. Y. 2011. "From Privileged Welfare to Civil Rights: Interpretation about the Principle of Universal Benefit Proposed in Proposals on Development of Early Childhood Education from the State Council." *Early Childhood Education (Educational Sciences)* 1 (2): 8. [In Chinese.]

Early childhood development in South Africa – progress since the end of apartheid

Eric Atmore

Department of Social Development, University of Cape Town, Rondebosch, South Africa

In April 1994, South Africa held its historic first democratic election. The African National Congress overwhelmingly triumphed and Nelson Mandela became the first president of a free and democratic South Africa. In this review, the situation of South Africa's young children under apartheid and the context of young children in South Africa in 2012 are described. A situation analysis of early childhood development (ECD) in South Africa was undertaken using South African government ECD policy and programme implementation reports, and the main challenges affecting children and the ECD sector in South Africa was investigated. There has been progress since 1994, both quantitatively and qualitatively. Children now have access to a Grade R year, government education and social development budgets have increased and a per capita subsidy is available to qualifying children at ECD centres nationally. More children are in provision and in better-quality provision than before. However, much still remains to be done before we can say with confidence that the needs of our youngest children are being met. This study identifies infrastructure, nutrition, ECD programmes, teacher training, institutional capacity and funding as the major gaps in ECD provision.

Introduction

South Africa lies at the tip of the African continent with a population of 50 million people from diverse religions, traditions, cultures, languages and backgrounds. Due to the policies of apartheid, ours has been a particularly oppressive country to live in for the majority of our people. For several hundred years, it was a country where quality of life depended on skin colour. Black South Africans' human rights were denied and young children lived a life of hunger and malnutrition; insecurity and trauma; instability, family breakdown and dislocation of communities; a lack of primary health care and educational opportunities; and the absence of adequate housing, electricity, running water and sanitation. This was the legacy of apartheid inherited by the newly elected government of President Nelson Mandela after the first democratic elections of April 1994.

Eighteen years after democracy, in 2012, the majority of young children in South Africa are still negatively impacted by a range of social and economic inequalities, including inadequate access to health care, education, social services and nutrition. This continues to undermine the development of our children. The South African constitution, through the Bill of Rights clause, makes provision for children's socio-economic rights, including the right to basic education and protection from neglect, abuse and exploitation. However, South Africa still has a long way to go to effectively meet the needs of the majority of children.

This paper provides an overview of the progress made in the early childhood development (ECD) sector in South Africa since 1994. It describes the context of children, what has been done in ECD and the challenges facing the ECD sector in six key areas, namely: infrastructure, nutrition, ECD programmes, teacher training, institutional capacity and funding.

ECD during the apartheid years

Children in South Africa have historically been neglected and abused by the political ideologies and structures of the apartheid government. Apartheid is the system of racial separation that was enforced by legislation in South Africa for over 100 years. The central thrust of apartheid education was best expressed in the 1950s by Minister of Bantu Affairs and later Prime Minister Hendrik Verwoerd, who justified apartheid by saying: 'There is no place for the Bantu in the European community above the level of certain forms of labour. What is the use of teaching the Bantu child mathematics when he cannot use it in practise?' (Clark and Worger 2004, 48). The result was an education system that provided compulsory education for white children and voluntary education for black children. Access to ECD programmes and services for black South African children was severely limited; by 1994, only 6% of black children attended an ECD programme (Padayachie et al. 1994, 6). For black children at primary school, retention rates were very low, with 25% of black children failing the first year of school and then dropping out of school permanently (Taylor 1989).

The lack of access to and the poor quality of ECD programmes and services resulted in low rates of primary school survival and in limited access to health services and nutritional intervention.

During the apartheid years, ECD in South Africa was described by Van Den Berg and Vergnani (1986) as:

- segregated as a matter of state policy;
- fragmented among a bewildering array of departments and bodies;
- totally inadequate;
- occurring inversely proportional to need, with the most resources provided for by far the most advantaged statutory population group;
- characterised by insistence on inflexible and unrealistic standards;
- lacking in co-ordination and co-operation;
- not seeking to provide a comprehensive and integrated service; and
- lacking in democratic participation.

ECD: progress since 1994

There has no doubt been progress in ECD since 1994, with significant initiatives directly affecting the lives of young children. Some have been very positive and others less successful. The successes include:

(1) The government signed the Convention on the Rights of the Child in 1995.
(2) Free medical and health care services are now available for all pregnant women and children from birth to six years of age.

(3) A Directorate for Early Childhood Development has been established within the national Education Department.

(4) A children's section has been established within the national Social Development Department.

(5) Education White Paper 5, on ECD, has been published, as well as a Welfare white paper with a section on ECD.

(6) Grade R[1] has been introduced, for children aged 5–6 years.

(7) A nationwide ECD Audit surveying 23,482 ECD sites was successfully completed in 2000.

(8) The nine provincial Social Development Departments now make ECD subsidies available for ECD sites each year.

(9) The nine provincial Education Departments make Grade R grants-in-aid available.

(10) A new Children's Act was passed by the parliament, including chapters that deal with ECD programmes.

(11) As of March 2012, 10.9 million children received social assistance through the Child Support Grant (South African Social Security Agency 2012, 18).

A picture of ECD in South Africa

In the year 2000, the author was contracted by the national Department of Education to manage a national study on ECD. This nationwide ECD audit (Department of Education 2001a) provided the first accurate information on the nature and extent of ECD provisioning, services and resources across the country. The audit of ECD in 2000 found in the following list:

- 23,482 ECD facilities across the country;
- 1,030,473 children enrolled in these centres;
- an even gender split between boys and girls;
- using the previous statutory population group definitions, 74% of children enrolled were black African, 10% were coloured, 2% were Indian and 14% were white;
- the majority of enrolled children spoke IsiZulu (24%), followed by IsiXhosa (19%), Afrikaans (14%) and English (12%);
- only 11,779 children (1.14%) were reported to have a disability;
- the teacher–child ratio was 1:19 nationally;
- 54,503 teachers were identified, 99% were female and fewer than 1% male;
- 68% of teachers were black African, 11% coloured, 2% Indian and 19% white;
- 3623 ECD facilities (17%) were school-based, 10,816 (49%) were community-based and 7453 (34%) were home-based;
- 49% were in urban areas, 11% in urban areas with wood and iron structure housing and 40% in rural areas;
- 53% of facilities had mains electricity, flushing toilets and piped water;
- 8% of facilities (1669) were not equipped with mains electricity, flushing toilets or piped water;
- 38% of facilities were registered with the Department of Education and 43% with the Department of Social Development, with some facilities having dual registration;
- fees paid by parents were the major source of income for ECD centres, with 90% of centres charging fees;

- 23% of adults working with young children had no training at all and only 12% had a Department of Education-recognised qualification;
- the non-profit organisation (NPO) sector trained most ECD teachers (43%), however, at that time such qualifications were not recognised by government;
- most teachers (44%) earned less than R500 per month (about US$60), with 74% earning less than R1500 per month (about US$180).

ECD policy priority

In 2001, the South African Department of Education released Education White Paper 5, which established a national system of provision, called Grade R, for children aged 5–6 years. This was to be progressively rolled out with full provision by the year 2010. This has been partially achieved, with enrolment at February 2012 standing at 767,865 children representing 63% of the eligible age cohort. Based on the Department of Education (2001b) statistics, 526,340 additional children entered Grade R in the first 11 years after the release of the 2001 White Paper on Education. The rate of take-up of Grade R places has continued thus:

- 37,201 in 2002;
- 36,661 in 2003;
- 41,100 in 2004;
- 48,710 in 2005;
- 36,444 in 2006;
- 45,884 in 2007;
- 56,274 in 2008;
- 76,424 in 2009;
- 86,980 in 2010;
- 27,451 in 2011; and
- 33,211 in 2012.

Realising that the target of full provision would not be reached by 2010, the government first revised the target date to 2014 and more recently to 2019.

Financial responsibility for Grade R lies with provincial education departments, and provision is made for subsidies to be paid to schools to allow them to establish Grade R facilities. Grade R programmes are expected to function at 'a cost considerably lower than primary school-based provision since the latter uses provincially-employed educators, whereas the practitioners at community-based sites are not employed by government and are paid considerably less' (Department of Education 2001b, 30).

Provincial Grade R spending was at R1.3 billion in 2008/2009. Provincial Grade R spending, as a percentage of total education spending, for all provinces was 0.74% in 2003/4 – that is, less than one per cent. Expenditure on Grade R by 2008/2009 had increased to 1.3% of the total education expenditure.

Challenges facing the ECD sector

Notwithstanding the progress made in ECD and Grade R provision since 1994, children in South Africa still face significant challenges, especially around infrastructure, nutrition, programme options, ECD teacher development, institutional capacity and funding.

Infrastructure

Infrastructure in ECD is a particular problem in the South African context. Many ECD facilities function without basic infrastructure such as running water, access to electricity or suitable sanitation. The nation-wide ECD audit of 2000 showed that about 8% of ECD centres in South Africa have none of these basic infrastructure requirements (Department of Education 2001a). The infrastructure in community-based facilities is of a poor standard, with a significant number of buildings in a bad or very bad condition.

A significant portion of ECD facilities had more than 40 children per playroom, whereas, the national Department of Education norms set for class ratios are 30 children per class for Grade R and 20 children per class for pre-Grade R. Many ECD facilities do not have any form of secure fencing around their premises, and in many, food is prepared in the same area in which children spend the majority of their time.

Poor infrastructure at ECD facilities not only presents significant health and safety risks to children attending these facilities, but can also point to poor quality ECD service provisioning. Furthermore, an unsafe and impoverished learning environment is often associated with substandard ECD.

Nutrition

For young children, hunger, malnutrition and food insecurity are significant challenges. The absence of adequate nutrition greatly affects a child's early development. The physical effects of inadequate nutrition are severe. Malnourishment can cause direct and irreversible structural damage to the brain; impair motor development; cause significant developmental retardation; affect cognitive development; impair exploratory behaviour; impair learning abilities and educational achievement; and can have long-lasting impact on a child's health (Duggan, Watkins, and Walker 2008; Victora et al. 2008).

In terms of learning, malnutrition and hunger have a profound affect on a child's ability to concentrate, focus attention and perform complex tasks (Wildeman and Mbebetho 2005). Therefore, children who lack certain nutrients or those who suffer from general malnourishment, or simply hunger, do not have the same readiness for learning as their healthy, adequately nourished counterparts. These negative consequences affect the child's ability to achieve their full potential, stunting not only the individual child's ability to flourish in adulthood, but also collectively limiting the country's human capital.

Interventions in nutrition at ECD centres are offered mainly by non-profit organisations and faith-based organisations. These interventions include school feeding schemes and the provision of food gardens. There have been no government interventions and the Primary School Nutrition Programme only includes children from Grade 1 upwards.

ECD programme quality

The ECD sector offers a number of ECD programme options to meet the needs of children and their caregivers. These include the traditional centre-based ECD model of provision, playgroups and family outreach programmes. However, the quality of much provision is poor.

Traditional provision involves the common practice of ECD teachers providing ECD care and education for a class of children, whose ages range from zero to six years. Classroom space is provided in an assortment of physical structures. These are situated in public schools (in the form of Grade R classes), and at community-based facilities (in pre-Grade R and Grade R classes). Community facilities are often based in private homes where an ECD practitioner converts a portion of her house to accommodate children, or classes can be provided at centre-based facilities where a community has a dedicated building for the children.

Family outreach programmes involve the provision of ECD services within a residential home. These outreach workers work with a number of families in a community and visit each one for a set amount of time each week or month, depending on the nature of the specific programme. During a home visit, the family outreach worker works directly with the caregiver by sharing knowledge on how to provide early learning stimulation and on various other important topics such as health, safety and nutrition. The family outreach worker also works directly with the children in their homes – demonstrating to the caregiver the various activities that can be done at home, and providing the children with a foundation for their early learning. These programmes empower parents and primary caregivers to provide early learning opportunities to their own children (Atmore, van Niekerk, and Ashley-Cooper 2012).

With informal playgroups, a fieldworker works on a session basis with a group of parents and children on early learning activities; this type of ECD contact can take place in a local park, a residential home or at a community hall. The activities focus mainly on the education activities that the parents can do in the home with their children.

ECD teacher development

Quality teaching and learning is essential for effective early development to take place. A good teacher can provide a learning environment in which a child can develop optimally and in a holistic manner. To produce quality ECD teachers, various training and education opportunities are made available through full ECD qualifications, as well as short skills programmes.

In South Africa, qualifications are established via the National Qualifications Framework by the South African Qualification Authority. Training in these ECD qualifications is offered mainly at Further Education and Training colleges and ECD non-profit organisations.

The Department of Social Development has minimum standards for ECD teacher requirements. The entry-level qualification is the Further Education and Training Certificate: ECD (Level 4), which provides ECD practitioners with the necessary skills to facilitate the holistic development of young children and to offer quality ECD services in a variety of settings.

In a recent study assessing the quality of ECD services in the Western Cape, researchers found that qualification level was not always associated with higher-quality outcomes, such as quality of care and learning (Human Sciences Research Council 2009). They also found that only 35% of practitioners responsible for infant and toddler classes had any form of ECD qualification, and only 47% of practitioners responsible for older children had any form of ECD qualification.

Institutional capacity

With regard to ECD facilities within the public school sector, the institutional capacities of public schools appear to be more sophisticated than those within community-based ECD centres and to have more structured governance and financial reporting systems.

This could be due to the fact that these ECD facilities form part of public schools and have close ties with the Department of Education's administration. With their superior institutional capacity, Grade R facilities in public schools are seen as the benchmark for community-based ECD facilities. Evidence indicates that within public schools, the school governing bodies are well established and have effective methods of accountability to parents.

However, for community-based ECD centres, proper administrative and management systems are lacking. For these centres to meet the minimum standards set by the Department of Social Development, specific processes and structures are required to be in place. However, the financial management of many of the community-based ECD facilities is poor; more than 50% of these centres do not have many of the necessary administrative documents and structures set up.

Funding

The largest portion of ECD centre funding nationwide is derived from parent fees. Government funding for ECD comes mainly from the provincial departments of Social Development and Education. The Department of Social Development in each province provides funding through a subsidy for registered ECD facilities, calculated at R15 per child per day (but varying by province) for those children from birth to four years of age. Only those children whose parents' or caregiver's income falls under a specific level, as assessed by an income means test, qualify for the subsidy. This means that only those ECD facilities that cater for the poorest of families benefit from this subsidy.

The funding and expenditure of various governmental departments and programmes show that funding for ECD facilities through the subsidy has increased over the last decade from R335 million in 2003/2004 to more than R1 billion in 2011/2012. While this increase is encouraging, there are significant disparities across the provinces in terms of the number of centres accessing the subsidy as well as the actual amount they receive, with many ECD centres not receiving any subsidy at all.

The provincial Departments of Social Development also provide funding for ECD, through targeted funding for NPOs aimed at a variety of ECD programmes. These are usually non-centre-based models of ECD provision, such as family outreach programmes, toy libraries, home visiting programmes and informal playgroups.

The Department of Education provides funding for Grade R programmes. The three primary channels of funding are: funding for Grade R in public schools; subsidies for registered community-based Grade R facilities and funding for training fees.

The ECD budget as a percentage of the total education expenditure has increased from 0.7% in 2006/2007 to 2% in 2012/2013. While this increase is encouraging, there are also significant variations in Grade R funding across the provinces, with most of the funding going towards Grade R facilities in public schools.

How government and donors can support the ECD sector in South Africa

With the preceding situation analysis as a basis for advancing the right of young children to quality ECD in South Africa, there are a number of options for government and the donor community to consider in supporting the ECD sector. These follow, in no particular order.

ECD centre infrastructure upgrades

Improvement of the ECD infrastructure through minor and major building upgrades is essential to increase access and improve quality. Infrastructure upgrades will ensure that our youngest and most vulnerable citizens receive a quality early learning programme in an environment that is safe, secure and hygienic.

Proper ECD infrastructure will also enable ECD centres to meet the minimum registration requirements and thus be eligible for the per capita ECD subsidy, which is available from the provincial Education and Social Development Departments. This will in turn increase the likelihood of the ECD centre being financially and educationally sustainable.

Nutrition support

Due to the extraordinarily high prevalence of poverty in South Africa, hunger, malnutrition and food insecurity are significant challenges facing children in communities across the country. Nutrition is a basic physical need that requires urgent attention; since the absence of adequate nutrition greatly affects a child's early development, which can lead to significant, negative adult outcomes such as reduced earning potential. These negative consequences affect children's ability to achieve their full potential, stunting not only the individual child's ability to flourish in adulthood, but collectively limiting the country's potential development.

An intervention in nutrition supplementation is critical and could include:

- school feeding schemes;
- the provision of deficient micronutrients through fortified sachet powders/pap to homes and community-based ECD facilities;
- skills development and training on nutrition; and
- establishing food gardens, allowing ECD centres to grow food for the children.

Education equipment provision

For optimal learning to take place at the ECD centre, it is necessary that sufficient age-appropriate education equipment is available for use by children. Age-appropriate education equipment at the ECD centre must be durable, safe to play with and fun. With proper teacher guidance, the equipment can be used to stimulate children's early learning with a focus on literacy, numeracy and life skills. The training of teachers in how to use education equipment appropriately is essential.

ECD teacher development

To offer an ECD learning programme which is efficient, sustainable and effective in educating and caring for young children, we need to ensure that ECD principals, supervisors, teachers and governing body members are appropriately trained. Teacher training on a wide range of topics, selected as they relate to a specific group of teachers/ practitioners, is essential. Amongst other aspects, this training can include: teaching practice, child development, financial management, fundraising, human resource man-agement and guidance on report-writing and registering with the provincial Departments of Social Development.

South Africa requires significant ECD teacher training and enrichment programmes that focus on the acquisition of essential skills for ECD teachers. These must be implementable over a short period of time and be of significant benefit to young children.

Literacy, numeracy and life skills programmes

There has been an under-emphasis on the development of the basic skills of reading, writing, numeracy and life skills at the early childhood and the formal Foundation phase (Grade R to Grade 3) levels. The very poor results achieved on the South African Annual National Assessments each year and the equally poor results of South African children on Grade 3 and Grade 6 assessments, when compared to other African countries, are indicative of this.

Quality literacy, numeracy and life skills programmes in the first six years of life (pre-Grade 1) are essential for the optimal social and educational development of young children. Such programmes provide children with innovative and interesting ways of acquiring literacy, numeracy and life skills and can also be used to encourage parents to be more involved in their children's early education and development.

Family outreach programmes

The majority of South Africa's children cannot access formal ECD provision (Department of Education 2001a), and as a result they are not exposed to quality early learning programmes prior to entering Grade 1. This means that our poorest children are generally not ready for formal education. These children enter Grade 1 not having experienced even one year of a structured learning programme and are poorly prepared for formal schooling.

In this programme option, family outreach workers partner with parents and caregivers in their homes to provide an early education programme which encourages parent-child interaction and learning through play. These home visits provide support, advice and hands-on, practical guidance and activities on various topics, including: health, nutrition, child safety, discipline, cognitive development, assistance with accessing social assistance grants and making educational toys and resources from recyclable materials.

Integrated ECD programmes

Integrated ECD programmes combine various programme options to serve an entire community. These programmes are comprehensive and provide quality ECD programmes by assisting ECD centres, ECD teachers and families through services that offer support, resources and skills training. Programmes can be structured to specifically and comprehensively meet the needs of local communities.

Funding

Increased national and provincial Social Development and Education Departments budget allocations are urgently required. Current allocation levels are inadequate for scaling-up ECD access and improving the quality of ECD and Grade R. Funding for new programme models, which target families and caregivers at a community and household level, are also needed. Private, donor and humanitarian funding for ECD programmes and services must also be increased.

Research

Quality research can assist the government, the donor community and ECD organisations in providing structured programmes that are more effective, serve those most in need and produce models that are cost-effective and easily replicable. With an investment in research, we can improve ECD programme quality and improve early learning opportunities for our youngest citizens.

Conclusion

There have been considerable improvements in ECD in South Africa since the fall of apartheid. The number of children in Grade R has trebled and the quality has improved slightly. Government expenditure on Grade R has increased three-fold since 2008/2009. The number of ECD centres registered with the national Department of Social Development has increased to 19,500 and there are currently approximately 836,000 children in a registered ECD centre, of which 488,000 (58%) received the ECD subsidy (Dlamini 2012, 1). Many more children are in unregistered ECD centres and no recent survey of ECD provision has been completed. However, it is correct to say that much work is still needed if we want to improve the quality of children's lives in South Africa. Given the critical importance of ECD in combating poverty and inequality, ECD must be an immediate priority for the South African government. Our youngest children deserve nothing less.

Note

1. Grade R is the year before entry into Grade 1 and is the first year of basic education provided to all children in South Africa. Beginning in 2001, compulsory coverage was envisaged for all children by January 2010. When this did not happen, the government revised the target date to January 2014.

References

Atmore, E., L. Van Niekerk, and M. Ashley-Cooper. 2012. Challenges Facing the Early Childhood Development Sector in South Africa. *South African Journal of Childhood Education* 2 (1): 139–158.

Clark, N. L., and W. H. Worger. 2004. *South Africa – The Rise and Fall of Apartheid. Seminar Studies in History.* Harlow: Pearson Education.

Department of Education. 2001a. *The Nationwide Audit of ECD Provisioning in South Africa.* Pretoria: Department of Education.

Department of Education. 2001b. *Education White Paper 5: Meeting the Challenge of Early Childhood Development in South Africa.* Pretoria: Department of Education.

Dlamini, B. 2012. "Keynote Address on the Occasion of the Early Childhood Development (ECD)." Conference at the International Convention Centre, East London, Eastern Cape, March 27.

Duggan, C., J. B. Watkins, and W. A. Walker. 2008. *Nutrition in Pediatrics: Basic Science, Clinical Application.* Hamilton: B.C. Decker.

Human Sciences Research Council. 2009. *Western Cape Department of Social Development 2009 Audit of Early Childhood Development Facility Quality.* Cape Town: Human Sciences Research Council.

Padayachie, R., E. Atmore, L. Biersteker, R. King, J. Matube, S. Muthayan, K. Naidoo, D. Plaatjies, and J. L. Evans. 1994. *Report of the South African Study on Early Childhood Development.* Johannesburg/Washington, DC: Centre for Education Policy Development/World Bank.

South African Social Security Agency. 2012. *Annual Report 2011/2012.* Pretoria: South African Social Security Agency.

Taylor, N. 1989. *Falling at the First Hurdle: Initial Encounters with the Formal System of African Education in South Africa.* EPU Research Report No. 1. Johannesburg: University of the Witwatersrand.

Van Den Berg, O., and T. Vergnani. 1986. *Providing Services for Preschool Children in South Africa.* Cape Town: University of the Western Cape.

Victora, C. G., L. Adair, C. Fall, P. C. Hallal, R. Martorell, L. Richter, and H. S. Sachdev. 2008. "Maternal and Child Undernutrition 2: Consequences for Adult Health and Human Capital." *Lancet* 371 (9609): 340–357. doi:10.1016/S0140-6736(07)61692-4.

Wildeman, R., and N. Mbebetho. 2005. *Reviewing Ten Years of the School Nutrition Programme.* Cape Town: An occasional paper for the Budget Information Service of Idasa.

Trends and tensions: Australian and international research about starting school

Sue Dockett and Bob Perry

School of Education, Research Institute for Professional Practice, Learning and Education, Charles Sturt University, Albury, Australia

This paper details and compares the discernable trends observed in a wide-ranging review of the recent starting school literature in Australia and beyond. More than half of the research reviewed considers children's readiness for school. This research is critiqued through a three-way view of readiness: child readiness, school readiness and support available through the family. Distinctions between transition to school and school readiness are made and the consequences of these are investigated for all key participants in the transition process: children, educators and families. The paper concludes with a critical consideration of tensions in the research around starting school.

Introduction

The significance of the early childhood years for later development and the importance of investing in high-quality early childhood education has promoted a great deal of interest in children's transitions to compulsory schooling. The impact of this interest can be seen in Australia across policy, practice and research in both government and non-government organisations.

At the level of national policy, the Australian government has committed to an early years reform agenda, incorporating the National Quality Framework (Department of Education, Employment and Workplace Relations [DEEWR] 2011) and the first national curriculum framework for early childhood education (DEEWR 2009). Accompanying these frameworks have been commitments to improving educational provision and outcomes for Indigenous children, promoting universal access to early childhood education in the year before school and strengthening the early childhood workforce. At the same time, the first national school curriculum (Australian Curriculum and Reporting Authority [ACARA] 2010) is being developed and will soon be implemented nation-wide.

Across these agendas, the transition to school has assumed educational significance as a potential connection between the two new curricula approaches, and social significance as a means of promoting ongoing, positive engagement with school. For example, a positive start to school education, leading to greater and ongoing connection with school, has been identified as a factor in disrupting cycles of social and economic disadvantage (Council of Australian Governments [COAG] 2009; Smart et al. 2008).

The national implementation of programmes targeting children's school readiness; such as the Home Interaction Programme for Parents and Youngsters (HIPPY; Dean and Leung 2010), and the funding of a population measure of children's readiness through the Australian Early Development Index (AEDI; Centre for Community Child Health [CCCH] and Telethon Institute for Child Health Research 2009) are further evidences of political interest. Underlying these policy approaches is the assumption that 'improved transition to school' leads to 'improved educational, employment, health and well-being outcomes' and that this, in turn, is linked to reducing 'inequalities in outcomes between groups of children' (COAG 2009, 4).

At the state and territory government level, school systems and early childhood organisations interpret Australian government policies in different ways. All Australian states and territories promote the importance of a positive transition to school but adopt different strategies to accomplish such transitions. An example is the Victorian initiative, Transition: A Positive Start to School (Department of Education and Early Childhood Development, Victoria 2012), which incorporates elements of research, policy and practice. In addition, state-based early childhood organisations provide a range of information and guidance for early childhood educators. At local levels, many schools and early childhood organisations have developed transition to school programmes. These vary considerably in terms of participants, programmes, location, length of time and outcomes.

Transition to school has also featured as a priority in the work of several other Australian organisations. Recent initiatives include linking a positive transition to school with children's mental health and well-being (Hirst et al. 2011); discussion papers and policy briefs exploring transition and school readiness (CCCH 2008; Farrar, Goldfeld, and Moore 2007), some with a particular focus on Indigenous children and families (Dockett, Perry, and Kearney 2010; McTurk et al. 2011); and the provision of a range of information for families in order to support a positive start to school.

The current focus on transition to school as a critical element of children's future school engagement and outcomes has emerged in Australia over the past two decades, informed by a range of Australian and international research. Starting around the 1990s, Australian researchers noted local interest in the age of school entry (Gifford 1992), as well as international attention to children's ability to 'settle in' to school (David 1990). This discussion was also informed by the National Education Goals Panel (1991) in the USA, and their focus on children starting school ready to learn. Since this time, there has been a steady increase in research investigating both the transition to school and school readiness. The influence of international issues and research has continued, with increasing interest in developing evidence, policy and practice that both reflects Australian contexts and positions Australia within international education debates.

In the remainder of this paper, we review recent research and identify a number of tensions emerging from the concerted focus on readiness and transition to school. We build on the review of trends in the conceptualisation of transition to school undertaken by Petriwskyj, Thorpe, and Tayler (2005), considering publications produced since this date. We draw only on English-language publications, and note that this provides a limited view of world-wide research. However, this is the research that is most accessible within Australia.

Research trends

The aim of the review is to map current trends in research related to transition to school, including readiness. The primary search strategy drew on PsycINFO and ERIC (Education Resources Information Centre) journal databases for the period 2005–2012. A range of key terms was used in the search, including transition, school, kindergarten, readiness, elementary school, early childhood, Australia and various combinations of these. This search was complemented by reference to commissioned reports, literature reviews, policy briefs and other documents featuring Australian research. The review identified 300 papers published in peer-reviewed journals, 56 of which used Australian data. The remaining articles were primarily North American ($n = 198$), though 46 articles reported research in Asia (11), Europe (13), Scandinavia (8), the UK (7), New Zealand (6) and Africa (1).

Up to three major foci were identified for each relevant paper. In practice, most papers were able to be allocated to one category. Twenty-five and 10 papers, respectively, were categorised as contributing to two or three foci. Frequency counts were the basis of categorisation according to the foci in Table 1.

Readiness

Readiness predominated in the research articles considered, with over 76% (228) of articles addressing some aspect of readiness. This compares with 25% (75) addressing transition. The same predominance is evident in Australian research, with 33 articles

Table 1.   Main foci of research articles exploring starting school, 2005–2012.

Focus	International ($n = 300$)	Australia ($n = 56$)
Readiness – assessment with Early Development Instrument (EDI)/Australian Early Development Index (AEDI)	59	11
Readiness – assessment, other	9	2
Readiness of children with special needs	30	5
Readiness of children living in disadvantage	13	3
Readiness of children with culturally and linguistically diverse backgrounds (CALD)	12	0
Readiness of Aboriginal/Indigenous children	6	4
Readiness of other children	3	1
Preschool and readiness	7	0
Readiness as a predictor of later school success	6	0
Programmes to develop readiness	4	0
Child factors in readiness	23	7
Ready schools	5	0
Curriculum areas and readiness	15	0
Educators' perspectives of readiness	13	1
Evaluation of readiness/transition programmes	23	0
Transition to school – practices and policies	25	6
Perceptions/expectations of parents/educators at transition	24	4
Children's perspectives of transition	10	5
Parent/family practices to support transition/readiness	16	0
Programmes for parents	4	4
Parent/family issues	3	0
Community/neighbourhood	7	1
Other	20	1

(59%) exploring readiness in some way. A substantial number of the articles about readiness have detailed the development, validation and implementation of the Early Development Instrument (EDI), with Australian research reporting the subsequent development and use of the Australian adaptation of the EDI, the Australian Early Development Index (AEDI), and comparison of data from Australia with other countries using the EDI. Special issues of the journals *Social Indicators Research* (Guhn et al. 2011) and *Early Education and Development* (Guhn, Janus, and Hertzman 2007) have featured this research. Relatively few articles have critiqued the EDI/AEDI (Agbenyega 2009; Li, D'Angiulli, and Kendall 2007) and these have questioned the developmental focus and its relevance for culturally and linguistically diverse populations. Such criticism has been rebutted and further research exploring the EDI in diverse contexts, with diverse populations, has been undertaken (Muhajarine, Puchala, and Janus 2011). Several other approaches to assessing readiness have promoted specific child measures (de Lemos 2008; Duncan and Rafter 2005), while others have considered the role of relationships in promoting readiness (Pelletier and Corter 2005).

The readiness status of specific groups of children also features heavily in the research reviewed. Groups identified in the international literature included children with special needs (30 articles), children living in disadvantage (13), children with culturally and linguistically diverse backgrounds (12) and Indigenous children (6). In many cases, children within these groups were considered to be 'less ready' for school than their counterparts from non-marginalised groups. They were deemed to face specific difficulties and/or challenges as they started school and, as a consequence, were described as requiring extra assistance or intervention in order to facilitate a positive start to school (Crosnoe and Cooper 2010; Daley, Munk, and Carlson 2011; Quintero and McIntyre 2011; Smart et al. 2008). In contrast, several Australian studies identified particular concerns related to inconsistent service provision (Dockett, Perry, and Kearney 2011) and the nature of inclusive pedagogy and practice as children started school (Petriwskyj 2010), or questioned current policy and practice agendas and the impact of these for specific groups of children (Taylor 2011). Most of the articles addressing the readiness of Indigenous children were Australian. While all of these acknowledged the relatively limited levels of educational engagement and outcomes from Aboriginal children nationally, a common theme across this research was the questioning of methods for assessing the readiness of Aboriginal children and the implications of using inappropriate measures for such assessment (Dockett, Mason, and Perry 2006; McTurk et al. 2011).

In the international literature, a number of child factors were related to readiness. These included the children's cognitive skills and motivation (Berhenke et al. 2011), and their behaviour (Eivers, Brendgen, and Borge 2010). Several Australian studies examined the knowledge and skills children possessed at the time of starting school (King and Boardman 2006; Wildy and Styles 2008). Connections between children's age and readiness have featured in some research, particularly around the issue of delayed kindergarten entry (Frey 2005). This research identifies initial performance gaps between older and younger children, but also notes that these level-off at middle school (Oshima and Domaleski 2006). While age of school entry has been a consistent issue in policy discussions around starting school (Gifford 1992), there has been relatively little Australian research investigating the role of children's age and readiness. From these few studies, and in keeping with international research, recent Australian studies have identified increasing trends for the practice of delayed school entry among some families

(Edwards, Taylor, and Fiorini 2011) and suggested that delayed school entry has little long-term effect (Martin 2009).

Reports of readiness that considered the role of preschool education in promoting children's readiness were absent from the Australian research reviewed. Four of the seven international studies that reported the generally positive effect of preschool attendance on children's readiness were from the USA (for example, Howes et al. 2008). The remaining three articles reported research in Turkey, Slovenia and China, indicating that focus on readiness is not confined to the English-speaking world.

Both Canadian and US research were reported in studies exploring connections between children's readiness and later academic and/or social outcomes (Sabol and Pianta 2012). North American research also featured in the description and/or evaluation of programmes designed to promote children's readiness. Several of the programmes reported were US state-based initiatives (Gormley and Gayer 2005), or evaluation studies (Clark and Zygmunt-Fillwalk 2008). The notion of ready schools that was highlighted by the National Education Goals Panel (1997) has also been discussed (Curtis and Simons 2008).

The contribution of literacy and numeracy to readiness was highlighted internationally (Fuchs et al. 2010; Yangin 2009), as was the reciprocal relationship between readiness and Australian children's early literacy and numeracy achievement (Murray and Harrison 2011). The role of arts and music curricula in boosting children's readiness for school was also explored (Phillips et al. 2010).

Studies of teacher beliefs or perceptions (Gill, Winters, and Friedman 2006), particularly about what constituted children's school readiness or the experiences most likely to prepare children for school (Lara-Cinisomo et al. 2009) were coded into the category of educators' perspectives. In several studies, these beliefs or perceptions were compared with those of parents, school administrators or, on rare occasions, children. The only Australian study explored the readiness perspectives of first-year-of-school teachers in one school, concluding that these teachers demonstrated a broad definition of readiness, incorporating child, family, community and school factors (Noel 2010).

Readiness assumed a great deal of importance in the Australian and international literature. The focus on assessing children's readiness has resulted in the development of a range of measures – including individual child and population measures – and these have been the subject of validation, application and evaluation. Some of these measures generate extensive data bases (such as the EDI/AEDI). Others draw on existing data, such as the USA studies using the Early Childhood Longitudinal Study-Kindergarten (ECLS-K), or Head Start programme data. Apart from the studies reporting the AEDI, much of the Australian research has involved smaller-scale, often qualitative, research. Considerable attention has been directed towards the readiness of children described as marginalised. Indeed, in their review of research, Rosier and McDonald (2011, 1) conclude that 'in Australia, the transition to school is likely to be more challenging for children from financially disadvantaged families, Indigenous families, families with children who have a disability and culturally and linguistically diverse (CALD) families', largely because of their levels of readiness. While there is some argument for a model of readiness based on relationships (Mashburn and Pianta 2006) that considers child, family, school and community factors (Dockett and Perry 2009), there remains a strong focus on the preparedness of individual children to start school.

Transition

Of the 65 articles primarily addressing transition, 38% (25) outlined transition practices and policies, reflecting a similar focus to that identified by Petriwskyj et al. (2005). Six Australian studies described specific transition programmes or practices (for example, Binstadt 2010; Margetts 2007). While reports of local transition practices are also evident in the international literature (Corsaro and Molinari 2008; Fisher 2011), larger-scale studies examining the use of transition practices and children's adjustment as well as academic outcomes also feature (Ahtola et al. 2011; Schulting, Malone, and Dodge 2005). Across these studies, there is consensus that transition practices can have a positive impact on children's adjustment to school, with greater effect noted when children participate in more, rather than fewer, transition practices.

The expectations of those involved in transition to school were explored in 24 studies. Reports of parent (Sanavagarapu and Perry 2005) and teacher expectations (Barblett et al. 2011; Gill, Winters, and Friedman 2006), and comparisons of these perspectives (Mirkhil 2010; Petrakos 2011), conclude that parents and teachers recognise the importance of working together to promote a positive start to school, while also noting that this does not always happen. The importance of home-school communication is also highlighted in other research (Rimm-Kaufman and Pianta 2005).

Five Australian studies reported children's perspectives of transition. These investigations recognise that young children are capable and competent narrators of their experiences and that much can be gained from the perspectives of those most directly involved in the transition to school (Jackson and Cartmel 2010; MacDonald 2009). In some instances, recognition of children's perspectives has led to changes in transition practices (Perry and Dockett 2011).

When compared with research on readiness, transition research was more likely to report small-scale, qualitative studies, detailing transition practices or programmes and/or considering the perspectives of a range of stakeholders. A number of these were descriptive or evaluative studies. The aim of many transition programmes was described as 'easing' or 'smoothing' the transition process, suggesting that the start to school was inherently challenging, particularly for children who were considered disadvantaged.

Parents, families and communities

Research examining parent, family and community issues as children start school was reported in 30 articles (10%). Five of these used Australian data. Apart from parents' beliefs about transition, which were considered above, parent behaviours and/or practices constituted the most common feature of this research. The stability of relationships within families (Cooper et al. 2011), parenting style (Walker and MacPhee 2011), parental attitudes and beliefs (Joe and Davis 2009), parents' own recollections and experiences of school (Miller, Dilworth-Bart, and Hane 2011; Turunen 2012), and their involvement in education (Crosnoe and Cooper 2010), all contribute to children's experiences of starting school. The nature of the home learning environment (Melhuish et al. 2008) and preparation activities (Quintero and McIntyre 2011), also are influential. The importance of the family context – including the neighbourhood or community in which families are located – is also noted as a contributing factor to children's transition to school (Nettles, Caughy, and O'Campo 2008).

Transition to school is also recognised as a time of potential stress for families (DeCaro and Worthman 2011; Griebel and Niesel 2009). This is the impetus for

Australian studies that report the development of parenting programmes with specific elements supporting parents as they manage the transition to school. Three programmes – the Pathways to Prevention programme (Freiberg et al. 2005), Transition to Primary School Parent Programme (Giallo et al. 2010) and Triple P – Positive Parenting Programme (Sanders et al. 2008) operate on the principle that supporting parents and enhancing their skills to manage interactions with their children, as well as schools, builds their capacity to support the children and promote a positive start to school.

The research trends identified in this review suggest that even when the terminology of transition is used, there remains an underlying focus on readiness, particularly children's readiness for school. A great deal of research attention has been directed towards the development and validation of measures to assess readiness, both at the individual and the population level. Less attention has been paid to measures examining the readiness of schools or educators. Recognition that specific groups of children may face significant challenges as they start school features strongly in the research. Australian research reflects these same trends. However, it also directs attention to the perspectives of those involved in transition, including children, as well as the principle of strengthening parent support and parenting as children start school.

Research tensions

The research reviewed also suggests a number of tensions. These are reported below as questions, with the aim of provoking discussion, rather than offering answers.

What is the role of readiness in transition?

The terms 'readiness' and 'transition' are often used together, yet, can be interpreted to mean many different things. In the research reviewed, the term 'readiness' is often used to describe characteristics of individual children or populations. While broad definitions of readiness have been promoted (Ackerman and Barnett 2005), there remains a focus on children's readiness, rather than on ready schools, families or communities.

With the prevalence of the focus on children's readiness, it is possible to consider children ready, or unready, for school. Coupled with the identification of specific groups as likely to experience challenges when starting school, there is the potential for children who have special needs, live in disadvantaged circumstances, are Indigenous or have diverse cultural and linguistic backgrounds to be considered unready. This situation can be exacerbated by the ways in which readiness is assessed and compounded by the nature of early school assessment.

The broader concept of 'transition' is usually applied to collections of practices or programmes. Often the focus of these activities is to build both familiarity and relationships around school. Transition programmes are usually contextually bound, though there are practices that are common to many programmes. While the nature of transition programmes varies considerably, they tend to extend over time rather than focus on the first day of school, reflecting the 'trend towards more complex under-standings of transitions emphasising continuity of children's experiences, partnerships with stakeholders and systems coherence, across extended time periods' (Petriwskyj et al. 2005, 1).

The role of readiness within transition programmes remains unclear, as does the contribution of transition programmes to perceptions of readiness. However, there is concern that focusing on narrow definitions of school readiness – typically involving academic skills – is contrary to the traditional holistic focus on early childhood programmes and may result in the pushing down of academic curriculum into the early childhood years (Centre for Equity and Innovation in Early Childhood 2008).

What counts as evidence to support evidence-based policy and practice?

A feature of much the US research relating to readiness is the use of large-scale data bases. As other countries embrace large-scale longitudinal studies – such as the Growing Up series of projects in Australia, New Zealand, Scotland and Ireland, and similar European studies – and as countries introduce population measures of readiness based on the EDI, the stage is set for even greater investigation of readiness in specific contexts, for specific groups and over time. In countries that operate regular national testing regimes, there is also the potential for data linkages. For example, in Australia, there is the potential for linkages between AEDI data, data from the Longitudinal Study of Australian Children (LSAC; Australian Institute of Family Studies 2012) and from the National Assessment Programme – Literacy and Numeracy (NAPLAN; ACARA 2012). Analysis of these linked data-sets can provide opportunities for sophisticated statistical analyses of quite specific research questions, and can contribute a range of evidence about specific populations. However, secondary data analysis also behoves questioning of the original sampling and purposes of data collection, recognising that the existing data-sets provide answers to some, but not all, research questions (Hussein 2011).

Smaller-scale, qualitative studies do not generate the explanatory power or generalisability of large-scale studies. However, they do contribute a great deal to our understanding of the experiences and expectations of those involved in transition and serve to remind us all that individuals, communities and contexts make a difference in all human endeavours. They also serve to remind us that there are multiple transitions, as no two children experience transition to school in exactly the same way: for each child, the transition to school is unique.

What is the connection between a positive start to school and educational outcomes?

It is clear that starting school is an issue that extends well beyond the educational community. In addition to educational journals, research reviewed was reported in economic, social policy, medical, psychology and family forums. One consequence is that a positive start to school is promoted as having a number of potential benefits in multiple areas – somewhat akin to the argument for investing in early childhood education. The existing research evidence does indicate that there are long-term implications from a positive start to school, across both academic and social outcomes (Entwisle and Alexander 1998). However, positioning a positive school start as a potential inoculation against future challenges could mean that later events are ignored or not supported. For example, some children will have a less than ideal start to school, yet, experience early school education that is supportive and challenging, and that promotes positive outcomes. Similarly, limited outcomes may be demonstrated by children who experience a positive transition to school, followed by a disengaging and non-supportive early school environment. In short, while the transition to school is important, so too is what happens once children are at school. Indeed, it is possible to argue that school readiness develops as children experience school and manage the various contexts and demands they encounter there. This view posits that school and classroom practices, as well as the context of school, shape experiences of school (Peters 2010).

What is the role of early childhood education in the transition to school?

Across much of the literature, there is support for the notion that participation in early childhood education settings facilitates a positive start to school. The reasons for this vary, but include opportunities afforded by these settings to engage in a range of preparatory social and academic activities and to experience new learning environments. While it is acknowledged that the quality of prior-to-school services is important in promoting a positive transition to school (Sylva et al. 2007), there appears to be the belief that 'attendance at early childhood education and care services is important for a successful transition to school' (Rosier and McDonald 2011, 3). This is particularly the case for children considered disadvantaged in some way. While the benefits of high-quality early childhood education have been reported widely (Sylva et al. 2007), the assumption that a successful transition to school is linked to participation in early childhood education leads to the corollary that those children who do not participate in early childhood education will have a problematic transition.

Should we promote seamless and smooth transitions?

The aim of many transition programmes was described as 'easing' or 'smoothing' the transition process, sometimes with the aim of promoting continuity between settings such as home or early childhood education and school. One way to promote continuity would be to have common curricula in the prior-to-school and early school years. However, any such move would be contested strongly by both sectors (Petriwskyj et al. 2005). Recent discussions argue for recognition of the differences across settings, accompanied by the provision of appropriate support to enable all involved (children, parents and educators) to navigate the challenges (Peters 2010).

There is consistent research evidence that children (and their families) encounter a number of changes as children start school. Marked discontinuities are reported between home, prior-to-school setting and school, notably across physical, social and philosophical dimensions (Fabian 2001). Several studies highlight these differences and call for greater continuity, particularly across prior-to-school and school contexts. However, an alternative approach acknowledges the changes encountered during the transition to school and recognises the strengths of children, families and communities as they navigate change and discontinuity. Appropriate support remains important, but this approach questions the assumptions that the transition to school is necessarily a time of challenge and problems for all, and that this is particularly the case for children and families from marginalised groups. In promoting a seamless approach to transition, we run the risk of removing many of the challenges and changes that children expect to encounter when they start school. A different question might be 'How do we promote both continuity and change as children start school?', recognising that both elements are integral to successful and positive transitions.

Is the transition to school a linear process?

There is considerable evidence that children have many different opportunities for learning, as well as access to different resources and experiences before school (Melhuish et al. 2008). Yet, a number of transition programmes and approaches to readiness imply that children have had similar experiences and opportunities and will build on these in particular ways as they make the transition to school.

The diversity of children's experiences is often not captured in programmes or practices which regard transition as a series of specific, 'discernable events, experienced in a linear sequence' (Ecclestone 2009, 19) and with predictable patterns and normative expectations. Considering transition to school as a linear process can influence decisions about what constitutes a successful transition and who is likely to make this. Alternative approaches to transition emphasise the processes of transition, particularly related to relationship-building, rather than the practices (Petriwskyj et al. 2005).

Conclusion

Analysis of the wealth of research investigating children's transition to school reveals a number of trends and tensions. While there seems to be a general commitment to promoting positive transitions to school for children, conceptualisations of transition – its nature, purpose and impact – differ. Far from being negative, this reflects the importance of varying contexts and approaches as well as multiple experiences of transition. However, one consequence of this is that the research evidence supporting particular approaches to transition is often descriptive or evaluative. This contrasts with much of the readiness research. While readiness itself remains a contested term, the research corpus identifies a number of factors and, from this, generates a set of conditions under which children are likely to experience a positive start to school.

The contrasting approaches contribute to the tensions identified in this paper. A focus on readiness, particularly on the readiness attributes of children, has the potential to narrow the scope of transition programmes, while focus on broad conceptualisations of readiness that incorporate child, family, school and community factors can, in turn, expand the focus of transition programmes and practices.

Recognising the diversity of experiences and backgrounds of children and their families is an important element of promoting a positive start to school. This can be hard to achieve if most attention is directed towards assessing children's skills in literacy and numeracy. It can be particularly hard if it is accompanied by expectations that children from marginalised groups have neither the skills nor the experiences to make the most of educational opportunities.

The current levels of social, political and educational interest in transition to school provide opportunities to boost recognition of the importance of high-quality early childhood experiences for all children. At the same time, this interest can also increase the pressure to identify 'what works'. Evidence from effective transition experiences suggests that there is no single best model. Rather, research emphasises the important of contextually and culturally relevant approaches that focus on relationship-building among all of those involved in the transition to school. At a time when we are becoming more aware of the complexity of transition, we need to be wary of attempts to simplify it by reducing it to a series of practices or actions.

In the past decade, a great deal of research has contributed to understandings of children's transition to school. In recognising this extensive range of work, we note consistencies and challenges, with the aim of providing guidance for future research and provoking discussion of its implications.

References

Ackerman, D., and W. Barnett. 2005. *Prepared for Kindergarten: What Does Readiness Mean?* NIEER Policy Report. http://nieer.org/resources/policyreports/report5.pdf.

Agbenyega, J. S. 2009. "The Australian Early Development Index, Who Does it Measure: Piaget or Vygotsky's Child?" *Australian Journal of Early Childhood* 34 (2): 31–37.

Ahtola, A., G. Silinskas, P.-L. Poikonen, M. Kontoniemi, P. Niemi, and J.-E. Nurmi 2011. "Transition to Formal Schooling: Do Transition Practices Matter for Academic Performance?" *Early Childhood Research Quarterly* 26 (3): 295–302. doi:10.1016/j.ecresq.2010.12.002.

Australian Curriculum and Assessment Reporting Authority (ACARA). 2010. Australian Curriculum, Canberra. http://www.australiancurriculum.edu.au/.

Australian Curriculum and Assessment Reporting Authority (ACARA). 2012. NAPLAN. www.naplan.edu.au.

Australian Institute of Family Studies. 2012. *Growing Up in Australia: The Longitudinal Study of Australian Children.* www.aifs.gov.au/growingup/.

Barblett, L., C. Barratt-Pugh, P. Kilgallon, and C. Maloney. 2011. "Transition from Long Day Care to Kindergarten: Continuity or Not?" *Australasian Journal of Early Childhood* 36 (2): 42–50.

Berhenke, A., A. L. Miller, E. Brown, R. Seifer, and S. Dickstein. 2011. "Observed Emotional and Behavioural Indicators of Motivation Predict School Readiness in Head Start Graduates." *Early Childhood Research Quarterly* 26 (4): 430–441. doi:10.1016/j.ecresq.2011.04.001.

Binstadt, M. 2010. "Ready Together – Transition to School Programme: Effecting Positive Outcomes for Children and Their Families in the Inala to Ipswich Area." *International Journal of Transitions in Childhood* 4: 37–44. https://extranet.education.unimelb.edu.au/LED/tec/journal_vol4.shtml.

Centre for Community Child Health (CCCH). 2008. *Rethinking the Transition to School: Linking Schools and Early Years Services.* Policy Brief no. 11. www.rch.org.au/emplibrary/ccch/PB10_Transition_to_School.pdf.

Centre for Community Child Health and Telethon Institute for Child Health Research. 2009. *A Snapshot of Early Childhood Development in Australia Australian Early Development Index (AEDI) National Report.* Canberra: DEEWR. www.rch.org.au/aedi/media/Snapshot_of_Early_-Childhood_DevelopmentinAustralia_AEDI_National_Report.pdf.

Centre for Equity and Innovation in Early Childhood. 2008. "Transition: A Positive Start to School" (Literature Review). http://www.eduweb.vic.gov.au/edulibrary/public/earlychildhood/learning/transitionliteraturereview.pdf.

Clark, P., and E. Zygmunt-Fillwalk. 2008. "Ensuring Readiness through Successful Transition to Kindergarten: The Indiana Ready Schools Initiative." *Childhood Education* 84 (5): 287–293. doi:10.1080/00094056.2008.10523026.

Cooper, C. E., C. A. Osborne, A. N. Beck, and S. S. McLanahan. 2011. "Partnership Instability, School Readiness and Gender Disparities." *Sociology of Education* 84 (3): 246–259. doi:10.1177/0038040711402361.

Corsaro, W., and L. Molinari. 2008. "Policy and Practice in Italian Children's Transition from Preschool to Elementary School." *Research in Comparative and International Education* 3 (3): 250–268. doi:10.2304/rcie.2008.3.3.250.

Council of Australian Governments (COAG). 2009. *Investing in the Early Years – A National Early Childhood Development Strategy.* http://acecqa.gov.au/storage/national_ECD_strategy.pdf.

Crosnoe, R., and C. E. Cooper. 2010. "Economically Disadvantaged Children's Transitions into Elementary School: Linking Family Processes, School Contexts, and Educational Policy." *American Educational Research Journal* 47 (2): 258–291. doi:10.3102/0002831209351564.

Curtis, P. A., and K. A. Simons. 2008. "Pathways to Ready Schools." *Child and Adolescent Social Work Journal* 25 (3): 171–183. doi:10.1007/s10560-008-0119-z.

Daley, T. C., T. Munk, and E. Carlson. 2011. "A National Study of Kindergarten Transition Practice for Children with Disabilities." *Early Childhood Research Quarterly* 26 (4): 409–419. doi:10.1016/j.ecresq.2010.11.001.

David, T. 1990. *Under Five – Under-Educated?* Philadelphia: Open University Press.

Dean, S., and C. Leung. 2010. "Nine Years of Early Intervention Research: The Effectiveness of the Home Interaction Programme for Parents and Youngsters (HIPPY) in Australia." *Learning Difficulties Australia Bulletin* 42 (1): 14–18. doi:10.1080/00094056.2008.10523026.

de Lemos, M. 2008. "Assessing Development and Readiness for School across Different Cultural and Language Groups." *Australian Journal of Learning Difficulties* 13 (2): 73–98. doi:10.1080/19404150802380597.

DeCaro, J. A., and C. M. Worthman. 2011. "Changing Family Routines at Kindergarten Entry Predict Biomarkers of Parental Stress." *International Journal of Behavioural Development* 35 (5): 441–448. doi:10.1177/0165025411406853.

Department of Education and Early Childhood Development, Victoria. 2012. *Transition to School.* http://www.education.vic.gov.au/earlylearning/transitionschool/.

Department of Education Employment and Workforce Relations (DEEWR). 2009. *Belonging, Being, Becoming: The Early Years Learning Framework for Australia.* http://www.deewr.gov.au/EarlyChildhood/Policy_Agenda/Quality/Pages/EarlyYearsLearningFramework.aspx.

Department of Education Employment and Workforce Relations (DEEWR). 2011. National quality framework. http://www.deewr.gov.au/Earlychildhood/Policy_Agenda/Quality/Pages/home.aspx.

Dockett, S., T. Mason, and B. Perry. 2006. "Successful Transition to School for Australian Aboriginal Children." *Childhood Education* 82 (3): 139–144. doi:10.1080/00094056.2006.10521365.

Dockett, S., and B. Perry. 2009. "Readiness for School: A Relational Construct." *Australasian Journal of Early Childhood* 34 (1): 20–27.

Dockett, S., B. Perry, and E. Kearney. 2010. *School Readiness: What Does it Mean for Indigenous Children, Families, Schools and Communities?* Canberra: Australian Institute of Health and Welfare. http://www.aihw.gov.au/closingthegap/documents/issues_papers/ctg-ip02.pdf.

Dockett, S., B. Perry, and E. Kearney. 2011. "Starting School with Special Needs: Issues for Families with Complex Support Needs as Their Children Start School." *Exceptionality Education International* 21 (2): 45–61.

Duncan, J., and E. M. Rafter 2005. "Concurrent and Predictive Validity of the Phelps Kindergarten Readiness Scale-II." *Psychology in the Schools* 42 (4): 355–359. doi:10.1002/pits.20096.

Ecclestone, K. 2009. "Lost and Found in Transition: Educational Implications of Concerns about 'Identity', 'Agency' and 'Structure'." In *Researching Transitions in Lifelong Learning* edited by J. Field, J. Gallacher, and R. Ingram, 9–27. London: Routledge.

Edwards, B., M. Taylor, and M. Fiorini. 2011. "Who Gets the 'Gift of Time' in Australia? Exploring Delayed Primary School Entry." *Australian Review of Public Affairs* 10 (1): 41–60. http://www.australianreview.net/journal/v10/n1/edwards_etal.html.

Eivers, A. R., M. Brendgen, and A. I. H. Borge. 2010. "Stability and Change in Prosocial and Antisocial Behaviour across the Transition to School: Teacher and Peer Perspectives." *Early Education and Development* 21 (6): 843–864. doi:10.1080/10409280903390684.

Entwisle, D. R., and K. L. Alexander. 1998. "Facilitating the Transition to First Grade: The Nature of Transition and Research on Factors Affecting It." *The Elementary School Journal* 98 (4): 351–364. doi:10.1086/461901.

Fabian, H. 2001. *Children Starting School.* London: David Fulton.

Farrar, E., S. Goldfeld, and T. Moore. 2007. *School Readiness (ARACY Topical Paper).* West Perth, Western Australia: Australian Research Alliance for Children and Youth.

Fisher, J. 2011. "Building on the Early Years Foundation Stage: Developing Good Practice for Transition into Key Stage 1." *Early Years* 31 (1): 31–42. doi:10.1080/09575146.2010.512557.

Freiberg, K., R. Homel, S. Batchelor, A. Carr, I. Hay, G. Elias, R. Teague, and C. Lamb. 2005. "Creating Pathways to Participation: A Community-based Developmental Prevention Project in Australia." *Children and Society* 19 (2): 144–157. doi:10.1002/chi.867.

Frey, N. 2005. "Retention, Social Promotion and Academic Redshirting: What Do We Know and Need to Know?" *Remedial and Special Education* 26 (6): 332–346. doi:10.1177/07419325050260060401.

Fuchs, L. S., D. C. Geary, D. L. Compton, D. Fuchs, C. L. Hamlet, and J. Bryant. 2010. "The Contributions of Numerosity and Domain-general Abilities to School Readiness." *Child Development* 81 (5): 1520–1533. doi:10.1111/j.1467-8624.2010.01489.x.

Giallo, R., K. Treyvaud, J. Matthews, and M. Kienhuis. 2010. "Making the Transition to Primary School: An Evaluation of a Transition Programme for Parents." *Australian Journal of Educational and Developmental Psychology* 10: 1–17. http://www.newcastle.edu.au/Resources/Research%20Centres/SORTI/Journals/AJEDP/Vol%2010/V10_giallo_et_al.pdf.

Gifford, J. 1992. *A Stitch in Time: Strengthening the First Years of School.* Canberra: Australian Government.

Gill, S., D. Winters, and D. S. Friedman. 2006. "Educators' Views of Pre-kindergarten and Kindergarten Readiness and Transition Practices." *Contemporary Issues in Early Childhood* 7 (3): 213–227. doi:10.2304/ciec.2006.7.3.213.

Gormley, W., and T. Gayer. 2005. "Promoting School Readiness in Oklahoma." *Journal of Human Resources* 40 (3): 533–558. http://ideas.repec.org/a/uwp/jhriss/v40y2005i2p533-558.html.

Griebel, W., and R. Niesel. 2009. "A Developmental Psychology Perspective in Germany: Co-construction of Transitions between Family and Education Systems by the Child, Parents and Pedagogues." *Early Years* 29 (1): 59–68. doi:10.1080/09575140802652230.

Guhn, M., M. Janus, and C. Hertzman. 2007. "Special Issue: The Early Development Instrument." *Early Education and Development* 18 (3): 369–374. doi:10.1080/10409280701610622.

Guhn, M., B. D. Zumbo, M. Janus, and C. Hertzman. 2011. "Opening Remarks to the Special Issue on Validation Theory and Research for a Population-Level Measure of Children's Development, Wellbeing, and School Readiness." *Social Indicators Research* 103 (2): 179–181. doi:10.1007/s11205-011-9840-7.

Hirst, M., N. Jervis, K. Visagie, V. Sojo, and S. Cavanagh. 2011. *Transition to Primary School: A Review of the Literature.* Canberra: Commonwealth of Australia.

Howes, C., M. Burchinal, R. Pianta, D. Bryant, D. Early, R. Clifford, and O. Barbarin. 2008. "Ready to Learn? Children's Pre-academic Achievement in Pre-kindergarten Programmes." *Early Childhood Research Quarterly* 23 (1): 27–50. doi:10.1016/j.ecresq.2007.05.002.

Hussein, S. 2011. *The Use of 'Large-Scale Datasets' in UK Social Care Research.* London: School for Social Care Research. http://www2.lse.ac.uk/LSEHealthAndSocialCare/pdf/SSCR%20Methods%20Review_5.pdf.

Jackson, A., and J. Cartmel. 2010. "Listening to Children's Experience of Starting School in an Area of Socio-economic Disadvantage." *International Journal of Transitions in Childhood* 4: 13–25. https://extranet.education.unimelb.edu.au/LED/tec/journal_vol4.shtml.

Taylor, A. J. 2011. "Coming, Ready or Not: Aboriginal Children's Transition to School in Urban Australia and the Policy Push." *International Journal of Early Years Education* 19 (2): 145–161. doi:10.1080/09669760.2011.602593.

Joe, E., and J. Davis. 2009. "Parental Influence, School Readiness and Early Academic Achievement of African American Boys." *The Journal of Negro Education* 78 (3): 260–276, 362–363. http://www.jstor.org/stable/25608745.

King, P., and M. Boardman. 2006. "What Personal/Social Skills are Important for Young Children Commencing Kindergarten? Exploring Teachers' and Parents' Insights." *Australian Journal of Early Childhood* 31 (3): 15–21.

Lara-Cinisomo, S., A. Fuligni, L. Daugherty, C. Howes, and L. Karoly. 2009. "A Qualitative Study of Early Childhood Educators' Beliefs about Key Preschool Classroom Experiences." *Early Childhood Research and Practice* 11 (1): 1–11. http://ecrp.uiuc.edu/v11n1/lara.html.

Li, J., A. D'Angiulli, and G. E. Kendall. 2007. "The Early Development Index and Children from Culturally and Linguistically Diverse Backgrounds." *Early Years* 27 (3): 221–235. doi:10.1080/09575140701594384.

MacDonald, A. 2009. "Drawing Stories: The Power of Children's Drawings to Communicate the Lived Experience of Starting School." *Australasian Journal of Early Childhood* 34 (3): 40–49.

Margetts, K. 2007. "Preparing Children for School – Benefits and Privileges." *Australian Journal of Early Childhood* 32 (2): 43–50.

Martin, A. J. 2009. "Age Appropriateness and Motivation, Engagement and Performance in High School: Effects of Age-within-cohort, Grade Retention and Delayed School Entry." *Journal of Educational Psychology* 101 (1): 101–114. doi:10.1037/a0013100.

Mashburn, A. J., and R. C. Pianta 2006. "Social Relationships and School Readiness." *Early Education and Development* 17(1): 151–176. doi:10.1207/s15566935eed1701_7.

McTurk, N., T. Lea, G. Nutton, and J. Carpetis. 2011. "Defining and Assessing the School Readiness of Indigenous Australian Children." *Australasian Journal of Early Childhood* 36 (1): 69–76.

Melhuish, E., K. Sylva, P. Sammons, I. Siraj-Blatchford, B. Taggart, and M. Phan. 2008. "Effects of the Home Learning Environment and Preschool Centre Experience upon Literacy and Numeracy Development in Early Primary School." *Journal of Social Issues* 64 (1): 95–114. doi:10.1111/j.1540-4560.2008.00550.x.

Miller, K., J. Dilworth-Bart, and A. Hane. 2011. "Maternal Recollections of Schooling and Children's School Preparation." *School Community Journal* 21 (2): 161–184. http://www.adi.org/journal/2011fw/millerDilworth-BartHaneFall2011.pdf.

Mirkhil, M. 2010. "Important Ingredients for a Successful Transition to School." *International Research in Early Childhood Education* 1 (1): 60–70. http://education.monash.edu.au/research/irecejournal/issues/2010/.

Muhajarine, N., C. Puchala, and M. Janus. 2011. "Does the EDI Equivalently Measure Facets of School Readiness for Aboriginal and Non-Aboriginal Children?" *Social Indicators Research* 103 (2): 299–314. doi:10.1007/s11205-011-9847-0.

Murray, E., and L. J. Harrison. 2011. "The Influence of Being Ready to Learn on Children's Early School Literacy and Numeracy Achievement." *Educational Psychology* 31 (5): 529–545. doi:10.1080/01443410.2011.573771.

National Education Goals Panel. 1991. *The National Education Goals Report.* Washington, DC: Author.

National Education Goals Panel. 1997. *Getting a Good Start in School.* Washington, DC: Author.

Nettles, S. M., M. O. Caughy, and P. J. O'Campo. 2008. "School Adjustment in the Early Grades: Toward an Integrated Model of Neighbourhood, Parental and Child Processes." *Review of Educational Research* 78 (1): 3–32. doi:10.3102/0034654307309917.

Noel, A. 2010. "Perceptions of School Readiness in One Queensland Primary School." *Australasian Journal of Early Childhood* 35 (2): 28–35.

Oshima, T. C., and C. S. Domaleski. 2006. "Academic Performance Gap between Summer-birthday and Fall-birthday Children in Grades K -8." *Journal of Educational Research* 99 (4): 212–217. doi:10.3200/JOER.99.4.212-217.

Pelletier, J., and C. Corter. 2005. "Design, Implementation and Outcomes of a School Readiness Programme for Diverse Families." *School Community Journal* 15 (1): 89–116. http://www.adi.org/journal/ss05/Pelletier%20&%20Corter.pdf.

Perry, B., and S. Dockett. 2011. "How 'Bout We Have a Celebration!': Advice from Children on Starting School." *European Early Childhood Education Research Journal* 19 (3): 373–386. doi:10.1080/1350293X.2011.597969.

Peters, S. 2010. "Literature Review: Transition from Early Childhood Education to School." Ministry of Education, New Zealand. www.educationcounts.govt.nz/publications

Petrakos, H. 2011. "Parents' and Teachers' Perceptions of Transition Practices in Kindergarten." *Exceptionality Education International* 21 (2): 62–73.

Petriwskyj, A. 2010. "Diversity and Inclusion in the Early Years." *International Journal of Inclusive Education* 14 (2): 195–212. doi:10.1080/13603110802504515.

Petriwskyj, A., K. Thorpe, and C. Tayler. 2005. "Trends in the Construction of Transition to School in Three Western Regions, 1990–2004." *International Journal of Early Years Education* 13 (1): 55–69. doi:10.1080/09669760500048360.

Phillips, R. D., R. L. Gorton, P. Pinciotti, and A. Sachdev. 2010. "Promising Findings on Preschoolers' Emergent Literacy and School Readiness in Arts-integrated Early Childhood Settings." *Early Childhood Education Journal* 38 (2): 111–122. doi:10.1007/s10643-010-0397-x.

Quintero, N., and L. L. McIntyre. 2011. "Kindergarten Transition Preparation: A Comparison of Teacher and Parent Practices for Children with Autism and Other Developmental Disabilities." *Early Childhood Education Journal* 38 (6): 411–420. doi:10.1007/s10643-010-0427-8.

Rimm-Kaufman, S. E., and R. C. Pianta. 2005. "Family-school Communication in Preschool and Kindergarten in the Context of a Relationship-enhancing Intervention." *Early Education and Development* 16 (3): 287–316. doi:10.1207/s15566935eed1603_1.

Rosier, K., and M. McDonald. 2011. *Promoting Positive Education and Care Transitions for Children.* Melbourne: Australian Institute of Family Studies. http://www.aifs.gov.au/cafca/pubs/sheets/rs/rs5.html.

Sabol, T. J., and R. C. Pianta. 2012. "Patterns of School Readiness Forecast Achievement and Socioemotional Development at the End of Elementary School." *Child Development* 83 (1): 282–299. doi:10.1111/j.1467-8624.2011.01678.x.

Sanavagarapu, P., and B. Perry. 2005. "Concerns and Expectations of Bangladeshi Parents as Their Children Start School." *Australian Journal of Early Childhood* 30 (3): 45–51.

Sanders, M. R., A. Ralph, K. Sofronoff, P. Gardiner, R. Thompson, S. Dwyer, and K. Bidwell. 2008. "'Every family': A Population Approach to Reducing Behavioural and Emotional Problems in Children Making the Transition to School." *Journal of Primary Prevention* 29 (3): 197–222. doi:10.1007/s10935-008-0139-7.

Schulting, A. B., P. S. Malone, and K. A. Dodge 2005. "The Effect of School-based Kindergarten Transition Policies and Practices on Child Academic Outcomes." *Developmental Psychology* 41 (6): 860–871. doi:10.1037/0012-1649.41.6.860.

Smart, D., A. Sanson, J. Baxter, B. Edwards, and A. Hayes. 2008. *Home-to-school Transitions for Financially Disadvantaged Children.* http://www.thesmithfamily.com.au/webdata/resources/files/HometoSchool_FullReport_WEB.pdf.

Sylva, K., E. Melhuish, P. Sammons, I. Siraj-Blatchford, and B. Taggart. 2007. *Promoting Equality in the Early Years.* www.ioe.ac.uk/projects/eppe.

Turunen, T. A. 2012. "Memories about Starting School: What is Remembered after Decades?" *Scandinavian Journal of Educational Research* 56 (1): 69–84. doi:10.1080/00313831.2011.567397.

Walker, A. K., and D. MacPhee 2011. "How Home Gets to School: Parental Control Strategies Predict Children's School Readiness." *Early Childhood Research Quarterly* 26 (3): 355–364. doi:10.1016/j.ecresq.2011.02.001.

Wildy, H., and I. Styles. 2008. "Measuring What Students Entering School Know and Can Do: PIPS Australian 2006–2007." *Australian Journal of Early Childhood* 33 (4): 43–52.

Yangin, B. 2009. "The Relationship between Readiness and Reading and Writing Performances." *Hacettepe University Journal of Education* 36: 316–326.

Educational innovation between freedom and fixation: the cultural-political construction of innovations in early childhood education in the Netherlands

Bert van Oers

Department Theory and Research in Education, VU University Amsterdam, Amsterdam, The Netherlands

As in many countries, in the Netherlands, governmental policy regulates the decisions of schools and care providers that concern and the control of the quality of education and care. Article 23 of the Dutch Constitution defines a fundamental right of freedom in matters of education within the context of institutions such as schools and other educational services that are under governmental control. Like freedom of speech, religion and association, the right to education and the freedom of education are deeply rooted values in the Dutch culture. This gives rise to serious tensions between schools, parents and the requirements determined by the government. This article explores these tensions by examining trends and innovations in the Dutch early childhood education and care (ECEC) services that have taken place over the past 20 years. In particular, the article outlines an approach to ECEC known as Developmental Education (DE). This initiative is unique in the Netherlands as it systematically implements the ideas about learning and development that stem from Vygotsky's cultural-historical account of children's development and learning. DE is evidence based and organised in a multidisciplinary, well-organised practical and research community. This community works at elaborating the concept of DE and contributing to permanent innovation of ECEC practices in collaboration with practitioners. In this article, I argue that DE and its associated community of practice offer a productive paradigm for future innovations in early childhood education and care.

Approaches in education in the Netherlands

The educational landscape in the Netherlands is diverse and heterogeneous with many movements, organisational set-ups and different categories of stakeholders. This applies not only to primary and secondary education but also to the preschool services for the 0- to 4-year olds. In this article, I will focus on some trends in the Dutch early childhood education and care (ECEC) services, which cater for children from 0 to 7 years. Institutionally in the Dutch system, this refers to the first three grades of primary school (4- to 6-year olds) and to preschool services for 0- to 4-year olds, such as day care centres and crèches. Considering the diversity of approaches, it will not be possible to present a systematic review of all initiatives and research projects here. I will confine myself to a few recent developments, which may be considered promising for the future of ECEC in the Netherlands.

It is impossible to understand the diversity in the Dutch ECEC services and the dynamics of innovation in the Netherlands without some understanding of the many deeply rooted cultural-political values, susceptibilities and regulations that influence provision of these services. Hence, a few preliminary words need to be said on this issue.

Anyone working in or with schools or ECEC services in the Netherlands will be familiar with article 23 of the Dutch Constitution. This article defines a fundamental right of freedom in matters of education within the context of institutions such as schools and other educational services that are under governmental control. Article 23 is meant to protect citizens and civil groups against authoritarian, unilateral state interference in pedagogical matters and schooling. Like freedom of speech, religion and association, the right to education and the freedom of education are deeply rooted values in the Dutch culture. The main consequences of this freedom are twofold: firstly, schools and ECEC services can choose their own pedagogical approach and can decide themselves how to organise their teaching in the classrooms or play centres; no national curriculum or testing procedure can be imposed on educational institutions. And secondly, any parent or group can decide to found a school or ECEC provision.

The diverse landscape of educational institutions and approaches in the Netherlands is a direct result of this freedom to found schools. Thus, in the Netherlands, one will find schools and ECEC provision based on a variety of ideological tenets. In addition to public schools, there are schools based on religious worldviews (e.g., Catholic, Protestant, Islamic, Jewish schools – see, for example, Rietveld-van Wingerden and Miedema 2003), and schools based on particular pedagogical approaches such as those of Montessori, Freinet and Steiner (called 'Free schools');[1] Petersen (called Jenaplan schools),[2] Parkhurst (called Dalton schools)[3], Vygotsky (called Developmental Education [DE] schools – see, for example, van Oers 2012a), and Laevers (called Experience-oriented schools – see, for example, Laevers and Heylen 2003). Finally, there are also schools based on more general principles or interests, such as the Leonardo schools for gifted children (see Hickey and Robson 2012 for a discussion), and democratic schools that follow the philosophy of the Sudbury school in America (see Trafford 2008 for a discussion). Although this is not a complete picture, it sketches the diverse Dutch educational situation quite well. Not every type of school is equally represented. In general, about 30% of the schools are public schools, and about 70% of the schools are denominational, concept-based or private.

Of course, in conjunction to the freedom of education and associated rights, there are a number of responsibilities and obligations that have to be met for schools to be accepted in the educational system and to obtain financial support from the government. These obligations are also established in the renowned article 23 of the Constitution. There must be a minimum number of pupils registered in the school, and all institutions have, of course, to abide by general civil law and guarantee children's rights, safety and hygiene. In addition, the government is very keen to ensure the adequacy of the pedagogical quality, the condition of the learning environment, the educational outcomes and the quality of the staff. It has formulated statutory objectives and standards concerning the curriculum content and expected levels of learning outcomes. These apply to all schools and school grades including the primary school grades 1, 2 and 3, which cover the education of 4- to 6-year-old children discussed in this article. The national Inspectorate strictly controls compliance with these standards. Similarly, in relation to ECEC provision, a number of (general) pedagogical standards have to be met as well. It is the pedagogical responsibility of the teachers and ECEC staff to decide freely how to meet these objectives and requirements.

In order to get a grip on the quality of institutional education establishments (publicly financed education and care), over the past decades a characteristic of governmental policy is that it has imposed increasingly more and more rules and standards for securing the quality of education and care. All schools and care provisions have to take these governmental quality requirements into account in order to accomplish their own programmes and innovations. It could be argued, therefore, that these institutions' attempts to integrate and reconcile the government's standards and requirements with their own pedagogical tenets, means that all educational practices should now be considered basically cultural-political constructions.

Tensions between freedom and fixations

As in many countries all over the world, in the Netherlands governmental policy regulates the decisions of the schools and care provisions that concern and the control of the quality of education and care. This gives rise to serious tensions between schools, parents and the requirements determined by the government. Two main policy issues can be distinguished in this respect:

(1) The application of evidence-based practices: this regards both methods and testing procedures. To an increasing extent, the government demands that programmes for the education of young children should demonstrate their effectiveness (particularly in the areas of language and emergent mathematical thinking) using evidence derived from psychometrically reliable and valid testing procedures. Although there is no denying the value of using reliable and valid methods (in matters of educating and testing), many workers in the early childhood education area feel that the type of 'evidence' that is acceptable to the government, does not do justice to the qualities of their work, which involves more than simply delivering children who can show acceptable scores on prescribed standardised tests. Although this is not the place for an extended discussion and critique of the advantages and disadvantages of evidence-based practice, it is apparent that this political tendency could seriously limit early childhood education practitioners' way of working and innovating. Also, there is a danger that this government requirement endangers the constitutional right of freedom of education. This problem is felt with regard to recommendations concerning the educational methods to be used, and even more acutely, with regard to prescribed ways of testing children's educational outcomes.

(2) The second issue is that ECEC is conceived as a policy instrument for addressing the problems of groups of children that enter the school system with considerable disadvantages (mostly language). Schools and early care providers are closely monitored and assessed on their successes in overcoming these disadvantages and stimulating young children's language development so that it reaches a particular normative level. ECEC providers are required to demonstrate that all children in their care can reach this level. Again: although nobody denies the importance of helping children to achieve a functional level of language proficiency, there is considerable debate about the methods used to achieve this and about how to measure the outcomes. For this reason, proponents of all educational innovations have to consider seriously whether these are likely to make a significant contribution to young children's language development, and how this can be demonstrated reliably.

Current government policy demonstrates a particular fixation with these points and takes every possible opportunity to reinforce the message that the 'core business' of any educational provider is the obligation to offer goal-directed teaching that will promote learning in the domains of Dutch language learning (vocabulary, reading, writing) and arithmetic. The government's current fixation on the need for children to demonstrate proficiency in the Dutch language and with literacy and numeracy development has had a significant influence on attempts to introduce innovation in ECEC practices. As a result, it is possible to identify several hot issues that, over the last decade, have increasingly determined (directly or indirectly) the debates on innovation of ECEC practices. These are as follows:

- The desire to implement nationwide testing of young children on initial entry to school (at four years of age); for example, one of the measures proposed by the government over the past decades is that children should be tested on their language ability at entry to primary school. Despite several government trials, however, and as a result of protests by parents, teachers and educational scientists, this proposal has not been implemented. The core arguments offered to counter this proposal are that it is impossible to test children of this age reliably and that these test results would be likely to stigmatise certain pupils from the start of their school career. The fact that successive governments have been trying to implement this idea, however, clearly shows that it can justifiably called a fixation.
- As a consequence of this instrumental conception of ECEC, the government tries to maximise the developmental effect of ECEC by lowering the school entrance age for children. Present law obliges parents to send their children to school at the age of five. In actuality, however, the majority of children enter school at the age of four. In 2010, the government's permanent advisory committee on educational matters (Onderwijsraad) suggested the need to introduce systematic education for three-year-olds. According to the committee, current educational provision for this age group is no longer sufficient for an effective start to statutory education. The proposal states that all three-year-olds should be offered 'a pedagogically rich school environment' where they can play and learn under the responsibility of a primary school, and that there should be an special focus on the promotion of language development (Onderwijsraad 2010). Although the committee's proposal for Dutch ECEC is not extraordinary when compared with many other countries in Europe, and although participation in this new scheme is voluntary for parents, the idea has encountered lots of critique. The debate about the entrance age in school has always been a delicate matter in the Netherlands, as parents and ECEC practitioners feel it as interference in their freedom of Education. Many of them fear that this proposal will finally result in an extension of the current primary school and that these young children will be subject to traditional scholarly instruction at a developmental stage where their main interest is play. Even though parents are free to choose whether or not to take advantage of this provision, many of them feel that they do not have much choice if they take their responsibility seriously to prepare children optimally for their future life. At the moment, there seems to be an impasse regarding the execution of this proposal, although this is mainly due to consideration of the financial consequences of its adoption (which should be met the government). The debate surrounding the proposal shows that most stakeholders take the quality of ECEC practices in the Netherlands seriously. It also reveals, however, that a programme-based approach focusing on specific

learning goals for three-year-old children is met with resistance on the part of many stakeholders.

- Employing product-oriented educational strategies: government policy lays heavy emphasis on the quality of the learning outcomes of the educational system. Basically, the government requires a systematic focus by ECEC providers on predefined learning outcomes (particularly in the area of emergent literacy development), as well as evidence of the effectiveness of this focus using reliable tests. As discussed above, although nobody rejects the idea of raising quality in ECEC, there is concern about the definition of what quality means, and how to achieve and to measure this in ECEC practices. The main concern of practitioners and parents is that the requirement for ECEC providers to focus on outcomes as a key measure of quality represents a limitation of their freedom to choose a way of educating young children that focuses on their developmental needs and possibilities, and that uses assessment procedures which offer a reliable overview of the real potentials of young children and their developmental progress that goes beyond performance on tests.
- The government's fixation on evidence-based practice has led to a bias towards specific types of evidence (standardised measurable outcomes), and as a result to programmes and research projects. This runs the risk of reducing the richness of the field and the exploration of alternative approaches. It also has the effect of limiting the concept of development to a set of narrow definitions based exclusively on cognitive performance. A recent critical analysis of the past 50 years of innovations in ECEC practice in the Netherlands was carried out by Janssen-Vos (2012). This analysis demonstrated that over the past three decades, decisions to adopt particular initiatives (and ways of gathering supportive evidence) have favoured innovations that accord with the government's demand for transmission type of ECEC practices and standardised testing on the basis of performances in limited domains. Fortunately thanks to Article 23, the government does not prohibit innovations that start out with other assumptions regarding children's development and good ECEC practice. In a political climate that is prejudiced towards standardised, norm-referenced measurement and randomised controlled trials in research, it is difficult to gain acceptance of initiatives and research that promotes the evaluation of young children's development using alternative means.

The permanent tensions that exist between these governmental fixations and pedagogically driven innovation in ECEC practices result in an unavoidable demand that all innovation initiatives must attempt to address. Several institutions and research groups in the Netherlands are conducting research that aims to contribute to this debate. In addition, many educational practices for the 0- to 7-year-old age group have been introduced that explore how new innovative ideas can benefit young children's development. In this paper, it is not possible to describe and evaluate all of these practices. Some focus on piecemeal research regarding the role of processes and mechanisms in young children's learning and development (see for example, Leseman, Rollenberg and Rispens 2001). Others are more broadly practice oriented in their research and innovations. These use an encompassing innovative strategy, which combines the elaboration of a specific ECEC approach (together with support that allows practitioners to implement the approach in their everyday practice), with research and the collection of evidence. Two of these approaches will be discussed in detail below: one focuses on children below the age of three, the other focuses on older children in the 3- to 7-year-old age group. First, however, we offer a brief overview of current innovations in the field of ECEC.

Innovations in early childhood education in the Dutch constellation
Preschool education initiatives

In the domain of ECEC, there are several alternative ways of working with young children from the age of three. Each of these approaches attempts to innovate and improve ECEC practices in the Netherlands, and attempts to achieve a balance between the demands of governmental policy and specific, theoretically informed pedagogical choices that offer a distinct view on young children's development.

In the Netherlands, the main integral approaches for the 3- to 7-year olds are the following: Piramide, Kaleidoscoop, Startblokken/Basisontwikkeling and Ervaringsgericht Onderwijs. To give a brief overview of the various initiatives in the field of ECEC innovation, these will be briefly characterised below.

Piramide

This is a thematic and strictly manual-driven programme for working with young children. Play episodes are alternated with thematic, instruction-based sessions. For children with developmental delays a special tutorial programme is available. This programme has been developed by the Dutch central institute for test development (Cito). The outcomes are evaluated by well-constructed, psychometric tests. There is a relationship between the aims of the programme and the tests. Theoretically, the programme is eclectic; although in the main, it is informed by Slavin's work on cooperative learning (e.g., Slavin 1996).

Kaleidoscoop

The Kaleidoscoop approach was originally based on the work of Hohmann and Weikart's (2002) High Scope programme and emphasises the development of the whole child. In the Netherlands, this programme has adopted an integral approach to teaching different developmental areas, although there is an emphasis on language development. It is a Piagetian-based approach based on the concept of 'active participatory learning'. It focuses on strengthening cognitive skills through active, hands-on learning experiences in different areas, such as language, mathematics and social interaction. The plan-do-review cycle is a core principle of this approach and is used to structure children's work where the teacher encourages children to plan the tasks they want to accomplish during free-choice time. After carrying out these self-selected tasks, children spend time later in the day reflecting on what they learned.

Startblokken/Basisontwikkeling (Starting blocks and Basic Development)

This approach is based on the Vygotskian concept of 'DE' (see van Oers 2012a). Children's development (in the broad sense) is stimulated through a thematic and play-based approach. Here, adults interact systematically with children to assess closely each child's potential for action and learning and promote his or her developmental steps within the appropriate zone of proximal development. In the initial stages, children's language and cognitive development is stimulated but the main focus is on their well-being, social interaction and emotional balance. The focus on communicative development increases over the years.

Ervaringsgericht Onderwijs (Experience-oriented education)

This approach was developed by Laevers and his team at the University of Leuven (Belgium) and was initially based on the ideas of Piaget and Rogers. More recently, it has been expanded to encompass notions of flow, sensitivity, experimentation and autonomy (see for example, Laevers 2011) The basic premise of the approach is that children's deep authentic involvement and experience of reality provides the motor for development, and this in turn triggers the need for learning.

There are many more initiatives. In the last decades, for example, there has been a growing interest in the implementation of (versions of) the Italian, Reggio Emilia approach. However, the next section focuses on two promising, innovative projects that have been originated in the Netherlands.

Preschool care initiatives

The government has recently propagated the idea that raising the quality of early care activities and of practitioners will improve early care provision for young children. In response to this, a remarkable initiative described by Elly Singer and Loes Kleerekoper (2009) outlines one attempt to contribute to the debate on the nature of excellent early care provision for 0- to 4-year-old children. In their booklet, Singer and Kleerkoper outline a pedagogical framework for working with 0- to 4-year-old children based on sound academic research and practical experience of working with young children. The framework is written as a detailed guide for practitioners that describes methods to improve the way they interact with these young children. The initiative is based on the idea that the development of young children's identity as humans is optimally stimulated when their potential is taken seriously and is identified as a starting point for further development. Singer and Kleerekoper argue that this development is best fostered in a rich and stimulating environment with adults who are sensitive to young children's needs and where there is a rich variety of peers.

The aim of this approach is to promote open and holistic interaction with children and their development. According to this perspective, early care should offer children a rich array of experiences through which adults can get to know their potential and their learning needs in the domains of social, emotional and personal competencies. Although the approach concentrates on the stimulation of these competencies, it essentially adheres to a holistic philosophy that conceives of children as integrated persons. A basic tenet is that rather than attempting to lead children's learning, adults should follow their spontaneous learning and offer stimulating interactions designed to expand this learning. In addition, adults should take care to ensure children's well-being at all times.

Most of the pedagogical suggestions given in the framework will be familiar to early care practitioners, but the important value of this pedagogical framework is that the authors offer a rich collection of practical suggestions of how to implement these starting points and how to embed active learning, play, communication and expression in everyday practices. Moreover, Singer and Kleerekoper (2009) have established a research foundation for their framework by consulting academic educationalists and researchers and also through their own research. Singer's own studies underpin and strengthen the approach for 0- to 4-year-old children as articulated by this pedagogical framework. Her research programme demonstrates how the spontaneous activities of children in everyday situations (like the sandpit) can be conceived of and developed as learning opportunities that early care practitioners can harness for the benefit of young children. The learning is focused on cognitive issues (e.g., van Schijndel et al. 2010), social-emotional issues such as conflict management among young children (e.g., Singer 2003), and young children's ways of dealing with diversity (e.g., de Haan and Singer 2010).

Singer and Kleerekoper's pedagogical framework does not only draw on scientific evidence for support but it also draws on social support by emphasising the benefits to children of collaborating with parents as educational partners. Although the framework proposed by Singer and Kleerekoper's will need further work if it is to be implemented on a large scale in early years care practices, importantly, their proposal combines a pedagogical view with appropriate empirical evidence, gathered in practices that can be considered paradigmatic for the approach. As such, it counters the political trend towards further advancing scholarisation of educational practices for young children. It can be seen as a starting point and an important innovation that will contribute to necessary improvement in the quality of early care practices in the Netherlands.

Innovating ECEC by implementing DE for young children

Another influential curriculum initiative for 3- to 7-year-old children currently operation in the Netherlands is known as DE. This approach is based on Vygotsky's (1978) writings on the cultural nature of human development. In the Netherlands, the DE approach is outlined in the practical guidelines for Startblokken (Starting blocks for Basic Development) and Basisontwikkeling (Basic Development). Starting blocks is implemented in about 25% of Dutch early education settings. The main ideas of DE (including its key concepts, recommended good practice and strategies for implementation) have recently been collected in an edited volume (van Oers 2012a).

The approach is unique in the Netherlands as it systematically implements the ideas about learning and development that stem from Vygotsky's cultural-historical approach. This conceives of human learning as a process of change in actions and/or activities, guided by more knowledgeable others (adults, peers, older children). According to this theory, learning will only optimally contribute to the broad development of cultural identity (not only focusing on cognitive performance but also including aesthetic, motivational, moral developments, etc.), when the learning is meaningful in a double sense: the learning content (goal) has cultural value, contributing to the learner's capacity to participate self-dependently in sociocultural practices, and the learning contents (goals) also have personal value (i.e., it make sense to the pupil as it relates to his personal feeling, emotions, motives and interests).

As El'konin (1972) has argued, during the preschool period, 3- to 7-year-old children relate playfully to their environment. Both he and Vygotsky identify play as the leading activity for young children. This means that through play children can easily make sense of the constraints and complexities of their environment and are most motivated to expand their abilities. According to Vygotsky, this is because play inverts the relationship between action and meaning:

> In play, meaning is going to dominate over real actions and objects. Meaning contextualised in an imaginary situation, regulates the real object-oriented and tool-mediated actions of the child and these actions produce new objects that may be a starting point for new explorations

of meanings and the production of new tools [...] The contradictions between the meanings in play (emerging from the imaginary situation) and the real actions are the main basis for children's development (van Oers 2008, 371).

DE has elaborated this cultural-historical conception of play by defining it as a possible format of cultural activities. All cultural activities can be carried out playfully when the actors abide by some of the constituting rules, enjoy some degrees of freedom for the interpretation and use of the rules, tools and goals, and are deeply engaged in the activity. Practitioners of DE systematically format the way children participate in a playful activity, as defined above.

The DE curriculum for young children is based on these starting points. It is thematic as it engages children in imaginary play that draws on meaningful activities that make sense to them in the context of their everyday lives such as going to the market, working in a vet's practice, gardening, buying new shoes (van Oers 2008). It is a consistent play-based curriculum as all activities for children are organised in a play format. This differs from other ECEC approaches that proclaim that 'play is an important element', but only schedule periods of free play activities in addition to 'work' or 'learning' activities. The DE curriculum is essentially play based as learning is always organised as a functional process in the context of playfully formatted activities (practices). van Oers (2012a) offers many examples of this kind of activity.

In ECEC settings that have adopted this curriculum, teachers take part in children's activities as more knowledgeable partners, taking care that the play character of children activity is not disturbed or replaced by a form of goal-directed instruction. It is important, however, to bear in mind that the teacher can have an intentional educational impact in the context of children's play, and that he or she is trained to promote children's development in a variety of domains without destroying play. By participating in, and engaging with children's play, the teacher can articulate new dimensions or needs within the activity. By so doing, the teacher creates zones of proximal development in which children eagerly learn new actions and tools.

To promote learning, the early years teacher has a number of stimulating tools at her disposal that encourage children to explore their own knowledge and skills and to expand these with new possibilities (actions, tools, rules, images, etc.). The tools the teacher employs to promote learning in the zone of proximal development are known as 'impulses'. 'Impulses' consist of a collection of strategies (such as orienting, structuring, reflecting) that allow teachers to elaborate children's activities into new meaningful actions that constitute a basis for further learning. These impulses (discussed below) are part of the expert teachers' repertoire (see Janssen-Vos 2008 and Janssen-Vos and Pompert 2012, for further explanation and examples).

Orienting

When using this collection of strategies, teachers explore situations and activities together with the children, and focus their attention on specific requirements. In role-playing a supermarket, for example, children are encouraged to focus on the details of such a practice: what is going on there? What kinds of things are involved? Which roles are involved? Through this orientation, children are encouraged to engage with sociocultural practices and scripts relevant to the situation. If necessary, the teacher assists children in this orientation by guiding questions or providing relevant words.

Structuring and deepening

Just providing a situation and tools is often not an optimal way of introducing productive play. Young children need open structures in order to get involved in role-play activities and to benefit from them. For example, the teacher develops a story with the children, by referring to a common story, or by opening the scene with a particular act. In the supermarket example, a teacher might enter the scene as a customer who needs some special commodity. This deepens the children's understanding by prompting them to consider, 'What we are going to do'? 'Is this available'? In general, the teacher tries to set the scene with the children by introducing a problem and discussing what is to be done or what is needed.

Broadening

This impulse is designed to connect the role-play activity with other activities and skills. In the supermarket, children are encouraged to think about the set-up of the shop and how to decorate it, for instance with leaflets, advertisements or informative posters and warnings. This activity harnesses early literacy skills by encouraging children to write and draw specific practice-related texts such as pricelists, for example. If it is to be successful, children should always experience the broadening of an activity as a contribution to their play. (A detailed example of how a play in a shoe shop can be broadened into arithmetical activities is described in van Oers 1998.)

Contributing

Significant innovations in play can be achieved by introducing new tools that answer the specific needs of children in a particular play situation. In role-play involving the school doctor, for instance, the children acting the parts of the doctor and her assistant might want to measure the height of all children in the class. They write down all the numbers on a paper and the teacher then introduces, or contributes a way of graphically representing the outcomes using lines of different lengths.

Reflecting

During any play activity, the teacher constantly gets the children involved in little moments of discourse about the on-going activity: 'How is it going, is this what you want'? 'Can you do it otherwise'? 'What does this mean'? 'Are you sure about this?' Such discourse stimulates children to think about their actions and to translate them into comprehensible narratives that include new questions. Not only do such reflections play an important function regarding the evaluation of the activity, they also start new orientations that in turn may lead to new (broadening, contributing, deepening) activities.

One of the teacher's main objectives when giving didactic impulses is to stimulate children's communicative activity (vocabulary acquisition, oral language, writing, drawing, graphing, etc.). Communicative activity is seen as the basis for all literacy practices and mathematical thinking (see van Oers 2003, 2012b, Fijma 2012).

To implement the ideas of DE in everyday ECEC practices, an extended network of educationalists (teachers, curriculum developers, teacher trainers, researchers) has been formed. This network is associated with a community for DE (www.OGO-academie.nl), which encourages innovation by fostering collaborations between practice and research. In addition, the DE organisation supports an influential institution that provides postgraduate training for teachers wishing to improve their expertise in DE (www.de-activiteit.nl).

Finally, DE is also a research programme (see van Oers 2012c). There are research groups at the VU University in Amsterdam and the Hogeschool Alkmaar (InHolland), doing research on learning in a play-based curriculum in order to elaborate theory and construct empirical evidence. Dorian de Haan (2012) has produced evidence that identifies the processes of young children's communicative learning taking place in a play-based curriculum. Similarly, van Oers and his colleagues have carried out several studies in order to find evidence for the effectiveness of DE that have identified many positive outcomes (see van Oers 2003, 2007, 2010a, 2010b, Peters and van Oers 2007, Poland, van Oers, and Terwel 2007, van Oers, and Duijkers 2012).

The constellation of this social network brings together different disciplines and a large number of ECEC practices and is quite unique in the Netherlands. Like Singer and Kleerekoper's pedagogical framework, research evidence suggests that existing preschool programmes based on the theoretical and practical framework offered by DE can be seen as a powerful starting point for large-scale implementation. It would be misleading, however, to suggest that all problems have been solved. In particular, resolving the tensions between the theoretical and pedagogical ideologies of the DE approach and the often-incompatible demands of the governmental fixations outlined at the beginning of this article will require further, serious consideration.

Future

The main ambition of all approaches to ECEC is to create circumstances that guarantee young children's well-being and at the same time optimally stimulate their development in a broad sense, so as to maximise their chances of participating autonomously in the sociocultural practices of their current and future life.

The legal right of freedom of education that exists in the Netherlands allows practitioners and parents to realise this ambition conscientiously in accordance with their own values and understandings (within the constraints set by the law regarding human rights and obligations). The government takes care that society as a whole provides the financial conditions to realise this ambition, but (justifiably) also sets standards that should be met in order to guarantee that (future) society as a whole can also benefit from the educational system. As explained above, the freedom of education and the government's responsibilities may cause tensions that have to be resolved by all institutionalised approaches to ECEC.

As discussed above, the various approaches to ECEC in the Netherlands all deal with these tensions in their own way. An important element of the strategy is to find ways to get parents involved. It is important that the pedagogical voices of the parents are negotiated in order to establish educational partnerships that will be of benefit to children. Currently, however, there is no 'best way' available that can create optimal parental involvement. This is a complex matter that all approaches are struggling with. It is clear that robust research is still needed to investigate the effects of parental involvement and to identify how best to negotiate pedagogical ideas with parents.

One of the vexing issues affecting the relationship between the proponents of pedagogical approaches to ECEC and the government (and the Inspectorate) is to decide what 'good education' is, and how this can be established by empirical evidence and persuasive argument. ECEC practitioners may maintain that their particular approach starts out from the whole child (as an integral identity). These assertions, however, lose credibility if practitioners nevertheless comply immediately, and without critical comment, with the government's fixation on a system of norm-referenced testing that employs decontextualising instruments and that focuses on limited dimensions of children's identity development.

In response to this criticism, the DE approach to ECEC has developed an instrument for assessing children's development as a holistic phenomenon. This instrument employs a systematic observation strategy that allows teachers to assess children's progress in relation to key developmental indicators in areas such as communication, problem solving, reflection and creative construction. Observations are carried out during the course of children's daily play activities. This observation strategy is known as HOREB, a Dutch acronym for Action-Oriented Observation, Registration and Evaluation in Basisontwikkeling (see E. van Oers 2012) Due to the efforts and negotiations of many people, the HOREB-instrument of Basic Development has been accepted by the Inspectorate as a valid assessment instrument. In addition, other teachers and researchers committed to DE are engaged in detailed efforts to elaborate reliable and valid instruments for Dynamic Assessment (Adan-Dirks 2012; van der Veen and Poland 2012). They argue that these instruments are directly related to other forms of criterion-referenced testing and that the instruments provide a more detailed and child-based view on a child's potential for learning in a specific domain. This is more consistent with the tenets of DE and should not be neglected in spite of the pressure for standardised, norm-referenced testing. As to the assessment of young children's development in different cultural domains, however, there is still a long way to go.

One of the political problems here is that the Inspectorates for schools and early care provisions are not independent institutions in the Netherlands: they are legally bound to refrain from pedagogical reflection, and their powers are limited to ensuring control of the quality of the Dutch schools and care settings. This makes the tensions between the freedom of education and governmental fixations even more difficult to solve. A more independent institute of quality control could potentially create a platform for a nationwide pedagogical discussion about the quality of education and might go some way towards mitigating the government's strong propensity to see education simply in economic terms.

For now, all approaches to ECEC have to follow their own choices regarding innovation in ECEC and achieving a balance between their pedagogical ideals and the government's educational fixations. Since the 1970s, the multidisciplinary theory-driven approach, DE, has proved to be an effective strategy for dealing with these governmental pressures without needing to renounce its pedagogical origins in cultural-historical theories of learning and development. DE is evidence based and organised in a multidisciplinary, well-organised practical and research community. This community works at elaborating the concept of DE and contributing to permanent innovation of ECEC practices in collaboration with practitioners. As such, it offers a productive paradigm for future innovations in ECEC.

Notes

1. For a brief history of the 'free school' movement inspired by the writings of Rudolf Steiner, see http://www.steinerwaldorf.org/whatissteinereducation.html
2. Jenaplan schools are based on the educational philosophy of Professor Peter Petersen (1884–1952) of the University of Jena. For details of this pedagogic approach, see http://www.jenaplan.nl/nl/jenaplanschools.html

3. For an account of the progressive educational philosophy of Helen Parkhurst (1887–1973) founder of the first Dalton school, see van der Ploeg, P. (2012). The Dalton Plan: recycling in the guise of innovation. *Paedagogica Historica* (ahead-of-print), 1–16.

References

Adan-Dirks, R. 2012. "Assessing Vocabulary Development." In *Developmental Education for Young children: Concept, Practice, Implementation*, edited by B. van Oers, 87–104. Dordrecht/ New York: Springer.

El'konin, D. B. 1972. "Towards the Problem of Stages in the Mental Development of the Child." *Soviet Psychology* 10: 225–251.

Fijma, N. 2012. "Learning to Communicate About Number." In *Developmental Education for Young Children. Concept, Practice, Implementation*, edited by B. van Oers, 253–270. Dordrecht and New York: Springer.

de Haan, D. 2012. "Learning to Communicate in Young Children's Classrooms." In *Developmental Education for Young Children: Concept, Practice, Implementation*, edited by B. van Oers, 67–86. Dordrecht and New York: Springer.

de Haan, D., and E. Singer. 2010. "The Role of Language in Young Children's Adaptive Modifying Strategies during Peer Conflicts." *First Language* 30 (3–4): 421–440. doi:10.1177/014272 3710370546.

Hickey, I., and D. Robson. 2012. *The Leonardo Effect: Motivating Children to Achieve Through Interdisciplinary Learning*. Abingdon: Routledge.

Hohmann, M., and D. P. Weikart. 2002. *Educating Young Children: Active Learning Practices for Preschool and Child Care Programs*. Ypsilanti, MI: High Scope Press.

Janssen-Vos, F. 2008. *Basisontwikkeling voor peuters en onderbouw [Basic Development for Preschool and the Early School Years]*. Assen: van Gorcum.

Janssen-Vos, F. 2012. *Baanbrekers en boekhouders. Herinneringen aan 50 jaar kleuters [Pioneers and Bookkeepers. Recollections of 50 Years of Young Children]*. Assen: van Gorcum.

Janssen-Vos, F., and B. Pompert. 2012. "Developmental Education for Young Children: Basic Development." In *Developmental Education for Young Children: Concept, Practice, Implementation*, edited by B. van Oers, 41–63. Dordrecht and New York: Springer.

Laevers, F. 2011. "Experiential Education: Making Care and Education More Effective Through Well-Being and Involvement." In *Encyclopedia on Early Childhood Development*, edited by Bennett, J., R. E. Tremblay, M. Boivin, R. de V., Peters, and R. G. Barr, 1–5. Montreal: Centre of Excellence for Early Childhood Development and Strategic Knowledge Cluster on Early Child Development. Accessed July 24, 2012. http://www.child-encyclopedia.com/documents/ LaeversANGxp1.pdf.

Laevers, F., and L. Heylen, eds. 2003. *Involvement of Children and Teacher Style: Insights from an International Study on Experiential Education (Studia Paedagogica)*. Leuven: University of Leuven Press.

Leseman, P. M., L. Rollenberg, and J. Rispens. 2001. "Playing and Working in Kindergarten: Cognitive Co-Construction in Two Educational Situations." *Early Childhood Research Quarterly* 16 (3): 363–384. doi:10.1016/S0885-2006(01)00103-X.

van Oers, B. 1998. "The Fallacy of Decontextualisation." *Mind, Culture, and Activity* 5 (2): 135–142. doi:10.1207/s15327884mca0502_7.

van Oers, B. 2003. "Learning Resources in the Context of Play: Promoting Effective Learning in Early Childhood." *European Early Childhood Education Journal* 11 (1): 7–26. doi:10.1080/ 13502930385209031.

van Oers, B. 2007. "Helping Young Children to Become Literate: The Relevance of Narrative Competence for Developmental Education." *European Early Childhood Education Research Journal* 15 (3): 299–312. doi:10.1080/13502930701679718.

van Oers, B. 2008. "Inscripting Predicates: Dealing with Meanings in Play." In *The Transformation of Learning: Advances in Cultural-Historical Activity Theory*, edited by B. van Oers, W. Wardekker, E. Elbers, and R. van der Veer, 370–380. Cambridge: Cambridge University Press.

van Oers, B. 2010a. "Children's Enculturation through Play." In *Engaging Play*, edited by L. Brooker and S. Edwards, 195–209. Maidenhead: McGraw Hill.

van Oers, B. 2010b. "The Emergence of Mathematical Thinking in the Context of Play." *Educational Studies in Mathematics* 74 (1): 23–37. doi:10.1007/s10649-009-9225-x.

van Oers, B., ed. 2012a. *Developmental Education for Young Children: Concept, Practice, Implementation.* Dordrecht and New York: Springer.

van Oers, B. 2012b. "How to Promote Young Children's Mathematical Thinking?" *Mediterranean Journal for Research in Mathematics Education* 11 (1–2): 1–15.

van Oers, B. 2012c. "Developmental Education: Reflections on a CHAT-Research Program in the Netherlands." *Learning, Culture and Social Interaction* 1 (1): 57–65. doi:10.1016/j.lcsi.2012.04.002.

van Oers, E. 2012. "Evaluation of Learning and Development." In *Developmental Education for Young Children: Concept, Practice, Implementation*, edited by B. van Oers, 223–238. Dordrecht and New York: Springer.

van Oers, B., and D. Duijkers. 2012. "Teaching in a Play-Based Curriculum: Theory, Practice and Evidence of Developmental Education for Young Children." *Journal of Curriculum Studies* 44 (1): 1–24. doi:10.1080/00220272.2011.637184.

Onderwijsraad. 2010. *Naar een nieuwe kleuterperiode in de basisschool [Towards a New Preschool Period in Primary School].* Den Haag: Onderwijsraad.

Peters, I., and B. van Oers. 2007. "Teachers' Action Strategies in Goal-Oriented Interactions with Young Children At-Risk." *European Early Childhood Education Research Journal* 15 (1): 121–136. doi:10.1080/13502930601161916.

Van der Ploeg, P. 2012. "The Dalton Plan: Recycling in the Guise of Innovation." *Paedagogica Historica: International Journal of the History of Education* 1–16.

Poland, M., B. van Oers, and J. Terwel. 2007. "Effects of Schematising on Mathematical Development." *European Early Childhood Education Research Journal* 15 (2): 269–293. doi:10.1080/13502930701321600.

Rietveld-van Wingerden, M., and S. Miedema. 2003. "Freedom of Education and Dutch Jewish Schools in the Mid-Nineteenth Century." *Jewish History* 17(1): 31–54. doi:10.1023/A:1021262227311.

van Schijndel, T. J. P., E. Singer, H. L. J. van der Maas, and M. E. J. Raijmakers. 2010. "A Sciencing Programme and Young Children's Exploratory Play in the Sandpit." *The European Journal of Developmental Psychology* 7 (5): 603–617. doi:10.1080/17405620903412344.

Singer, E. 2003. "The Logic of Young Children's (Non)Verbal Behaviour." In *Narratives of Childhood*, edited by B. van Oers, 68–80. Amsterdam: VU University Press.

Singer, E., and L. Kleerekoper. 2009. *Pedagogisch kader Kindercentra 0–4 [A Pedagogical Framework for Early Care 0–4].* Maarssen: Elsevier gezondheidszorg.

Slavin, R. 1996. *Education for All: Contexts for Learning.* Lisse: Swets and Zeitlinger.

Trafford, B. 2008. "Democratic Schools: Towards a Definition." In *The Sage Handbook of Education for Citizenship and Democracy*, edited by J. Arthur, I. Davies, and C. Hahn, 410–424. London: Sage. doi:10.4135/9781849200486.n33.

van der Veen, C., and M. Poland. 2012. "Dynamic Assessment of Narrative Competence." In *Developmental Education for Young Children. Concept, Practice, Implementation*, edited by B. van Oers, 105–120. Dordrecht and New York: Springer.

Vygotsky, L. 1978. *Mind in Society: The Development of Higher Psychological Processes.* Cambridge, MA: Harvard University Press.

Promoting critical awareness in the initial training of preschool teachers in Greece: resistance and perspectives

Evangelia Kourti and Alexandra Androussou

Department of Early Childhood Education, University of Athens, Athens, Greece

This article focuses on the development of future preschool teachers' critical awareness through the introduction of two 'new' subjects – intercultural education and media education – in the curriculum of an early childhood department in Greece. The current social and political context, the structure of preschool teachers' training in Greece and the design and evaluation of the operation of these courses that are designed to raise students' critical awareness are discussed. Particular attention is given to students' resistance to the specific issues taught, which appears to result from their personal beliefs and the institutional inertia of the education system.

Introduction

If we accept that the educational process is a 'political act' (Freire 1973), teachers must be trained in order to 'act' and to take into consideration the social and cultural background of children in their classroom and society at large. Thus in order to respond to the new challenges for education at the pedagogical, political and social levels (Jacquinot-Delaunay 2001), it is not only necessary to introduce new courses but also to develop future teachers' 'critical awareness' (Mayer 1986), which will enable them first to read and analyse social reality, and then to act using this theoretical knowledge as a tool (Cochran-Smith 2005). We will argue that preschool education today must respond and adapt to new social and political circumstances and technological progress and discoveries (Yelland 2005a), both at local and international levels.

In this article, we reflect on tensions and dissonance experienced between traditional curricula and pedagogy and alternative educational perspectives based on the introduction of two courses, intercultural education and media education, in the Department of Early Childhood Education at the University of Athens in Greece. These courses, which deal with critical issues for current early childhood education at an international level, are at the forefront of contemporary discussion occurring in Greece (Rhedding-Jones 2005; Rowan and Honan 2005; Yelland 2005b; Robinson and Diaz 2006).

The social and political context in Greece relative to these courses is discussed first, followed by an outline of the institutional framework of preschool teachers' initial training in order to clarify the educational context in which these courses were designed.

Subsequently, the common elements found in the design of these courses are underlined, and an assessment is made of their functioning and the resistances that emerged, whether from students' personal perceptions or from the institutional inertia of the educational system. Finally, concerns over the introduction of such courses into university curricula in the current political and social context are discussed.

Migration and media issues in Greek society

Having experienced (for historical, political and social reasons) migration as a sending country until the late twentieth century, in recent decades, Greece has been confronted with the reverse experience, receiving successive waves of immigration at a tremendous pace – initially from the Balkans, then from Asia, Eastern Europe, the Middle East and Africa (Damanakis 1997; Triantafyllidou and Maroukis 2010). As a result, the country's demography has changed, and the immigrants now represent a significant proportion of the Greek population. In the 2001 census, people of foreign nationality accounted for 7% of the population (Kotzamanis 2008).[1]

Immigrants settled both in big cities and in rural areas, turning a society that had been used to being mono-cultural into a multicultural community (Androusou 2005). In turn, this led to significant challenges for the Greek education system that have profound implications for how teachers are trained. Approximately 10% of the total student population in Greek compulsory education today is made up of children of immigrants, and this proportion is higher in schools in large urban centres (Toura 2009). The integration of immigrants into the society is a difficult process; it creates inequality, social segregation, racism and phobic reactions, especially in this time of severe economic crisis.[2] Future teachers need to be aware and alert to these issues (Androusou and Askouni 2011).

Like other European countries, Greece has experienced rapid technological change in the last decades. In addition to traditional media, the Internet has become important in daily life, education, work and participation in society. This has led to problems related to inequalities concerning access to and the use of media by different social groups and a growing digital divide. The need for media education (that is, learning about 'reading' and 'writing' in relation to diverse media) seems more and more important as digital media become the primary means of delivering information, entertainment and knowledge. Media education, therefore, needs to be considered as seriously as formal education. In turn, this means that schools have to reduce the distance that separates them from their social environment, to recognise (without an alarmist or over-optimistic attitude) media as an element of culture in today's world and make explicit attempts to connect with children and young people's media cultures. This requires teachers who dare to move beyond standard schooling, who adopt a reflective stance on their own relationship with the media and on the role of media in society and in the lives of young people. Teachers, instead of undermining children's media culture, need to use it as a starting point (Jacquinot-Delaunay 2001).

In order to address these issues, two courses – intercultural education and media education[3] – were introduced into initial teacher-training programmes of the Department of Early Childhood Education of the University of Athens in the mid-2000s. These courses cover different topics and social needs but are related, as media contributes to the representation of migrants and otherness in Greek society. It was anticipated that their introduction into the curriculum of initial teacher training would prepare teachers to deal with the new situation in Greek schools and to educate their pupils as active citizens able to 'read' social reality and demonstrate critical thinking. These concepts are rooted in the logic of critical pedagogy:

> Critical pedagogy opens up a space where students should be able to come to terms with their own power as critical agents; it provides a sphere where the unconditional freedom to question and assert is central to the purpose of the university, if not democracy itself. (Giroux 2007, 1)

Clearly, these two 'new' subjects are certainly not neutral, since over and above their scientific and educational dimensions, they have an ideological and political dimension that largely contrasts with the prevailing conceptions of the issues they are dealing with. Intercultural education refers to diversity, otherness and immigration – crucial issues in today's Greek society. Media education focuses on the social and cultural dimensions of the relationship with (old and new) media rather than just the development of technical skills on how to use ICT, which is the prevailing practice in Greek education. It should be noted that in the last Greek elections (May and June 2012), although the main thrust of the election campaign was the economic situation of the country, the public debate among political parties focused almost exclusively on immigration and the impact of the presence of immigrants on Greek society and economy. The role of media in this debate was influential.

Their content apart, these courses require a different way of teaching, which reinforces critical thinking and students' active participation, in order for them to make the connection between course form and course content.

Early childhood teacher training in Greece: from vocational schools to university

For the past 25 years, the initial training of teachers has occurred in university Teacher Training Departments, which admitted their first students in 1984. Prior to that, primary school teacher training was conducted at Pedagogic Academies or, for preschool teachers, at Nursery Teacher Schools. These were vocational educational establishments with a two-year programme of studies. Their curricula included mainly psychology courses, with an emphasis on children's individual characteristics, pedagogy and practical application in various subject matters. Students' studies were not oriented towards the sociological dimension, educational politics or the analysis of educational practices. The rationale of these educational establishments was to prepare 'practical teachers' for the profession through the transfer of professional 'know how' and through 'scientific analytical training'. The educators in these Pedagogic Academies were mostly school counsellors, in-service teachers and artists (Androusou, Dafermou, and Tsafos 2012a). A detailed account of the history and evolution of the Educational Departments in Greece is offered by Stamelos (1999) and Bouzakis and Tzikas (1998).

From 1984 to 1988, eight university departments were established in Greece to train primary school teachers (for children aged 6–12), and eight more departments were created to train preschool teachers (for children aged 4–6). In these departments, initial teachers' training lasts four years. The distinction that existed under the previous regime between primary school and preschool teachers was maintained. Departments that train primary school teachers attract a diverse student body; in Departments of Early Childhood Education, however, the student body is much more homogenous. The students are almost exclusively women. According to data from a survey carried out by Androusou, Dafermou, and Tsafos' (2012b), the majority of students at the Early

Childhood Education Department of the University of Athens are of low- or middle-class background and are born and raised in small towns or villages. The educational level of their parents is that of secondary education.

The curriculum of university Departments of Early Childhood Education is largely dominated by a focus on pedagogy and educational sciences. Students attend courses on general pedagogical knowledge, i.e. teachers' pedagogical knowledge of classroom management, on subject-specific pedagogies (for example, environmental education, special needs education and the didactics of science and mathematics) and on questioning and planning, as well as courses on psychology, social psychology, sociology, history of education and educational politics. This knowledge is usually transmitted using a conventional, didactic approach in lectures where educators talk and students listen. This way of transmitting knowledge is commonly described as 'banking education' (Raths and McAninch 1997; Gordon 2007). This tradition does not allow for the kind of personal reflection likely to lead to developmental change in trainee teachers' understanding of teaching and learning. Nevertheless, education students are expected to assimilate new ideas and processes that relate to educational theory and practices. At the same time, they are expected to change deeply held personal views and prejudices that have been shaped during their own 12-year experience of schooling.

Continuing in the traditions established by the old Pedagogic Academies and Nursery Teacher Schools (Law No. 1268 of the year 1982 and Presidential Decrees[4] No. 320 of the year 1983), it is clear from the course descriptions and practicum programmes of some university departments that pedagogical knowledge is still perceived as knowledge that future teachers will need in order to deal with classroom problems. Despite the efforts of some progressive educational departments to reinforce students' knowledge and understanding of educational theory, amongst the general public, the Ministry of Education and even some teacher educators, the stereotype of teachers that persists widely is one where practitioners are only considered effective when they are able to demonstrate the skills necessary to perform routine, prescribed tasks. As a result a teacher-centred pedagogy and 'conservative' approach to teacher training remain prevalent, in line with the overall Greek educational system. This system is centralised and bureaucratic (Sofou and Tsafos 2010), with the teacher's role limited to the strict application of a closed curriculum. This curriculum is decided centrally by the Ministry of Education and is applied throughout the country, even in private schools (Katsarou and Tsafos 2009). Despite two recent curricula reforms, a recent analysis shows that school curricula at all levels remain largely closed and only include a few references to intercultural education and media education issues (Katsarou and Tsafos 2010).

Intercultural education and media education from a critical awareness perspective

'Intercultural education' and 'media education' courses are two new additions to the curricula of University Preschool Departments. These were introduced in response to a major wave of migration to Greece and new discussions about the importance of ICT in education (Aslanidou 2008). Nevertheless, these courses are regarded as a somewhat peripheral part of the curricula, and even today, there are departments where these courses are not taught at all. This attitude contradicts the importance attached to these issues in public debate and national politics. From our examination of the course descriptions of the different Preschool Department's Study guides, one can discern a variety of scientific and pedagogical approaches to teaching these courses. It is apparent that each educator is allowed to make his/her own choices concerning the content, method of delivery and theoretical approach. Thus, one finds a range of courses from the more traditional to those that adhere to a critical approach and even those that subvert the dominant narrative. It could be argued, therefore, that these are essentially ideological and political choices that reflect those educators' own stance on these issues. Nevertheless, as reported above, the intention in introducing these courses was that they should cover internationally critical issues that challenge not only long-established beliefs but also traditional practices in early childhood education (Yelland 2005a). As such, the topics they address go 'against the tide' and challenge the dominant perception of what is adequate and appropriate to teach in preschool, where it is commonly assumed that young children's education should steer clear of politics and technology.

At the University of Athens, future preschool teachers' 'critical awareness' of the social, political and educational dimensions of the issues raised in these courses is achieved through the content, the teaching methodology and the theoretical approaches adopted. It is our common belief that preschool teachers' training should aim to create reflective practitioners and teacher-researchers who adopt an enquiry-based approach to their practice rather than professionals who simply apply pre-designed activities (Zeichner and Liston 1996; Gordon and O'Brien 2007).

In the context of a reflective approach, the main objective of the educator is to enable future teachers to work on their own perceptions of diversity and the role of the media and also to encourage them to examine critically any stereotypical notions they might have about the nature of childhood and children's learning. This is because at the stage when students first enter the Department of Early Childhood Education, their knowledge of what they consider 'appropriate to teach' to this specific age group (i.e. whether issues such as racism or the media are of concern to young children), will largely determine their attitude to these courses. From our point of view, a reflective approach is the only one that will enable students to recognise and acknowledge their own stereotypes and to move forward, through reflection, to a balanced understanding of the social, political and educational aspects addressed in these courses. We also hope that encouraging reflection may, at a later stage, lead students to question the dominant pedagogical practices of the Greek preschool education, and that, in turn, this will later permit them to design educational interventions that take into account the social and political context.

We are aware that the introduction of these two courses in this specific educational context contradicts students' educational memory and prior experience (Nelson and Harper 2006). This requires us to offer students a work pattern that creates a de facto breakthrough in their way of thinking. We see this as necessary in order to reverse taken-for-granted knowledge and promote a form of 'social literacy' (Baynham 1995; Street 1995) that also takes into consideration the students' gender and social background.

As mentioned previously, students enter the university having had experience of a school system that is highly centralised. The courses are taught through textbooks (the same ones for the whole country), approved by the Ministry of Education. The prevailing way of working in the classroom is teacher-centred, with an emphasis on learning courses taught as discrete modules. Thus there is little intention on the part of the school to develop critical thinking or interdisciplinarity; rather the aim is verbatim memorisation of curriculum content (Hopf and Xohellis 2003). The university admission process reinforces this style of teaching. Success in the Panhellenic exams requires literal reproduction of the textbook material. As a result, for almost all students, the preparation for these exams is undertaken by 'frontistiria', a parallel system of private schools, which operate after high school hours. Frontistiria seek to replicate and consolidate students' acquisition of the official course content in a mechanical way. Additionally, many schools are governed by an ethnocentric perception that does not recognise cultural diversity (Frangoudaki and Dragona 1997). Thus, although in their daily school and social life students have lived alongside an ever-increasing number of immigrant children, it is not surprising that they see issues relating to diversity through stereotypical lenses constructed by society and the educational system.

Similarly, although our students consume many forms of technology on a daily basis (e.g. PCs, mobile phones, social networks, Internet and games) and live in an environment of 'technological optimism' promoted in recent years by the Greek educational system, they ignore the economic, political and social dimensions of using this technology. The rhetoric developed by the Ministry of Education and the practices pursued recently in the 'Digital Classroom Action' – e.g. offering a laptop to each student in the first year of Gymnasium (junior high school) – exemplifies recently observed trends that appear to consider the accumulation of information as knowledge. Somehow this deification of the tool to which magical powers are attributed assumes that access to ICT alone is enough to solve all the problems of education (Kourti 2012a).

Our pedagogical approach for teaching both courses, therefore, has been to adopt methods that require active participation and encourage critical thinking. We have designed a 'thematic week' for intercultural education and a workshop in media education (see Kourti and Leonida 2007 and Kourti 2012b). The 'thematic week' is an innovatory crash-course that uses teaching methods based on the principles of experiential learning, representing a significant new practice for the University of Athens, Department of Early Childhood Education. The next section outlines our approach in more detail and offers a critical evaluation of the courses based on the findings of an action research study.

Description and evaluation of the courses
Content, pedagogic rationale and mode of delivery

Both courses attempt to highlight the complexity of the issues addressed and the necessity of reading a situation at many levels with many tools. Through the elaboration of students' experiences and their personal involvement, the positive aspects of diversity and media are also illuminated. This contrasts with current public discourse, where the emphasis is mostly on the negative aspects. In this way, we hope to encourage students to take a scientific, objective approach to issues relating to their daily lives. We want to enable our students (especially in the current time of great tension and crisis) to examine these issues from a certain distance and to give them comprehensive consideration. Broadly speaking, in moving students away from an approach to learning based on memorisation and by encouraging reflective learning, we also aim to familiarise them with new ways of teaching that could be used in future in their own teaching practices.

The pedagogical rationale that informs these courses is that in order for students to achieve cognitive understanding of these issues, initially we need to work to uncover their existing perceptions and stereotypes. The most appropriate way to do this, in our view, is to create pedagogical situations that introduce them to the process of questioning 'their own truths' so that they really understand the 'new knowledge' through action. In order for students to become open to new ideas, it is necessary to create a state of conflict that challenges their existing preconceptions. Our approach is based mainly on sociocognitive theories of learning (Doise 1985; Weil-Barais 1985; Bednarz and Garnier 1989) that argue that learning takes place when new ideas conflict with prior knowledge. As resolution of this conflict requires modification of existing knowledge to accommodate the new knowledge, further progression in thinking is usually achieved, together with a change in individual perspectives and the way reality is understood. Both courses employ experiential learning techniques to motivate students' participation and to challenge their existing knowledge. Later, students are required to read relevant texts, attend lectures and complete assignments that recontextualise and support this experiential learning both theoretically and cognitively.

Approximately, 60 students at a time take part in the Intercultural Education course. Using experiential workshops and discussion, the objective of the Intercultural Education thematic week is to enable students to negotiate issues of intercultural education using as triggers films, theatre and visual arts happenings and new teaching practices. In this course, the learning dynamic is reinforced by the alternation between the experiential approach used with small groups of 20 individuals and the theoretical elaboration that takes place in plenary sessions. In this course, intercultural education issues are not approached as pedagogical applications, as our primary aim is for students to develop an understanding of the conditions of migration and its social and historical dimensions. We then focus on work in the kindergarten and the issues that might arise in relation to the teacher's management of a heterogeneous class.

The aim of the media education workshops, which 20 to 30 students participate in at a time, is to activate the knowledge they have acquired already through their everyday experience with the media and to encourage the development of a more systematic and critical understanding of how the media operates (Buckingham 2007). Students work in small groups of three to five people. Each group undertakes the production of a specific project, which consists of the construction and operation of a blog throughout the semester on a theme of a broader educational interest agreed by its members. Each group must upload relevant written and audio-visual texts and is committed to producing at least one audio-visual text (video). In our view, this direct experience of media production promotes a more reflective use of the media and sensitises students to the techniques, practices and language used by media professionals in their attempt to recreate reality.

Evaluation of the course aims, content and pedagogy

In order to evaluate the progress of these two courses, both in terms of content and the adopted format of teaching, we have conducted a long-term action-research project (Norton 2009; McIntosh 2010) to record their evolution. We have kept detailed, reflective diaries over the past six years. In addition, we kept and analysed the feedback from our students in the form of their written work and media productions. Examining these outputs allowed us to evaluate the quality of students' understanding and critical reflection. In addition, every year, students are asked to give a systematic evaluation of these courses. Year-on-year, the nature of this evaluation varies slightly as it corresponds to modifications to the course content and way of working as suggested by the previous year's student evaluation.

More specifically, for the Intercultural Education course, students' written work includes a diary where they are asked to record what they felt, what they considered as new learning and what they found difficult during the thematic week. They are also required to provide a brief written self-evaluation that documents how their thinking and understanding evolved during this week, as well as their evaluation of the organisation and content of the course. To assess their theoretical understanding, we require students to choose a text from a bibliography given to them in class, to analyse this and identify how it can be integrated into the problematic of intercultural education. This means that in each student's work, one can find both reflective elements and evidence about how they recontextualise knowledge and link theory with practice. For the Media Education course, at the end of the semester, each group of students is expected to produce a portfolio that offers a detailed record of the evolution of the tasks in the workshop, the theoretical and practical issues they encountered concerning their use of media and media-related language and their own preoccupations and the progress of their group. Furthermore, outside the workshop, each group is required to enrich the portfolio with supplementary material from the Internet or other media on issues that relate to the objectives of the workshop and their own media production (for example, articles on social networks, etc.). Like the written work associated with the Intercultural Education course, therefore, this portfolio material offers us insights into how students collect and compile relevant data on the media as well as on their efforts to reflect on their group's creative processes. How well the groups of students implement this task, therefore, demonstrates their understanding of and capacity to synthesise the set of concepts outlined in the workshops that relate to media education. At the end of the semester, students produce a short report on their experience and on how well the course corresponded to their expectations. Again, these reports are scrutinised to determine what students have learned, how this compares with their preconceptions about media and what this reveals about their needs concerning theory and practice.

In the next section, we present insights gained from a thematic content analysis of this material, offering points of comparison concerning the design of the courses, the difficulties we experienced relating to their implementation and the resistances we encountered on the part of the students.

The fragile process of change

Every year, students' evaluations identify their participation in these courses as a very fruitful experience. Overall, our evidence suggests that students actively participate: they state that they 'have learned things', that 'several perceptions of foreigners are overturned' and that their attitudes to media in everyday life and conceptions of the educational process have changed.

Our observations over the years of the gradually increasing active participation by students and positive reception of initiatives undertaken in the different activities of the courses attest that the courses reinforce students self-confidence and ability to generate, discuss and listen to points of alternative views and positions expressed in public, regardless of whether these are compatible with, provocative or even subversive in terms of their own position. It seems that empowerment through group work offers a kind a springboard that allows for a more active and effective presence in society, and thus it may lead students to a new understanding of the teacher's role in society. At the same time, students become more self-confident in creating educational material using a variety of media. In the future, this self-confidence in analysing and creating educational material will help them to have a better awareness of the likely ideological impact of the different kinds of media used in the classroom.

Our data show, however, that although this perspective on education and its way of teaching supports a critical approach, at the same time, it meets serious resistance from students. This resistance is related to their experiences of course content, the ideology of the Greek school on diversity issues and innovation and what is considered as proper 'school knowledge'. Every year in their assignments, though these are largely reflective and characterised by a critical disposition, in various ways students also express doubts about how to apply what they have learned to their future work. It appears that their experiences on their practical placements in various kindergartens highlight an evident contradiction between current educational reality and the approach and outcomes of these courses.

Students' ability to understand and reflect on the critical issues covered by these courses is a cause for concern, however, and calls into question the long-term effectiveness of introducing students to new educational practices if, at the same time, they are confronted with traditional educational practices on a daily basis. It seems that our pedagogical approach, which promotes investigation and processing of context-sensitive parameters, creative solutions, flexibility and constant adaptation, causes considerable turmoil as it challenges long-established experience and certainties. This contradiction seems to destabilise students and creates uncertainty about their ability to escape from the influence of previous educational experiences that have allowed them to be subjected to, and moulded by, a homogenised view of knowledge and knowledge transmission. Thus, although students experience a different, more radical, approach through our courses and teaching (and assess this positively), they find it quite hard to make it their own, to disengage from the security of long experience and the theoretically and empirically formed perception that pedagogy is pure application. Our evidence seems to indicate that once they qualify and become teachers, compliance with what they already know has a good chance of prevailing. This might be described as an example of the inability to make the leap from empirical to scientific knowledge that often leads to a sort of 'amnesia of theory' (Baton-Hervé 1999). This impression is reinforced by the fact that in students' written assignments and, also, in their audio-visual productions, we frequently discern stereotypical views and opinions that testify to the power of empirical knowledge (acquired through personal experience and observation) over the 'scientific' knowledge of educational theory and practice that is acquired as a result of formal learning experiences (Frangoudaki 2008). The issues presented in both courses are familiar to everyone, and everyone has positions and points of view about these issues shaped by the personal values, the media and the society at large. It seems that this daily and intimate experience easily counters any exposure to scientific information that we might offer our students.

Thus, despite the fact that students' evaluations of the two courses are positive, both in terms of their cognitive content and the method of teaching and that their contribution to the students educational training is recognised, this alone is not enough to enable them to challenge their lived experience and preconceptions about education acquired over many years of schooling.

Discussion

Our experience of delivering these courses suggests that if we want to find sustainable solutions to the issue of preschool teachers' initial education and promote critical awareness as an essential tool for their educational practice, we need to focus on how these resistances are formed by the current educational system and formulate proposals that can create a dynamic and conditions for change.

Beyond individual resistances, it seems also useful to consider the context which defines the training of future preschool teachers in order to analyse and understand the limits and contradictions of the educators' intervention and of the institutional framework as it stands today in Greece. The history of preschool teachers' initial training in Greece, and the transition from Pedagogical Academies to Universities, has led to a contradictory situation. From vocational schools we now have a university-scientific training aimed at both academic/scientific formation and professional preparation. Achieving this mix is a challenge for all Greek preschool education departments from the first day of their establishment, and for every teacher educator individually. In our own practice and the design and delivery of the courses analysed above, we have attempted to build this bridge between theory and practice (Gordon 2007). Yet the pedagogic approach we advocate is not very apparent in the development of new models of teacher training at university level. As yet, these are still not well defined (Guibert and Troger 2012). This situation is reflected in the curriculum of the Education Departments. Differences can be discerned in the balance between scientific–analytical and vocational–applied approaches. Thus, the bridging between theory and practice (Allsopp et al. 2006) that students are called upon to achieve as a result of a university education is somehow 'undermined' from the outset by inherent weaknesses in different departments' curricula to practically implement this and also by some educators' willingness to understand and achieve it.

As far as these two courses are concerned, it is evident that their content and teaching methodology are not reflected in wider education policy. Paradoxically, the Ministry of Education, while implementing various actions through European programmes on these two topic areas,[5] does not give equal emphasis to them in the official curricula in schools. Nevertheless, this curriculum content is taught in the pedagogical courses at the university. As students have experienced the limited application of these curriculum areas during their practical placement in Greek national kindergartens, by the time they enrol in our courses[6] their opinions about the everyday educational reality and lack of priority given to these curriculum areas has already been formed.

Considering the above contradictions, one might wonder why such a superficial approach to the issues of cultural diversity and media persists, given the explicit requirements for these issues to be included as a distinct part of a kindergarten's official curricula content. At this particular historical moment, recent surveys suggest that issues of diversity (Parekh 2000; Ladson-Billings and Gillborn 2004) and the need to adopt a critical approach to the media (Carlsson et al. 2008) should be key priorities for educational policy.

In Greece, the state education system's choice to support educational policies and practices that mostly concern the use of ICT in education rather than to train future teachers in media education means that a critical approach to the use of different forms of media is largely ignored. It could be argued that in the context of a conservative educational system, media education that enables students to question the educational material proposed by the state might occasion a redefinition of the educational process. At this point in time, it appears that this is something that the state does not want to risk. Similarly, as far as diversity issues and otherness are concerned, despite the attempts for change in recent years (in terms of textbooks and curricula), the national education offered in Greek schools is based mainly on a non-historical conception that over its long history, the nation has remained homogenous, with unchanged cultural characteristics. This emphasis on homogeneity, even as a value, encourages xenophobia in the name of the preservation of 'authentic' national characteristics from 'alien' influences and does not leave space in the school for those who do not identify with this 'pure' national standard. As a result, the 'other' becomes either invisible or treated with a folkloric approach. The dominant narrative of the Greek school is threatened by an intercultural approach that adopts a critical view and questions the value of homogeneity in the context of accounts of the historical, social and political dimensions of Greek society.

As it currently stands, therefore, the situation we have described above could be interpreted as a lack of political will to state or to take a position on these critical issues. Consequently, it is not hard to understand why the subject matter of courses on intercultural and media education do not become legitimised in the consciousness of future and in-service teachers' minds and why they remain invisible in the daily ritual of schools. Unless this situation changes, this can only be to the detriment of the education of young children growing up as media consumers in an increasingly diverse, multicultural society.

Conclusion

The aim of this article was to discuss the findings of a systematic evaluation of the introduction of two courses into the University of Athens's curriculum for initial preschool teacher's training. As detailed above, these courses have been designed to respond to some urgent needs in modern Greek society. As a result of this process, we have come to realise that, apart from the ideological issues raised by the subject matter of these two courses, concerns about their successful implementation revolve around issues and broader questions about the nature of initial teacher training (Darling-Hammond and Bransford 2005; Cochran-Smith, Feiman-Nemser and McIntyre 2008), especially how to link theory and practice. The main question remains: 'How should we train teachers in Greece today?'

In the relevant literature and corresponding practices, two main trends in initial and in-service teacher training can be discerned. The first of these supports teaching as a reflective process and prevails in most European countries. The second of these treats teaching as 'instrumental', where the emotional and educational dimension is margin-alised. For example, in the UK and the USA recent curriculum 'reforms' (Guibert and Troger 2012) have attempted to reassert traditional, conservative values. The perspective we have adopted follows the first trend. At this historical moment where a clear conservatism of the Greek educational system is observed, our goal remains to empower teachers through educational processes that enable them to activate their theoretical knowledge and learn how to build a bridge between theory and practice. In this way, we hope to raise preschool teachers' awareness so that they become alert to, and can meet current demands for educational reforms. In this way, we hope to protect them from the constant frustrations they experience. Rather than constituting the 'weak link' in the system, we argue that the systematic strengthening of the country's future teachers should act as a lever to change the system from the bottom up. To achieve this will require collaboration amongst all university departments in order to elaborate a common perception about the content and the delivery of initial training for preschool education programmes. Nowadays, achieving this consensus appears to be increasingly crucial if we are to make changes in teacher education and create in our universities the conditions that can 'persuade' future teachers to move beyond the current rigid point of view that 'teaching means just transmitting knowledge' and to assimilate the view that 'teaching means acting politically' and reflexively.

Currently, although each university department has its own curriculum, progress has been made with the creation of a network of educators from preschool education departments. Over the past four years, members of this network have been meeting to discuss and search for consensus on teacher education issues, with the main axis being the connection between theory and practice. Meetings are organised at different universities, and the exchange of experiences among educators is creating a community of learning and practice (Kimble, Hildreth, and Bourdon 2008). The exchange of 'good practices' helps to develop a kind of common code between the departments, which is then transferred to their students. The example of working in thematic weeks, which was designed and implemented for the first time in the Department of Early Childhood Education of the University of Athens for the course on intercultural education, has so far been adopted by three other departments in their curricula. Within the network, it is clear that the process of reflecting on our own academic work and practices is highly fruitful; it creates the dynamic conditions where critical awareness may flourish, despite the difficulties encountered in changing the Greek Educational system. As we have argued above, this bottom-up effort to change the status quo should allow future teachers to develop a critical stance towards the system itself as well as the current practices adopted by the formal school system. Our hope is that the new generation of preschool teachers will be able to recognise and exploit the opportunities given by the system every time that it attempts to introduce changes or reforms to its education policy.

The intercultural and media education courses discussed in this article represent an attempt by members of the Department of Preschool Education at the University of Athens to reflect on and incorporate recent educational issues into its initial teacher training programme. As has become apparent, however, where planned reforms simply follow or just obey European education policy imperatives under specific programmes and are implemented solely at the level of teachers' in-service training, this is unlikely to meet with success. Instead, it results in localised production of alternative educational materials and isolated actions by individual university departments. The course production processes and educational expertise developed does not feed into the educational system in a systematic way in order to achieve change, although some teachers and collectives have benefited from these actions and have attempt limited-scale interventions (sometimes, of course, at a cost).[7] Even if the scope of these interventions is limited, however, they certainly create breakthroughs in the system and help register in the collective unconscious the feasibility of such innovations. The current economic crisis in Greece is likely to divert attention away from the need to create a more inclusive educational system and to offer its youngest citizens a programme of media education fit for the twenty-first century. At this moment in time, therefore, it is clear that there is an urgent need for more than isolated initiatives and actions.

It would be illusory to believe that it is possible to achieve the goal of having teachers with critical awareness only through a reform of initial teacher training. There is a need for a synergy involving the state, universities and preschool teachers themselves. It is essential that the dialogue between teachers and researchers, universities and schools, becomes more systematic and dynamic, with the Greek educational system meeting the new demands of the society and creating institutional conditions that will allow teachers to act differently in schools. Finally, since the work of the professional teacher is learnt gradually, given the complexities of the immersion in a field of practice that takes place over time, a continuous participatory in-service training programme that meets the evolving demands of teachers will also be necessary.

Notes

1. Data from the 2011 Census is not yet available.
2. At the end of 2009, the Greek economy faced the highest budget deficit and government debt to GDP ratios in the European Union. This, and rising debt levels, led to rising borrowing costs, resulting in a severe economic crisis and a crisis in international confidence in Greece's ability to repay its sovereign debt. In May 2010 the International Monetary Fund and other Eurozone

nations agreed a rescue package. Greece was required to adopt harsh austerity measures to bring its deficit under control. The economic and political situation in Greece is extremely complex. In 2013, the Greek economy remains in deficit, stringent austerity measures continue to be imposed and there is considerable political unrest amongst its citizens.

3. The media education course is described in the curriculum as 'Issues on Audiovisual Communication'.
4. Presidential Decrees are regulations voted in Parliament and signed by the President of the Hellenic Republic, in order to acquire the status of a law.
5. Since 1997, the Ministry of Education through European funding programs has run under NSRF (National Strategic Reference Framework) four major educational programs – interventions targeted at 'vulnerable groups' (immigrants, gypsies, Muslim minority in Thrace, Greek immigrants abroad). Also, in recent years the Ministry of Education has promoted activities that encourage students and teachers to engage with media education. The recent proposal for a media education curriculum (called Audiovisual Expression) in the broader context of Aesthetic Education for all levels of compulsory education (2011), demonstrates that the Recommendation of the European Commission (20 October 2009) is accepted by the Greek State.
6. These courses are optional and can be chosen by the third year (intercultural education) or fourth year (media education) students. Thus, students have already attended – according to the Department curriculum – the theoretical courses related to the official curriculum and have been trained for at least two semesters in kindergartens.
7. See the case of the 132nd Primary School of Athens where there is an important number of migrant children. The school is renowned all over the country as un example of educational methods directed towards respect and integration of different school populations, students' achievement, participation of parents and antiracist education despite the lack of support, strong distrust and polemic by populist press and political parties or part of the educational authorities (Varnava-Skoura 2008). The example of '132' illustrates the contradictions of the Greek system: while this effort was also opposed by the education authorities, simultaneously it received a award from the Children's Ombudsman for educational proposals against discrimination (2011) and was presented in Brussels as a Greek 'good practice' in a relevant conference (see the published report 'Good Practice Exchange Seminar', 2012, on Public Policies on combating discrimination and fostering diversity in education, and the school web site www.132grava.net).

References

Allsopp, D. H., D. DeMarie, P. Alvarez-McHatton, and E. Doone. 2006. "Bridging the Gap between Theory and Practice: Connecting Courses with Field Experiences." *Teacher Education Quarterly* 33 (1): 19–35. http://www.teqjournal.org/Back%20Issues/Volume%2033/VOL33%20PDFS/33_1/07allsoppetal-33_1.pdf.

Androusou, A. 2005. "Working with Others: Facets of an Educational Experience." *Pedagogy, Culture and Society* 13 (1): 87–108. doi:10.1080/14681360500200217.

Androusou, A., and N. Askouni. 2011. *Cultural Diversity and Human Rights: Challenges for Education.* [In Greek.] Athens: Metaixmio.

Androusou, A., Ch. Dafermou, and V. Tsafos. 2012a. "Educating Teachers: Observation of a Classroom's Framework as Part of the Student Teachers' Education." *The International Journal of Learning* 18 (8): 191–212.

Androusou, A., Ch. Dafermou, and V. Tsafos. 2012b. "Preschool Teacher's Education: the Reflective Teacher in the Framework of Pedagogical Theory and Educational Practice." [In Greek.] In *Education and In-service Training of Teachers*, edited by V. Oikonomidis, 543–560. Athens: Pedio.

Aslanidou, S. 2008. "A propos de l'éducation aux medias en Grèce: le cas d' *A.S.P.E.T.E* [On Media Education in Greece: The Case of A.S.P.E.T.E]." In *Des jeunes et des medias en Europe*, [In French.], edited by G. Jacquinot-Delaunay and E. Kourti, 221–231. Paris: L'Harmattan.

Baton-Hervé, E. 1999. "Les enfants téléspectateurs: Prégnance des répresentations médiatiques et amnésie de la recherche [Children Viewers of Television: Pervasiveness of Media Representations and Amnesia of Research]." *Réseaux – Dossier: Les jeunes et l'écran* [In French.] 17 (92–93): 205–217.

Baynham, M. 1995. *Literacy Practices*. London: Longman.

Bednarz, N., and C. Garnier, eds. 1989. *Construction des savoirs, obstacles et conflits*. Ottawa: CIRADE/Agence d'Arc.

Bouzakis, S., and Ch. Tzikas. 1998. *The Period of Pedagogical Academies and Nursery Teacher Schools 1933–1990. Vol. B of Training Primary and Nursery School Teachers in Greece*. [In Greek.] Athens: Gutenberg.

Buckingham, D. 2007. "Digital Media Literacies: Rethinking Media in the Age of Internet." [In Greek.] *Zitimata Epikoinonias* (Special Issue on media education) 7: 13–30.

Carlsson, U., S. Tayie, G. Jacquinot-Delaunay, and J. M. Pérez Tornero, eds. 2008. *Empowerment through Media Education. An Intercultural Dialogue*, 59–63. Göteborg: International Clearinghouse on Children, Youth and Media.

Cochran-Smith, M. 2005. "The New Teacher Education: for Better or for Worse?" *Educational Researcher* 34 (7): 3–17. doi:10.3102/0013189X034007003.

Cochran-Smith, M., S. Feiman-Nemser, and M. McIntyre, eds. 2008. *Handbook of Research on Teacher Education: Enduring Questions in Changing Contexts*. New York: Routledge and the Association of Teacher Educators.

Damanakis, M. 1997. *The Education of Repatriate and Foreign Pupils in Greece*. [In Greek.] Athens: Gutenberg.

Darling-Hammond, L., and J. Bransford, eds. 2005. *Preparing Teachers for a Changing World*. San Francisco: Jossey-Bass.

Doise, W., ed. 1985. *Psychologie sociale du développement cognitif* [Social Psychology of Cognitive Development]. [In French.] Berne: Peter Lang.

Frangoudaki, A. 2008. *Study Guide of the Thematic Unit 'Cultural Diversity and Social Inequalities'*. [In Greek.] Patra: Hellenic Open University.

Frangoudaki, A., and Th. Dragona, eds. 1997. *What is Our Country?: Ethnocentrism in Education*. [In Greek.] Athens: Alexandria.

Freire, P. 1973. *Pedagogy of the Oppressed*. New York: Seabury Press.

Giroux, H. 2007. "Democracy, Education and the Politics of Critical Pedagogy." In *Critical Pedagogy: Where Are We Now?*, edited by P. McLaren, and J. L. Kincheloe, 1–5. New York: Peter Lang.

Good Practice Exchange Seminar (Public Policies on Combating Discrimination and Fostering Diversity in Education). 2012. In Brussels, March 26–27. Hosted by Norway, Brussels: GEG Contributions, 34–37.

Gordon, M. 2007. "How Do I Apply This to my Classroom?" In *Bridging Theory and Practice in Teacher Education*, edited by M. Gordon, and T. O'Brien. Rotterdam: Sense Publishers.

Gordon, M., and T. O'Brien, eds. 2007. *Bridging Theory and Practice in Teacher Education*. Rotterdam: Sense Publishers.

Guibert, P., and V. Troger. 2012. *Peut-on encore former des enseignants?* [Can We Still Train Teachers?] [In French.] Paris: Armand Colin.

Hopf, D., and P. Xohellis. 2003. *High-school and Lyceum in Greece*. [In Greek.] Athens: Ellinika Grammata.

Jacquinot-Delaunay, G. 2001. "The Teacher and the Media: Towards a New Professional Identity?" [In French.] Accessed February 10, 2012. http://spme2008.free.fr/formation/conferences/Jacquinot.ppt.

Katsarou, E., and B. Tsafos. 2009. "Dominant Discourses vs. Students' Subjectivities in Greek L1 Curriculum." *International Journal of Learning* 16 (11): 35–46.

Katsarou, E., and B. Tsafos. 2010. "Multimodality in L1 Curriculum: The Case of Greek Compulsory Education." *Critical Literacy: Theories and Practices* 4 (1): 48–65.

Kimble, Ch., P. Hildreth, and I. Bourdon, eds. 2008. *Communities of Practice: Creating Learning Environments for Educators*, Vol. 1. Charlotte, North Carolina: Information Age Publishing.

Kotzamanis, B. 2008. "Foreigners in Greece: A Preliminary Analysis of their Geographical Dispersion and their Contribution to the Population Changes of the Last Decade (1991–2001)." [In Greek.] In *Volume 1 of Migration in Greece: Experiences – Policies – Perspectives*, edited by Tz. Kavounidi, A. Kontis, Th. Lianos, and R. Fakolias, 12–37. Athens: IMEPO.

Kourti, E., ed. 2012a. *Childhood and Media, Vols. 1 and 2*. [In Greek.] Athens: Herodotos.

Kourti, E. 2012b. "Social Media and Media Education during Initial Teacher Training." In *VIDEOMUSEUMS: Recording Traces of our Subjective Culture*, edited by N. Govas, 113–120. Athens: Directorate of Secondary Education of Eastern Attica.

Kourti, E., and M. Leonida. 2007. "From Spectators to Producers. Media Literacy and Audio-visual Production." [In Greek.] *Zitimata Epikoinonias* (Special Issue on Media Education) 7: 88–102.

Ladson-Billings, G., and D. Gillborn, eds. 2004. *The Routledge Falmer Reader in Multicultural Education.* London: Routledge Falmer.

Mayer, J. 1986. "Teaching Critical Awareness in an Introductory Course." *Teaching Sociology* 14 (4): 249–256. doi:10.2307/1318382.

McIntosh, P. 2010. *Action Research and Reflective Practice: Creative and Visual Methods to Facilitate Reflection and Learning.* London: Routledge.

Nelson, C., and V. Harper. 2006. "A Pedagogy of Difficulty: Preparing Teachers to Understand and Integrate Complexity in Teaching and Learning." *Teacher Education Quarterly* 33 (2): 7–21. http://files.eric.ed.gov/fulltext/EJ795203.pdf

Norton, L. S. 2009. *Action Research in Teaching & Learning: A Practical Guide to Conducting Pedagogical Research in Universities.* London and New York: Routledge.

Parekh, B. 2000. *Rethinking Multiculturalism: Cultural Diversity and Political Theory.* New York, NY: Palgrave.

Raths, J., and A. McAninch. 1997. *What Counts as Knowledge in Teacher Education.* Stamford: Ablex Publishing Corporation.

Rhedding-Jones, J. 2005. "Questioning Diversity." In *Critical Issues in Early Childhood Education,* edited by N. Yelland, 131–145. London: Open University Press.

Robinson, K., and C. J. Diaz. 2006. *Diversity and Difference in Early Childhood Education: Issues for Theory and Practice.* London: Open University Press.

Rowan, L., and E. Honan. 2005. "Literarily Lost: The Quest for Quality Literacy Agendas in Early Childhood Education." In *Critical issues in Early Childhood Education,* edited by N. Yelland, 197–223. London: Open University Press.

Sofou, E., and B. Tsafos. 2010. "Preschool Teachers' Understandings of the National Preschool Curriculum in Greece." *Early Childhood Education Journal* 37 (5): 411–420. doi:10.1007/s10643-009-0368-2.

Stamelos, G. 1999. *University Departments of Pedagogy: Origins – Current state –Potential.* [In Greek.] Athens: Gutenberg.

Street, B. 1995. *Social Literacies.* London: Longman.

Toura, K. 2009. "Education of Foreigners and Emigrants in the Greek Educational System." [In Greek.] *Greek Society* (Research Centre of the Athens Academy) 89: 311–336.

Triantafyllidou A., and Th. Maroukis, eds. 2010. *Migration in 21st-century Greece.* [In Greek.] Athens: Kritiki.

Varnava-Skoura, G. 2008. *Pedagogical Actions and Didactical Approaches in a Multicultural Context: The Case of 132 Primary Schools of Athens.* [In Greek.] Athens: Doudoumis.

Weil-Barais, A. 1985. "L'étude des connaissances des élèves comme préalable à l'action didactique [Study of Children's Level of Knowledge as Preliminary to Didactic Activities]." *Bulletin de Psychologie* 368: 157–160.

Yelland, N. 2005a. "Curriculum, Pedagogies and Practice with ICT in the Information Age." In Critical issues in Early Childhood Education, edited by N. Yelland, 224–242. London: Open University Press.

Yelland, N., ed. 2005b. *Critical Issues in Early Childhood Education.* London: Open University Press.

Zeichner, K., and D. Liston. 1996. *Reflective Teaching: An Introduction.* New Jersey: Lawrence Erlbaum Associates.

Preschool a source for young children's learning and well-being

Sonja Sheridan and Ingrid Pramling Samuelsson

Department of Education, Communication and Learning, University of Gothenburg, Gothenburg, Sweden

This article aims to examine dominant discourses and changing paradigmatic views on children's learning and well-being in preschool in relation to theories on learning and research on quality and policy in Sweden. The key question: what are the main changes in policy, pedagogy and views of children's learning? The article builds on research that has been carried out by the research group in early childhood education at the University of Gothenburg. The results of these studies are analysed here through four dimensions of quality. The theoretical framework is based on interactionist perspectives, which bring together theories of learning in which individuals and the environment influence and are influenced by one another in continuous interaction and communication. The results demonstrate the interdependence and reciprocity between policy, views on children's learning, children's perspectives and preschool pedagogy. The results show that high-quality preschool is a product of the combined efforts of stakeholders on different system levels, confirming the significance of a comprehensive perspective when researching conditions for children's learning in preschool.

Introduction

This article aims to examine dominant discourses and changing paradigmatic views on children's learning and well-being in preschool in relation to theories on learning and research on quality and policy in Sweden. Education starts at birth and is a question of laying a broad foundation for children's lives in terms of well-being, values, attitudes, play, learning and creativity. From an early age, 87% of Swedish children are involved in preschool, which constitutes the first step of the educational system and embraces children from one to five years of age. The Swedish preschool should offer an enjoyable, secure and rich learning environment, aiming to give children a good start in life by applying a holistic approach to promoting their lifelong learning and development (Ministry of Education and Science 2010). All activities in preschool must be carried out in accordance with fundamental democratic values, enabling children to acquire an understanding of the values upon which Swedish society is based.

The preschool curriculum is composed of goals within a broad range of content areas, within which children's social and cognitive learning are integrated and viewed as of equal importance (Ministry of Education and Science 2010). For example, in preschool, children are expected to develop social competence, acquire knowledge of mathematics and science and learn how to play and cooperate with peers. Research clearly shows that in working with content such as literacy, mathematics and scientific issues, it is of fundamental importance that such activities take place in natural and meaningful contexts in which children can obtain concrete experiences (Sylva et al. 2010; Sheridan, Pramling Samuelsson, and Johansson 2009). This is in line with the intentions in the Swedish preschool curriculum, which states that the goals are to be integrated with one another and worked with as themes (Ministry of Education and Science 2010) using preschool didactics[1] (Pramling and Pramling Samuelsson 2011). Thus the quality of a preschool, referring to the conditions created for children's learning about different contents, is dependent on how pre-schoolteachers work with the goals in the curriculum.

Longitudinal research shows that the quality of preschool makes a difference to children's learning, affecting a wide range of cognitive, social and emotional outcomes in children's learning and development (Ceglowski and Bacigalupa 2002; Sylva et al. 2010). Preschools of high quality can significantly benefit children's learning, academic achievements, self-esteem and attitudes towards lifelong learning (Burchinal et al. 2000; Clifford and Bryant, 2003; NICHD 2005; Schweinhart, Barnes, and Weikart 1993; Sheridan, Pramling Samuelsson, and Johansson 2009; Sylva 1994; U.S. Department of Education 2000).

Variations in the quality of preschools can be described as the fit or the lack of fit between pedagogical intentions; the uses of material resources, contents, activities, teachers' learning strategies, communication and interplay with children and children's learning and experience of participation and influence, documentation and evaluation (Sheridan 2009). In high-quality preschools these aspects are intertwined, shaping and constituting each other. In low-quality preschools they seem to be separate constructs and situations. For example, the curriculum goals seem to have no influence on ongoing activities, which in turn are not related to documentation and children's learning in the preschool (Sheridan 2009).

The quality of a preschool is dependent on the influences of culture, context and dominant discourses relating to the child and childhood (Moss 2004), as well as to policy and societal and educational intentions for preschool (Sylva et al. 2010). This implies that the quality of preschool – and by 'quality' we mean the conditions for children's learning in terms of goals, content, pedagogical processes, communication, interaction and participation – has to be studied from a comprehensive perspective and in the light of those changes in preschool policy, pedagogy and views on children's learning that have taken place over the last decade. Questions at issue are:

- What are the main changes in policy?
- What are the main changes in pedagogy?
- What are the main changes in views and understandings of children's learning?

Theoretical framework

The article presented here is based on interactionist perspectives, which bring together theories of learning in which individuals and the environment influence one another in continuous interaction and communication (Ball 2006; Bronfenbrenner 1979, 1986; Bruner 1996; Vygotsky [1934] 1986). Children's learning is seen as a change of perspective that results from experiencing, acting and communicating with the environment, which, in turn, interacts with children in various ways (Sommer, Pramling

Samuelsson, and Hundeide 2010; Vygotsky [1934] 1986). The development of cognitive, social and emotional aspects cannot be separated; together they constitute an integrated whole.

The interactionist perspective that we adopt draws on Urie Bronfenbrenner's ecological systems theory (1979, 1986) as extended by James Garbarino (1992) and by Miller, Dalli, and Urban (2012), who advocate a critical ecology of the early childhood profession, as well as of theories of children's learning (Vygotsky [1934] 1986; Pramling 1994) and a perspective based on four dimensions of pedagogical quality (Sheridan 2009). Together these theoretical perspectives contribute to the understanding of relationships between policy issues and educational goals, and of how these affect the conditions for children's learning in preschool.

When applying ecological systems theories and the four dimensions of pedagogical quality, children's learning in preschool is examined in terms of different interrelated strata – namely macro-, exo-, meso-, micro- and chrono-system levels. In this article, they are used to highlight how, on different levels, systems interact, constitute and transform dominant discourses and paradigmatic views on children's learning and well-being in preschool.

This article is based on a perspective on pedagogical quality as constituted by four interacting dimensions. These are (1) society, (2) teachers, (3) children and (4) learning contexts. Each dimension is constituted by aspects/qualities that are unique to that dimension and that can be related to structures, processes, contents and results (Donabedian 1980; Sheridan 2009). Depending on how the dimensions interact with one another, learning environments of different quality are created.

The core of pedagogical quality lies in the interplay between the teacher and the child. This means that pedagogical quality does not exist in itself, but takes shape and develops in pedagogical processes through the interaction and communication between children and teachers, and through children's interactions with objects in preschool contexts (Sheridan 2001; Sheridan, Pramling Samuelsson, and Johansson 2009).

Design

This article is based on research that has been carried out in our research group at the University of Gothenburg. The results of these studies are analysed here through the four dimensions of quality. *The main focus in this article is the dimension of the child*, while the other dimensions are used as analytical lenses through which central aspects in the overall preschool context can be discerned and understood.

To highlight dominant discourses and changing paradigmatic views on children's learning and well-being in preschool – in relation to theories on learning and research on quality and policy in Sweden – the analytical process was conducted in two steps. Initially each dimension was used independently as a solitary analytical lens. Finally all of these dimensions have, in an integrated way, been taken into consideration and positioned in relation to the focus of analysis.

Analytical studies

The first analytical study is *Children's Early Learning*, which was conducted in Gothenburg (Sheridan, Pramling Samuelsson, and Johansson 2009). The aim of this study was to grasp the complexity of pedagogical quality as an educational phenomenon and the relationships between preschool quality and the conditions for children's learning.

A stratified sample of eight districts was chosen in order to represent diverse geographical areas and living conditions, as well as ethnic and socio-economic backgrounds. Within these districts a random sample of 38 preschools was selected. A total of 230 children between one and two years of age, their parents and 120 pre-schoolteachers participated in the study.

The data were generated using a mixed-methods approach. Preschool quality was evaluated using a revised version of the Early Childhood Environment Rating Scale (ECERS) (Harms and Clifford 1980; Sheridan 2007). The preschools were externally evaluated and related to the teacher's self-evaluations on the ECERS. The evaluations of quality on the ECERS were analysed statistically using SPSS. The external evaluations have a mean value of 4.44 and a range from 2.90 to 6.24 (1.00 – 7.00 = min–max). The mean values for the self-evaluations are higher (5.19) and range from 3.41 to 7.00. The results reveal differences among the teachers' self-evaluations. Whilst teachers in preschools externally evaluated as being of low or good quality tend to evaluate their own preschool quality as high, teachers in preschools of high quality seem to underestimate their own quality (Sheridan, Pramling Samuelsson, and Johansson 2009).

To capture the relationships between preschool quality and conditions for children's learning, new methods for the observation, analysis and evaluation of children's learning were developed. For example, video observations were used to document children's mathematical understanding during a structured situation characterised by play and talk (Doverborg and Pramling Samuelsson 2009). Video observations were also used to document children's communication during a situation in which a teacher read a story to a number of children individually and then each child retold the story with the help of different artefacts (Mellgren and Gustafsson 2009). The study of *Children's Early Learning* has been analysed through each of the four dimensions, and then through the four dimensions together.

The second focus of analysis was a group of studies in which children's meaning-making about various contents was the core of attention. Characteristic of these studies is that, as researchers, we decide what we want to study with the help of the teachers. This means that we work in partnership with the teachers, bringing them into a kind of collaborative in-service training wherein they have to read texts, participate in seminars and have us, as researchers, follow their work in practice. The in-service training is based on a specific theoretical perspective called developmental pedagogy, where play and learning are integrated. (For further reading, see Johansson and Pramling Samuelsson 2009). In practice it is the researcher who video-records the communication and interaction between pre-schoolteachers and children, while they are working in the agreed content. The teachers continually get feedback on their growing skills in communication and challenging children in creating meaning about the object for learning. The focus of analysis is children's meaning-making (Pramling Samuelsson and Pramling [accepted for publication]). These studies have been analysed first through the dimension of the child and then through all four dimensions together.

Results

The results of the analyses are here presented in relation to each of the four dimensions of quality. First we present three dimensions – which in this article are to be seen as contextual dimensions – and then the dimension of the child, which is, as we pointed out earlier, the main focus of analysis in this article.

The dimension of society

This dimension focuses on societal intentions related to views of the child, childhood and preschool. This dimension provides knowledge of policy and the overall goals for preschool and reveals how these goals are implemented in practice as values, content and activities. The focal points of analysis are the conditions for children's learning as they appear in the relationships between the intentions expressed in overall goals and children's learning. Therefore, for this article, the analysis through the dimension of society focused on how dominant discourses and changing paradigmatic views on children's learning and well-being in preschool are related to policy and educational goals in the preschool curriculum in Sweden.

In Sweden, over the last decade, preschool has been the focus of policy changes. In 1998, a national curriculum was introduced and this was revised in 2010 (Ministry of Education and Science 2010). The political intention behind this revision of the preschool curriculum was to make preschool more pedagogical. The goals and content related to language and communication, mathematics, science and technology were developed and strengthened, and a new area of evaluation and development of preschool quality was introduced. In order to avoid dichotomies between so-called 'academic' and 'social' learning, all curriculum goals and values must, according to policy, be integrated in children's play and learning. The ambition is to develop a pedagogy that can be described in terms of a Nordic perspective on preschool didactics (Pramling and Pramling Samuelsson 2011). Since the education act passed in 2010, preschool has also been recognised as a distinctive kind of school within the Swedish educational system (Ministry of Education and Research 2010).

The dimension of learning contexts

The dimension of learning contexts highlights the observable aspects of quality in preschools. It shows how teachers, children and (learning) objects interact and are related to one another in practice. The dual focus of this dimension is on how

(1) contents, pedagogical processes, communication and interaction are formed into a learning environment and
(2) this environment supports and challenges children's learning and development and enables them to participate and influence ongoing processes and activities in preschool.

In this dimension, analyses focus on the range of aspects within the four dimensions and consider how they interact with one another, to gain an understanding of the conditions for children's learning and development in preschool (Sheridan 2009).

Let us first examine the evaluations of preschool quality gained from the ECERS in the study of *Children's Early Learning* (Sheridan, Pramling Samuelsson, and Johansson 2009). The results highlight three qualitatively different learning environments, namely *Separating and Limiting environments*, *Child-centred Negotiating environments* and *Challenging Learning environments*. The variety of learning environments of low, good and high quality created different conditions for children's learning in preschool.

Low-quality preschools can be characterised by their limitations in space, material resources and restricted accessibility for the children. The results demonstrate how low-quality preschools are characterised by few reciprocal encounters, poor interaction and communication between teacher and child and few opportunities for children's participation in and learning of different content. Further, in such preschools, although teachers are present physically, they seem most frequently to focus on keeping control and maintaining order. Teachers and children appeared to follow parallel but separate paths that never actually merged. They seemed to have different intentions and/or were unaware of each other's intentions; as a consequence, they gained different experiences.

In preschools externally evaluated as being of high quality, the learning environment seemed to be rich in challenges and learning opportunities. During observations, the children participated in ongoing activities and the teachers focused on their interests, experiences and knowledge-formation in relation to the overall goals for preschool. They communicated and seemed to focus on and share similar learning objectives. The teachers interacted with the children in the 'here and now' by being present physically, emotionally and cognitively in communicating about issues in the past, present and future (Sheridan, Pramling Samuelsson, and Johansson 2009). The analyses show that the participating preschools varied in quality, indicating that the children had unequal conditions for learning.

The dimension of teachers

The focus of this dimension is teachers' professional competence. The dimension encompasses teachers' knowledge, skills, beliefs, values and their views of the child, knowledge and learning. A central feature of this dimension is the teachers' perspectives of the child and the ability to understand the child's own perspectives in terms of strategies, approaches, communication and interplay. It is a question of being part of the child's learning processes and combining the child's interests and intentions for learning with the goals in the preschool curriculum.

In this article, the analyses aim to highlight how the teachers approach the children in their learning processes, the strategies the teachers use, their knowledge of different educational content and their competence in sharing and communicating leaning objectives with the children (Sheridan et al. 2011)

The results of several studies (Sheridan 2001; Sheridan, Pramling Samuelsson, and Johansson 2009) highlight variations in teachers' approaches and identify different strategies/teaching orientations. These are *abdication, dominance, negotiating* and *learning-oriented* approaches. One main difference between these approaches is teachers' understanding of how children learn and make meaning about different contents, situations and phenomena. In the first three approaches (*abdication, dominance* and *negotiating*), it seems as if teachers believe that children learn by just doing things and participating in different activities. In the *learning-oriented* approach, teachers create conditions for learning by directing the child's attention towards a specific and shared learning objective in relation to the child's participation and relevant activities.

The results of the study *Children's Early Learning* show that teachers' knowledge seems to be generalised. This means that the teacher's knowledge – or lack thereof – encompasses different contents, areas and situations. Consequently, low quality in preschool encompasses more or less all contents and ongoing activities in preschool, and vice versa when the quality is high. The results show that the teacher's professional approach and competence are decisive for what children learn in preschool.

A study of pre-schoolteacher competence (Sheridan et al. 2011) highlights that the meaning given to teacher competence can be related to the continuous socio-political changes that have taken place over the past decade in Swedish society (Bronfenbrenner 1979, 1986; Garbarino 1992). In this study three intertwined dimensions of teacher competence were identified. Two of these dimensions identify competence in terms of knowledge of what, how and why – which seem to be definitions of competences that commonly emerge in most research on teacher competence. The third dimension is rather unique and can be related to current research in which teacher competence is regarded as interactive and transactional (Brostrøm and Veijleskov 2009; Sommer 2011), situational and relational (Dalli 2008; Miller, Dalli, and Urban2012; Pramling and Pramling Samuelsson 2011; Sommer, Pramling Samuelsson, and Hundeide 2010). Thus teacher competence is seen in terms of dialogical qualities and interactive, relational and transactional competences (Sommer) that are expressed though care, communication and interplay with the children, colleagues, parents, etc.

More specifically the results show that the participating teachers have a broad multidisciplinary knowledge, which needs to be deepened within specific areas such as, for example, mathematics, ICT, science, etc. Teachers place a high value on social competence, both in their own profession and as a focus for children's learning and development. They emphasise the importance of being a good role model who communicates intentions and democratic and ethical values, and who aims to take the perspective of the child into consideration, creating positive conditions for children's learning and development. Their view of the child seems to be focused more on becoming rather than being, as teachers often talk about what children need to learn in order to grow up to become democratic citizens. The teachers relate children's learning to everyday-life situations, taking children's interests as the points of departure for learning. The teachers reflect continuously on preschool practice, ongoing activities and upon their own knowledge in order to make improvements in line with changes in society (Sheridan et al. 2011).

Another study, focusing on documentation and evaluation in preschool, shows that preschool teachers seem to be at the intersection of conflicting paradigmatic views on children's learning and development (Sheridan, Williams, and Sandberg 2013). The results highlight that a more traditional psychological developmental approach can be discerned, in that the focus in documentation is often on what the child can or cannot do, blended with a more sociocultural approach in which children's learning processes are documented in relation to conditions created for their learning in preschool. Thus the results show how different paradigmatic views – about which aspects of children's learning and development should be documented and followed up, and how, when evaluating the quality of preschools – seem to exist parallel to one another and/or integrated together in ideologies, policy and preschool practice.

The dimension of the child

Children are, in this dimension, seen as subjects with voices of their own. Central aspects of this dimension are children's meaning-making, communication and interaction, both with one another and with pre-schoolteachers. The focus of research is on children's well-being, learning and development. Participation is studied from a child perspective. It is based on a desire to understand children's intentions and expressions of meaning in relation to a specific content, a certain situation and a particular context. Documentation and evaluation provide means to support and challenge children in their learning, as well as to enhance preschool quality (Sheridan 2009).

Let us begin with the discourse and fact that children of today are considered to have rights just like adults, pointed out, for example, in the UN Convention on the Rights of the Child (1989). Adults should not only do what they think is best for a child, but let children's own voices come through, and be listened to and taken notice of, in everyday-life situations (Shier 2001). In the field of early childhood education, the ambition for child-centred pedagogy has – in different ways and for various reasons – always existed. This could be because the children in question are younger than school age and need to change activities often, or could also be due to the fact that the content has been related to children's experiences in the family – like cooking, gardening, carpentry, etc. Child-centeredness has also been adapted to concrete activities that young children are believed to enjoy and in which they can be involved (Pramling Samuelsson and Asplund Carlsson 2007). In preschool, teachers have tried to do what they think is best for children, in comparison with school where the needs of the labour market and of society have been guiding principles. Both as a research and practical field, early childhood education has always been close to children's perspectives and their needs. This may be even more evident today, as the democratic aspect of trusting all human beings as being capable of representing what things mean to them has reached early years education. There are two main reasons for children's perspectives and voices to be brought into education: (1) to honour the idea of democracy, and (2) because learning is defined as making sense of things – that is, the sense children make of the content that they learn about (Sommer).

Behind the idea of children as subjects with voices of their own is the view of children as competent and not only vulnerable. This change in the view of childhood psychology, seeing the child as competent, can be related to the fact that children now live in a wider world and enter into numerous relationships from infancy. Children are presented as less fragile than earlier developmental psychologists asserted, and also as more resilient. It is the dynamic between the two phenomena that better describes the child of today. The same dual notions refer to children as novices or as competent; both sides have to be included in the view of modern children (Sommer).

Sommer's book *A Childhood Psychology* (2012) has had an enormous impact on early childhood education in Sweden. He describes children's development as linked to socio-emotional questions rather than as pure cognitive development – which, however, is not excluded. Throughout the book two leading standpoints are expressed: (1) young children are relatively socially competent, and (2) knowledge about children has to be embedded in historical and cultural contexts.

Children are active agents in their own learning and meaning-making. This premise has guided our research team at the University of Gothenburg. When analysing the study *Children's Early Learning* (Sheridan, Pramling Samuelsson, and Johansson 2009), through the dimension of the child, it is obvious that we tried to find evaluation tasks that met the same standard, to give voices to children's ideas and meaning-making. In this study, play situations with small animals and other props were arranged, allowing children and the researcher to play and communicate in order to evaluate the participating children's understanding of some important basic mathematical concepts. Six tasks embracing different aspects of basic mathematics were presented to the children in a playful manner with a lot of space for children's acting and communicating. The results describe what the children revealed about their perspectives, in accordance with their meaning-making. The results show that in young children experience grows with encounters and age, and that the teacher's knowledge of basic mathematics and ability to challenge children in their understanding are vital (Doverborg and Pramling Samuelsson 2009). The results highlight that the quality of the preschool in which the children were involved set the frame for their meaning-making. That is, children in preschools with higher quality created more advanced meanings than did other children (Doverborg 2011).

In the same study, Mellgren and Gustafsson (2009) evaluated children's knowledge and experience in language and communication. The teacher read a story to each individual child. The child then retold the story with the help of different artefacts symbolising the content of the book. Video observations focused on the relation between the teacher and the child: how the teachers interacted with the children while reading to them, what they did and said and how they approached the child during the retelling session. The results highlight four hierarchical categories, showing qualitative steps in the children's behaviour during the book-reading situation. These categories were labelled awareness, acting, inference and integration, and they represent various ways children relate themselves to the story reading. In this way we could see both each child's intellectual ability to make sense of the story and also the ways in which the teacher and child interacted, indicating how the teacher's ways of interacting with the child and the text created different conditions for the children to make sense of or to retell the story.

The other studies that our research team have worked with extensively relate to children's learning about specific aspects of the world around them in terms of creating understanding. This perspective challenges the tradition of early childhood education where social relationships and acting have been the key notions. The studies aim to examine what children are able to grasp or make sense of in relation to specific contents, and not in an abstract way. However, curriculum goals in early education are often focused on children's cognitive or social development, or on children's self-confidence, bodily awareness, etc. Children's developments in relation to these kinds of goals are hard to evaluate in everyday work. If we look at it from another perspective, children have to create meaning – a meaning that can then be built on to create a more advanced meaning. Children need, for example, to be able to understand numbers before they can begin to handle subtraction and addition of numbers. In every area of learning, one can find key notions or ideas that are critical for taking a new step in the learning process (Pramling and Pramling Samuelsson 2011).

In these studies the research team has worked in various content areas. Let us look at one of the most recent studies, wherein we have focused on aesthetics (dance, poetry and music). Aesthetics is an area frequently used in early childhood education, but most often with the intention to teach children something other than aesthetics. Often teachers say that they use music and singing with the children in order to create something joyful or a feeling of belonging. Children also clap their hands to music to learn how to count or to become aware of their bodies, or teachers use such movements as a preparation for children to be able to sit still and concentrate (Asplund Carlsson, Pramling, and Pramling Samuelsson 2008). Instead of using aesthetics as a method for learning something else, we asked, what does it mean to become skilled in music, dance and poetry? What are the possible learning objectives in music, dance and poetry? That is, what is it possible for young children to make sense of, and what do we want them to become aware about in the world around them? This means that a goal related to aesthetics could be to become interested in music, while a learning objective could be to discern time (metre) in music, for example – for the child to develop the ability to discriminate between 2/4 and 3/4 time, or in dance to become able to distinguish between soft and hard movements, or free movement in comparison with movement coordinated with someone else (Pramling Samuelsson et al. 2009).

By having teachers who knew and could teach the building blocks of poetry, children from three years of age were able to become skilled in writing poetry. The building blocks used in the study were simile (e.g., 'the star is like an aquarium'); metaphor (e.g., 'the moon is a necklace in the sky'); synaesthesia, or the blending of senses (e.g., 'warmly brown'); line breaks and what they do to the sound (and sense) of the text when read aloud; onomatopoetic words (e.g., 'brrrr', 'bang') and repetition (like a refrain in music). These were all aspects that could be employed to make children aware of how to create poetry (Pramling 2009, 2010).

Another example is work with rhyming (Pramling and Asplund Carlsson 2008). When a group of children had to rhyme by pairing cards with various pictures, it became obvious that children thought of rhyming in four qualitatively different ways: (1) a sense relationship (shoe-foot, cow-pig); (2) ending sound, but only for words also related in sense (hear-ear); (3) sound-based relationship, irrespective of sense (riil-niil) and (4) some children were able to take a meta-perspective and explain the principle of rhyming. By learning from how children made sense, the teachers acquired tools to deal with the problems that the children faced and were then equipped to challenge the children to think and talk about the learning objective.

With the examples above we have tried to show how research can highlight children's meaning-making within various content areas. Here these are narrowed down to learning objectives in order to both influence children's learning and to be able to trace the results in terms of what children have learnt. This, we claim, is a new way of looking at children's learning in early childhood: not in terms of more general psychological development, and not in terms of traditional academic skills, but in terms of children's meaning-making in various content areas. This approach can be viewed as a Nordic perspective of didactics – that is, understanding how the interaction between children, the teacher and the content (learning objective) comes about in children's minds. (For further reading, see Pramling and Pramling Samuelsson 2011).

Conclusions

In this article, changing paradigmatic views on children's learning in preschool were examined in relation to policy issues in Sweden. The knowledge generated by analyses using the four dimensions of quality in this study is of importance to research on early childhood education at both a national and international level. The result provides knowledge of how both changes in policy and views on the child and learning affect preschool pedagogy, and gives additional evidence that children's conditions for learning depend on the quality of preschool (Sheridan, Pramling Samuelsson, and Johansson 2009). The results of this study also highlight that high-quality preschools for all children are dependent on and result from joint efforts and shared intentions between preschools and stakeholders at different system levels. Analyses through the four intertwined dimensions also strengthen the link between the quality of a preschool and children's learning of different content areas.

What are the main changes in policy?

In Sweden, over the last few decades, preschool has been a significant part of the political agenda. Numerous decisions and reforms have, over the years, built up a model of preschool provision that is integrated in both the social welfare and educational systems. Recent reforms have made preschool free for 15 hours a week for children from three years of age, and a maximum fee has been introduced for full-day education and care. In order to provide each child with a place from one year of age, preschool provision is being continuously increased in all municipalities. Together the reforms make Sweden the only country to have achieved the highest score of a benchmarking system that compares standards of early childhood education and care in 25 OECD countries (UNICEF 2008).

These reforms also indicate that on a societal level there seems to be an overall consensus on the allocation of economical resources, the formulation of policy, juridical issues and pedagogical intentions related to preschool. This consensus on a societal level has made it possible to organise preschool provision with high pedagogical intentions, embracing nearly all of the children in Sweden. This has created a workable system of provision that also helps to support a flexible and available workforce; this improves parents' gender equality and equity (Tallberg-Broman, Rubinstein-Reich, and Hägerström 2002) and positively affects children's lifelong learning (Ministry of Education and Science 2010). The deep integration of preschool in society and in people's daily life tends to make preschool a universal issue of concern.

In Sweden preschool is seen as a right of the child. Since 1998, preschool has been part of the educational system with a national curriculum (Ministry of Education and Sciences 1998). In 2010 preschool became a distinct form of school, being regulated by the Education Act (2010). Based on the intentions of making preschool more pedagogical, the curriculum was also revised in 2010. The idea behind this is the growing knowledge of young children's learning potential and the importance of an early comprehensive education that gives children a good start in life. There is also a political ambition to provide preschools of high quality, giving all children in Sweden equal conditions for learning.

There has also been a focus on the competence of pre-schoolteachers. The Swedish government financially support both directed in-service training and research training for pre-schoolteachers up to a licentiate degree, which is beyond a master's degree and equivalent to half a doctoral degree. Municipalities are also encouraged to employ pre-schoolteachers with a licentiate degree. Judging by this, the political intentions for preschool provision are high. One might say that they are in line with research and theories on learning emphasising the importance of early years education.

However, the arenas of policy-making and implementation do not always work hand in hand. In practice there is still variety in the quality of preschools, giving children unequal conditions for learning (Sheridan 2001; Sheridan, Pramling Samuelsson, and Johansson 2009). There is still a long way to go before all personnel in preschool are educated pre-schoolteachers. Today about 54% have a pre-schoolteacher education. In some parts of Sweden there are preschools staffed only by childcare attendants while, on the other hand, some preschools employ three pre-schoolteachers with university degrees.

What are the main changes in pedagogy?

In Sweden a new pedagogical approach is being developed. This play- and learning-oriented pedagogy combines the so-called academic and social-pedagogical approaches into a new integrated approach, creating conditions for children's holistic learning across a broad spectrum of areas. This approach requires teachers to have a range of professional competences including, among other things, an understanding of preschool pedagogy and a depth of content knowledge. However, it is not an easy task to change a system from one approach to another.

Since Froebel's time (Johansson 1992) preschool has mainly been based on a social-pedagogical approach. In this approach the pre-schoolteachers seem to be one step behind the children – waiting for the child's initiative, giving support and creating activities for them. In the play- and learning-oriented approach now being developed, the pedagogical intention can be described as a joint journey; either the child takes initiatives, which the pre-schoolteacher tunes into and challenges, or the teacher takes initiatives and inspires children to deal with content areas identified in the preschool curriculum.

The approach developed in Reggio Emilia preschools is one that many preschools are fascinated by and claim to work with. Their philosophy is 'the pedagogy of listening' (Åberg and Taguchi 2005). Listening is an important aspect in any pedagogy, but is not in itself sufficient for creating high-quality pedagogy. This approach requires pre-schoolteachers to be interactive partners in young children's play and learning (Pramling and Pramling Samuelsson 2011). In this interactive approach, pre-schoolteachers need to create a balance between guidance and responding to children's meaning-making. If teachers lack pedagogical competence, this approach can easily turn into a pedagogy where the pre-schoolteacher forgets the wholeness and becomes too instructive, leading the children to a 'correct answer' without giving them possibilities to create meaning, which is contradictory to the intentions in the Swedish preschool curriculum (Pramling Samuelsson and Pramling 2008). In spite of a specific emphasis on early mathematics, literacy, technology and science, the intentions in the Swedish preschool curriculum are that the work should be organised thematically and not approached as separate school subjects (Ministry of Education and Science 2010).

Research on quality and children's learning has directed focus onto the importance of teachers' interactive presence – that is, being 'here and now' physically, emotionally and cognitively – and onto communication, interaction and sharing learning objectives. However, this is not enough. Teachers also have to go beyond the 'here and now', and look at pedagogy as a series of events around which children can talk and reflect and be challenged to relate earlier experiences or similar phenomena to the here and now (Pramling and Pramling Samuelsson 2011).

Summarising, one might say that the main change is from a pedagogy based on a Froebelian tradition to a pedagogy based on new theories and empirical research. In practice this means a change from a pedagogy of keeping young children busy with various activities to a pedagogy that has interaction and communication as core elements. This interactive pedagogy puts new demands on the competences of pre-schoolteachers in terms of being able to engage in goal-directed communication with children (Doverborg and Pramling Samuelsson 2012; Sheridan, Williams, and Sandberg 2013) and to have knowledge about the content they are communicating about (see e.g. Pramling Samuelsson et al. 2009).

What are the main changes in views on children's learning?

Based on modern theories, there is a growing belief in young children's abilities to learn and create meaning from early in life. The metaphor of the child as a scientist in the crib, which is the title of a book by Gopnick, Meltzoff, and Kuhn (1999), is characteristic of modern views of children as being eager to learn by systematically scrutinising objects and testing ideas from their early years. Or, expressed in another way, children are competent to learn as much as their environment can provide (Sommer).

At the same time, today we know that exposure to experiences and support and challenge from the world around the child are vital for their learning. We posit that there is an acceptance today, that young children in preschool are much more capable than we used to believe (Lindahl 2002), but at the same time children are vulnerable and dependent on support and care. Children are both beings and becomings, and they are at a developmental level at the same time as they are in a continuous developmental process, taking various positions in their daily life in preschool (Bjervås 2011). That is why it becomes so important to observe, interact and communicate with children to become aware, as an adult, of each child's experiences and ideas – ideas that have to be both the means for learning and the results of learning.

The Swedish School Inspection (2012) has recently published an evaluation of the quality of preschools, with a focus on how they work with the new goals and a brief to evaluate preschool quality in the revised preschool curriculum. The three notions linked together are documentation, evaluation and development (improvement of the pro-gramme). It is obvious that there is a lack of understanding of how to deal with the fact that it is not children who are going to be evaluated, but the preschool as a whole. Pre-schoolteachers also raise questions about documentation as it takes a lot of time, preventing them from being together with the children (Bjervås 2011). Results from a recent study show that pre-schoolteachers seem to hold conflicting and changing views on the focus for evaluation, from the child to the quality of the preschool (Sheridan, Williams, and Sandberg 2013).

In a way, Sweden is in a time of change, with a strong emphasis on a higher quality of preschool; with more focus on content, interaction and communication and based on the belief that early education lays the foundation both for the child as an individual and for benefits for society (OECD 2012). These intentions can also be seen in the new form of pre-schoolteacher education, which is more focused on various content areas (see further Pramling Samuelsson and Sheridan 2010).

Taken together, the results of this study provide knowledge of the interdependence and reciprocity between policy, views on the child, preschool pedagogy and conditions for children's learning in preschool. The results also highlight that high quality in preschool is an issue of combined efforts, shared intentions and collaboration among stakeholders on different system levels, strengthening the significance of a comprehens-ive perspective in research on conditions for children's learning in preschool.

Note

1. Didactics' from a European/Continental and Nordic perspective means not instruction, but a communicative preschool pedagogy – child-centred and with content described in terms of learning objects (i.e., items which children are supposed to make sense of).

References

Åberg, A., and H. Lenz Taguchi. 2005. *Lyssnandets pedagogik. Etik och demokrati i pedagogiskt arbete* [The Pedagogy of Listening. Ethics and Democracy in Pedagogical Work]. Stockholm: Liber.

Asplund Carlsson, M., N. Pramling, and I. Pramling Samuelsson. 2008. "Från görande till lärande och förståelse. En studie av lärares lärande inom estetik." [From Doing to Learning and Understanding: A Study of Teacher's Learning in Aesthetics]. *Nordisk barnehageforskning* 1 (1): 41–51. http://www.nordiskbarnehageforskning.no/

Ball, S. J. 2006. *Education Policy and Social Class: The Selected Works of Stephen J. Ball.* London: Routledge.

Bjervås, L.-L. 2011. *Samtal om barn och pedagogisk dokumentation som bedömningspraktik i förskolan: en diskursanalys* [Teachers' View of Preschool Children in Relation to Pedagogical Documentation – A Discourse Analysis]. Studies in Educational Sciences. Göteborg: Acta Universitatis Gothoburgensis.

Bronfenbrenner, U. 1979. *The Ecology of Human Development: Experiments by Nature and Design*. Cambridge, MA: Harvard University Press.

Bronfenbrenner, U. 1986. "Ecology of the Family as a Context for Human Development: Research Perspectives." *Developmental Psychology* 22 (6): 723–742. doi:10.1037/0012-1649.22.6.723.

Brostrøm, S., and H. Veijleskov. 2009. *Didaktik i børnehaven: Planer, principer og praksis* [Didactics in Preschool: Plans, Principles and Practice]. Fredrikshavn, Denmark: Dofolo.

Bruner, J. S. 1996. "Frames for Thinking: Ways of Making Meaning." In *Modes of Thought: Exploration in Culture and Cognition*, edited by D. R. Olson and N. Torrance, 93–105. Cambridge: Cambridge University Press.

Burchinal, M. R., J. E. Roberts, R. Riggins, S. A. Zeisel, E. Neebe, and D. Bryant. 2000. "Relating Quality of Centre-based Child Care to Early Cognitive and Language Development." *Child Development* 71 (2): 339–357. doi:10.1111/1467-8624.00149.

Ceglowski, D., and C. Bacigalupa. 2002. "Four Perspectives on Child Care Quality." *Early Childhood Education Journal* 30 (2): 87–92. doi:10.1023/A:1021245017431.

Clifford, R., and D. Bryant. 2003. *Multi-state Study of Pre-kindergarten*. National Center for Early Development and Learning. Chapel Hill: University of North Carolina.

Dalli, C. 2008. "Pedagogy, Knowledge and Collaboration: Towards a Ground-up Perspective on Professionalism." *European Early Childhood Education Research Journal* 16 (2): 171–185. doi:10.1080/13502930802141600.

Donabedian, A. 1980. *The Definition of Quality and Approaches to its Assessment. Vol. 1 of Explorations in Quality Assessment and Monitoring*. Ann Arbor: Health Administration Press.

Doverborg, E. 2011. "*Att utveckla de yngsta barnens matematiklärande i förskolan – vad krävs av läraren?* [To Develop the Youngest Children's Mathematical Learning in Preschool – What is Required of the Teacher?]" In *Barns lärande i ett livslångt perspektiv* [Children's Learning in a Lifelong Perspective], edited by P. Williams and S. Sheridan, 64–76. Stockholm: Liber.

Doverborg, E., and I. Pramling Samuelsson. 2009. "Grundläggande matematik [Fundamental Mathematics]." In *Barns tidiga lärande: En tvärsnittsstudie om förskolan som miljö för barns lärande* [Children's Early Learning: A Current Study of Preschool as an Environment for Children's Learning], edited by S. Sheridan, I. Pramling Samuelsson, and E. Johansson, 125–150. Göteborg: Acta Universitatis Gothoburgensis. http://hdl.handle.net/2077/20404

Doverborg, E., and I. Pramling Samuelsson. 2012. *Att förstå barns tankar: Kommunikation med barn* [To Understand Children's Thoughts: Communication with Children]. 4th ed. Stockholm: Liber.

Garbarino, J. 1992. *Towards a Sustainable Society: An Economic, Social and Environmental Agenda for our Children's Future*. Chicago: The Noble Press.

Gopnik, A., A. N. Meltzoff, and P. K. Kuhn. 1999. *The Scientist in the Crib: Minds, Brains and How Children Learn*. New York: William Morrow.

Harms, T., and R. Clifford. 1980. *The Early Childhood Environment Rating Scale*. New York: Teachers College, Columbia University.

Johansson, J.-E. 1992. *Metodikämnet i förskollärareutbildningen* [The Methodology Subject in Preschool Teacher Education]. Göteborg: Acta Universitatis Gothoburgenses.

Johansson, E., and I. Pramling Samuelsson. 2009. "To Weave Together – Play and Learning in Early Childhood Education." *Australian Research in Early Childhood Education Journal* 16 (1): 33–48. http://www.tandfonline.com/doi/abs/10.1080/13502930802689053#.UhjTQYXV1vY.

Lindahl, M. 2002. *Vårda – Vägleda – Lära: Effektstudie av ett kompetensutvecklings-program för pedagoger i förskolemiljön* [Care – Supervise – Learn: Effect Study of Competence Development by Pedagogues in Preschools]. Göteborg: Acta Universitatis Gothoburgensis.

Mellgren, E., and K. Gustafsson. 2009. "Språk och kommunikation." [Language and Communication]. In *Barns tidiga lärande: En tvärsnittsstudie om förskolan som miljö för barns lärande* [In Children's Early Learning: A Current Study of Preschool as an Environment for Children's Learning], edited by S. Sheridan, I. Pramling Samuelsson, and E. Johansson, 151–183. Göteborg: Acta Universitatis Gothoburgensis. http://hdl.handle.net/2077/20404

Miller, L., C. Dalli, and M. Urban. 2012. "Early Childhood Grows Up: Towards a Critical Ecology of the Profession." In *Early Childhood Grows Up: Towards a Critical Ecology of the*

Profession, edited by L. Miller, C. Dalli, and M. Urban. Heidelberg: Springer Dordrecht (Ch. 1).

Ministry of Education and Sciences. 1998/2010. *Curriculum for Preschool, 1 to 5 Years of Age*. (Revised 2010). Stockholm: Skolverket.

Ministry of Education and Research. 2010. *The New Education Act – For Knowledge, Choice and Security*. Govt. Bill 2009/10:165.

Moss, P. 2004. "Setting the Scene: A Vision of Universal Children's Spaces." In *A New Era for Universal Childcare?*, edited by Daycare Trust, 19–23. London: Daycare Trust.

NICHD (The National Institute of Child Health and Human Development). 2005. *Child Care and Children's Development: Results from the NICHD Study of Early Child Care and Youth Development*. New York: Guilford.

OECD. 2012. *Starting Strong III: A Quality Tool Box for Early Childhood Education*. Paris: OECD.

Pramling, I. 1994. *Kunnandets grunder: Prövning av en fenomenografisk ansats till att utveckla barns förtåelse för sin omvärld* [The Foundations of Knowing: Test of a Phenomenographic Effort to Develop Children's Ways of Understanding the Surrounding World]. Göteborg: Acta Universitatis Gothoburgensis.

Pramling, N. 2009. "Introducing Poetry-making in Early Years Education." *European Early Childhood Education Research Journal* 17 (3): 377–390. doi:10.1080/13502930903101578.

Pramling, N. 2010. "The Sound and the Sense: Exploring the Collaborative Construction of Free-form Poetry in the 6-year-old Group." *Contemporary Issues in Early Childhood* 11 (2): 156–174. doi:10.2304/ciec.2010.11.2.156.

Pramling, N., and M. Asplund Carlsson. 2008. "Rhyme and Reason: Developing Children's Understanding of Rhyme." *Contemporary Issues in Early Childhood* 9 (1): 14–26. doi:10.2304/ciec.2008.9.1.14.

Pramling, N., and I. Pramling Samuelsson, eds. 2011. *Educational Encounters: Nordic Studies in Early Childhood Didactics*. Dortrecht, Holland: Springer.

Pramling Samuelsson, I., and M. Asplund Carlsson. 2007. *Spielend lernen: Stärkung lernmethodischer Kompetenzen* [The Playing Learning Child in a Developmental Pedagogical Theory]. Troisdorf: Bildungsverlag EINS.

Pramling Samuelsson, I., M. Asplund Carlsson, B. Olsson, N. Pramling, and C. Wallerstedt. 2009. "The Art of Teaching Children the Arts: Music, Dance, and Poetry with Children 2–8 Years Old." *International Journal of Early Years Education* 17 (2): 119–135. doi:10.1080/09669760902982323.

Pramling Samuelsson, I., and N. Pramling. 2008. *Didaktiska studier från förskola och skola* [Didactic Studies from Preschool and Primary School]. Malmö: Gleerups.

Pramling Samuelsson, I., and N. Pramling. 2013. "Orchestrating and Studying Children's and Teachers' Learning: Reflections on Developmental Research Approaches." *Educational Inquiry* 4 (2): 1–18.

Pramling Samuelsson, I., and S. Sheridan. 2010. "A Turning-point or a Backward Slide: The Challenge Facing the Swedish Preschool Today." *Early Years* 30 (3): 219–227. doi:10.1080/09575146.2010.513328.

Schweinhart, L., H. Barnes, and D. Weikart. 1993. *Significant Benefits: The High/Scope Perry Preschool Study through Age 27. No. 10 in Monographs of the High/Scope Educational Research Foundation*. MI: The High/Scope Press.

Sheridan, S. 2001. *Pedagogical Quality in Preschool: An Issue of Perspectives*. Göteborg: Acta Universitatis Gothoburgensis.

Sheridan, S. 2007. *En svensk version av the Early Childhood Environment Rating Scale (ECERS): Reviderad version av Harms and Clifford, 1980; Kärrby 1989*. [A Swedish version of the Early Childhood Environment Rating Scale (ECERS), Harms and Clifford, 1980] Göteborg: Göteborgs Universitet, Institutionen för pedagogik och didaktik.

Sheridan, S. 2009. "Discerning Pedagogical Quality in Preschool." *Scandinavian Journal of Educational Research* 53 (3): 245–261. doi:10.1080/00313830902917295.

Sheridan, S., I. Pramling Samuelsson, and E. Johansson, eds. 2009. *Barns tidiga lärande: En tvärsnittsstudie om förskolan som miljö för barns lärande* [Children's Early Learning: A Current Study of Preschool as an Environment for Children's Learning]. Göteborg: Acta Universitatis Gothoburgensis. http://hdl.handle.net/2077/20404

Sheridan, S., P. Williams, and S. Sandberg. 2013. "Systematic Quality-work in Preschool." *International Journal of Early Childhood* 45 (1): 123–150.

Sheridan, S., P. Williams, A. Sandberg, and T. Vuorinen. 2011. "Preschool Teaching in Sweden – A Profession in Change." *Educational Research* 53 (4): 415–437. doi:10.1080/00131881.2011.625153.

Shier, H. 2001. "Pathways to Participation: Openings, Opportunities and Obligations." *Children and Society* 15 (2): 107–117. doi:10.1002/chi.617.

Sommer, D. 2011. "Læring og barnperspektiv." [Learning and child perspective] In *Barns lärande i ett livslångt perspektiv* [Children's Learning in a Lifelong Perspective], edited by P. Williams and S. Sheridan, 88–100. Stockholm: Liber.

Sommer, D. 2012. *A Childhood Psychology: Young Children in Changing Time*. Hampshire: Palgrave Macmillan.

Sommer, D., I. Pramling Samuelsson, and K. Hundeide. 2010. *Child Perspectives and Children's Perspectives in Theory and Practice*. New York: Springer.

Sylva, K. 1994. "School Influences on Children's Development." *Journal of Child Psychology and Psychiatry* 35 (1): 135–170. doi:10.1111/j.1469-7610.1994.tb01135.x.

Sylva, K., E. Melhuish, P. Sammons, I. Siraj-Blatchford, and B. Taggart. 2010. *Early Childhood Matters: Evidence from the Effective Pre-school and Primary Education Project*. London: Routledge.

Tallberg-Broman, I., L. Rubinstein Reich, and J. Hägerström. 2002. *Likvärdighet i en skola för alla. Forskning i fokus, nr 3* [Equality in a School for All: Research in Focus No. 3]. Skolverket. Stockholm: Fritzes.

The Swedish School Inspection. 2012. *Förskola, före skola – lärande och bärande* [Preschool, Before School – Learning and Bearing]. Kvalitetsgranskningsrapport om förskolans arbete med det förstärka pedagogiska uppdraget. Skolinspektionen, Rapport 2012:7. www.skolin spektione.se

UN Convention. 1989. *The UNConvention on the Rights of the Child*. New York: United Nations.

UNICEF. 2008. *The Child Care Transition: A League Table of Early Childhood Education and Care in Economically Advanced Countries*. Florence, Italy: UNICEF Innocenti Research Centre.

U.S. Department of Education. 2000. *Building Strong Foundations for Early Learning: The U.S. Departments of Education's Guide to High-Quality Early Childhood Education Programs*. http://www.ed.gov/offices/OUS/PES/whatsnew.html

Vygotsky, L. [1934] 1986. *Thought and Language*. Cambridge, MA: MIT Press.

Mothers' experiences with a mother–child education programme in five countries

Sevda Bekman[a] and Aylin Atmaca Koçak[b]

[a]Department of Primary Education, Boğaziçi University, Istanbul, Turkey; [b]Student Counseling & Guidance Centre, Boğaziçi University, Istanbul, Turkey

Although previous quantitative studies have demonstrated the effectiveness of the mother–child education programme (MOCEP) that originated in Turkey in 1993, the study reported here uses a qualitative approach to gain an in-depth understanding of mothers' views of the outcomes of the programme. The study was conducted with 100 mothers from five different countries (Turkey, Belgium, Switzerland, Bahrain and Saudi Arabia) and designed to investigate their perceptions of the effects of the programme, and the essential factors in its effectiveness. In-depth interviews were used for data collection. The findings revealed that participant mothers perceived changes in their child's overall development and in the mother–child relationship, and indirect effects in their relationship with the child's father and the father's relationship with the child. Mothers also reported that the group meetings attended by all the mothers, the characteristics of the teacher and the curriculum of the cognitive education programme were important factors in the effectiveness of the programme. The results of the study regarding what mothers experienced and perceived as changes in children and in themselves were similar to the results obtained from previous quantitative research carried out to evaluate MOCEP. The present study, however, provides new information about how the programme works, why the mothers attended the programme and their experiences with their environment regarding the programme.

Introduction

As is now well understood, the basic building blocks for the child's physical, cognitive, social and emotional development are set in the early years of life, and the family is the principal context in which this development takes place (Bronfenbrenner 1979; Sameroff 1975). A stimulating environment (Coleman 1990), involvement in educationally enhancing activities such as reading and exposure to written materials (Bradley et al. 1994; Pfannenstiel, Seitz, and Zigler 2003) and use of language that is complex in structure and elaborated in content (Hart and Risley 1995) are all considered to be important positive features of family environments that enable children's development. There is ample evidence, however, regarding the negative effects on children's development and educational outcomes of risk factors in the family environment (Engle and Black 2008; Murnane 2007). Where family environments lack the positive features identified above, children tend to lag far behind their peers in their overall development (Lamb et al. 2005) and, as exposure to environmental risk factors is cumulative, (Evans 2004), this developmental gap expands in later years (Schweinhart et al. 2005).

The cognitive and social development of children from at-risk environments can be enhanced, and the developmental gap reduced through increased intellectual stimulation and by strengthening the developmentally appropriate characteristics of the environment through intervention programmes (Campbell and Ramey 1994). The shared goal of early intervention programmes for children from at-risk environments is to promote a healthy overall development, which will enable a successful transition to school, and in the long run, to contribute to school adjustment and success. In this article, we discuss new research on mothers' perceptions of a long-standing intervention programme, the mother–child education programme (MOCEP) that has been designed to minimise potential risk factors.

In Turkey in recent years, a consensus has emerged concerning the benefits of early intervention. Numerous studies have demonstrated that at-risk children are more successful at school and adapt better to the society as a result of intervention programmes undertaken in Turkey (Bekman 2007; Kagitcibasi, Sunar, and Bekman 2001; Kagitcibasi et al. 2009). In the USA, evaluations of programmes such as High Scope (Schweinhart et al. 2005), the Chicago Longitudinal Study (Reynolds and Ou 2004), the Infant Health and Development Program (McCormick et al. 2006) and the Abecedarian Project (Campbell et al. 2002), also underline the effectiveness of early intervention on later school success and adaptation to school (Blok et al. 2005).

As a result of increased awareness of the impact the environmental context has on development, early childhood intervention programmes now adopt an ecological approach (Bronfenbrenner 1979). Rather than focusing exclusively on the child, the emphasis is on the interrelationships between the child, the family and social support systems (Reynolds 1999). Transactional interpretations of development (Sameroff, 1975) and Bronfenbrenner's (1979) view of the family as a system embedded in a larger ecological framework of systems, constitute the underlying philosophy of intervention programmes, where the goal is to give equal attention to the child and to his/her environment.

Understanding the parents' role in attaining positive child outcomes in the intervention process needs attention, and can be approached from three different aspects: parenting, the home–school relationship and responsibility for learning outcomes (Harvard Family Research Project 2006). A number of studies have examined the contribution of traditional parental involvement activities to the academic development and achievement of children from socially and educationally at-risk groups (Bohon, Macpherson, and Atiles 2005; St Clair and Jackson 2006). Children whose parents were involved in their education were found to perform better in reading and writing (Reutzal, Fawson, and Smith 2006; Senechal 2006) and were better supported in terms of their learning and achievement (Gonzalez-DeHass, Willems, and Doan Holbein 2005). Chang et al. (2009) studied the effects on children's cognitive outcomes of three different types of parental involvement: parenting classes, group socialisation and parental support groups. All three activities led to increase in parental involvement in language and cognitive stimulation at home, in parental supportiveness and to decrease in parental intrusiveness.

Involvement in intervention programmes can also lead to positive changes for parents as well as children, such as increases in consistent maternal behaviour and maternal sensitivity (Asscher, Hermanns, and Deković 2008), and a reduction in maternal stress (Conners, Edwards, and Grant 2007). Intervention programmes are known to have positive effects on maternal employment, maternal education, mother–child interaction (Benasich, Brooks-Gunn, and Chu Clewell 1992), maternal competence and parental attitudes and behaviour more generally (Pehrson and Robinson 1990). To date, however, researchers have seldom considered how parents themselves perceive the impact of these programmes on their children's development, on their own personal growth and family relationships. In this article, we present the findings from a recent study that attempts to address this gap. We present mothers' narrative accounts of their experiences of the MOCEP in order to understand their perceptions of the programme's impact and how the programme worked from their point of view.

The mother–child education program

Aim and content

MOCEP targets the child and the child's immediate environment, especially the mother, rather than the child alone. It reaches out to children of 5- to 6-year olds and their parents. The programme has two main elements: the cognitive education program (CEP) and the mother support program (MSP).

The primary aim of the CEP is to prepare children for school by stimulating pre-literacy and numeracy skills, eye-hand coordination, sensory discrimination, language development, classification, seriation, concept formation (direction, size and place), learning of colours and shapes, problem solving skills and general ability. Eight picture storybooks are used to develop listening comprehension, verbal expression, vocabulary, question–answer activities and reasoning skills. There are 25 workbooks, 20–25 pages each. The workbooks for each week contain various daily exercises that mothers and children will carry over five days. It takes about 15–20 minutes per day to complete the exercises.

The MSP aims to increase the mother's sensitivity to the child's cognitive, social and emotional development and to assist her in preparing a home environment that will support the child's development. It also has the purpose of supporting parents to create a consistent and positive mother–child interaction.

Process

Mothers attend weekly group meetings for 25 weeks in adult education centres, community centres and primary schools. The week's topic of the MSP is determined in advance, so that teachers are prepared, and discussed during the first hour and a half of each meeting. Some meetings are devoted to discussing the mother's feelings about being a woman and a mother. Group dynamic techniques are used to support mothers' active participation. Mothers are encouraged to ask questions, express their opinions and share ideas and experiences.

In the second part of the meeting, mothers are asked to form groups of five or six, and using 'role play', they learn the CEP exercises that they will later carry out with their children at home. The whole meeting lasts about three hours and each group consists of 20–25 mothers.

MOCEP is now an international programme and operates in Europe (Belgium, France, Germany and Switzerland), in Saudi Arabia where it employs Turkish with

Turkish immigrant mothers and Arabic with native mothers in Saudi Arabia, Bahrain and Lebanon. Before its implementation in a particular country, the programme is modified to meet local needs. To date MOCEP has reached about 8000 children and mothers outside Turkey. Mothers with children who meet the age requirement can enrol in the programme by applying to the programme centre in their country.

Staff

The qualifications of staff members who lead the programme show differences within countries. Some are paraprofessionals at a local Non Governmental Organization (NGO), some are Turkish social sciences and psychological guidance teachers sent abroad by the Turkish government and some are adult education teachers. Except in Bahrain, local staff are trained by the Mother-Child Education Foundation (ACEV). In Bahrain, the local partner institution trains the staff.

Previous research to evaluate MOCEP – A longitudinal study taking place over 24 years has been the main quantitative evaluation of the programme to date. This investigation used an experimental design that randomly selected and assigned mothers and children to an intervention or a control group. The immediate effects of the intervention on children were measured just before the termination of the programme. The first follow-up effects were measured seven years after the termination of the programme.

The immediate and the follow-up effects indicated substantial differences between the children and mothers who had and had not attended MOCEP. The performance of children in the trained group exceeded that of the control group on all measures of cognitive, social and emotional development (Bekman 2007; Kagitcibasi, Sunar, and Bekman 2001). Furthermore, mothers who attended the programme formed closer relations with their children and provided a more stimulating environment. There were differences in child-rearing attitudes of the mothers in the control and intervention groups and for mothers in the intervention group their status as the woman within the family improved, as did their powers of decision-making. They also had a more optimistic outlook for their future life (Bekman 2007; Kagitcibasi et al. 2009).

A second follow-up study, carried out 19 years later when the original child participants had reached adulthood, indicated that adults whose parents had attended the programme had more years of education, worked in higher-quality jobs and used computers and credit cards more than adults whose parents had not attended the programme (Kagitcibasi et al. 2009).

A separate evaluation using a quasi-experimental design took place when the programme was implemented at scale throughout Turkey. This measured outcomes immediately after the end of the programme, and one year later, when the children completed their first year of formal schooling (Bekman 1998). The findings of this study were similar to those reported for the longitudinal research.

The five-country study

In this article, we report the first qualitative evaluation of MOCEP and the first evaluation of its international implementation across all five countries where MOCEP was in operation at the time of the study (Turkey, Saudi Arabia, Switzerland, Belgium and Bahrain). This new evaluation makes a significant contribution to the knowledge obtained from the previous quantitative evaluations as it allows the voices of the mothers to be heard. In addition, the evaluation provides new evidence about the transferability of a programme to different contexts in other countries.

Aim and method

The aim of this study was to answer the questions: 'What are the perceived effects of the programme as reported by the mothers?' and 'What are the mothers' perspectives on what makes the programme work?' A narrative inquiry method using structured, in-depth interviews was used to explore these questions with mothers who had taken part in the programme.

Participants

One hundred mothers, 20 from each of the five countries, took part in this study. Mothers in Turkey and Bahrain were living in their own country; the mothers in Belgium, Switzerland and Saudi Arabia were Turkish emigrants. Mothers who had completed the programme were invited to attend local meetings that outlined the aims of the research and what was expected out of volunteers. To be included in the sample, mothers had to have participated in and completed MOCEP during the previous two years. Research participants were chosen randomly from mothers who volunteered and who met this criterion. The demographic characteristics of these volunteers were similar to those of the original population.

Characteristics of the participants

Mothers were between 22 and 48 years of age, (mean age, 33 years). Forty-four were high school graduates, 21 were working at the time of the study and 26 had previously worked, but were no longer working. Among the working mothers, 12 were skilled and 9 were unskilled workers.

Fathers' ages ranged from 28 to 52 years (mean age, 38 years). Forty-seven were high school graduates. Eighty-two were working; 59 were skilled workers and 15 were unskilled and 8 owned their own business. Only two of the families consisted of divorced parents. The children from these families were all seven years old. Forty-five were girls and 55 were boys.

Between country differences in participants' characteristics

In terms of educational level, the majority of the mothers in Bahrain (65%) and Turkey (60%) were high school graduates, whereas the majority of the mothers in Saudi Arabia (60%) had graduated from primary school (see Table 1). As Table 1 illustrates, the household size was largest in Bahrain, followed by Saudi Arabia. Most of the mothers in Turkey and Saudi Arabia did not have any work experience.

Procedure

Trained interviewers carried out structured, in-depth interviews in the mothers' first language, usually in the mother's home. The interview schedule consisted of 73 open-ended questions designed to investigate mothers' experiences before joining the MOCEP as well as their experiences during its implementation. Interviews lasted between one-

Table 1. Demographic characteristics of the participants.

Characteristics	Belgium		Switzerland		Bahrain		Turkey		Saudi Arabia	
	N	%	N	%	N	%	N	%	N	%
Can read and write	1	5.0	0	0.0	0	0.0	0	0.0	1	5.0
Primary school	9	45.0	7	35.0	0	0.0	5	25.0	12	60.0
Middle school	3	15.0	3	15.0	4	20.0	2	10.0	3	15.0
High school	7	35.0	8	40.0	13	65.0	12	60.0	4	20.0
University	0	0.0	2	10.0	3	15.0	1	5.0	0	0.0
Household size	4	20.0	4	20.0	8	40.0	4	20.0	5-6	30.0
Number of children in family	2	10.0	2	10.0	3	15.0	2	10.0	3	15.0
With work experience	11	55.0	12	60.0	12	60.0	7	35.0	5	25.0
No work experience	9	45.0	8	40.0	8	40.0	13	65.0	15	75.0

and-a-half to two hours. Mothers' views on the programme, their experiences of the group process with the teacher and CEP implementations and their views about the information provided were also interrogated. Finally, for mothers living outside Turkey, the interview included questions about the benefits of the programme that were specific to them. The questions were neutral and were designed to elicit accounts of both negative and positive experiences. All interviews were transcribed for analysis. The interviews in Bahrain were translated from Arabic into Turkish. Examples of the interview questions are as follows:

- Do you think that this programme (MOCEP) has affected your life?
- How do you feel about having attended such a programme when you consider all your experiences after participating in the programme?
- Do you believe that your participation in the programme affected your relationship with your child? (If yes) How?
- Have there been differences in your behaviour towards your child after attending the programme?
- If you were able to change certain things in the programme to make it a better one, what would you change?
- You discussed many things in the programme such as how to talk to a child, discipline, nutrition, health, play, toilet training, women's health. What was the topic/information from which you benefited the most?
- What was the topic/information from which you benefited the least?
- What could have been omitted?

Interviewers also kept detailed field notes of observations they made during their interviews with the mothers.

Analysis

Both researchers analysed the interview data using the method of constant comparison and each transcript was read many times until first familiarity was established. Next, significant statements that could answer the research questions were extracted and statements on similar topics were grouped into categories and subcategories (see Table 2). All interview data were then classified according to these categories. Simultaneously, we

Table 2.   List of categories and subcategories in the study.

Categories	Subcategories
Perceived direct effects on children	Cognitive development
	• Learned new concepts
	• Improved concentration
	Social development
	• More social
	• Higher self-confidence
	• Better organised
	Physical development
	• Better small muscle use
Perceived direct effects on mothers	Self-perception
	• Perception of motherhood changed
	• Felt more conscious about child-rearing practices
	• Felt more valuable
	• Had more self-confidence
	• Felt beneficial
	Mother–child relationship
	• More knowledgeable about child development
	• Decreased use of negative discipline methods
	• More tolerant and understanding
	• Spent more time with the child
	• Better communication
Perceived changes in the father–child relationship	• Acted with more awareness
	• Spent more time and had closer relationship with the target child
	• Had closer relationship with other children
What makes the programme work according to the mothers	The group process
	• Felt a sense of belonging
	• Felt relief and psychological support
	• Learned from other people's experiences
	• Felt that she was not the only one experiencing problems
	• Felt valuable as she was listened to
	Cognitive education program
	• Contributed to the child's development
	• Helped the child to be more responsible
	• Better mother–child relationship
	• Mother felt proud of herself
	Teacher
	• Her mastery in implementing the content
	• Her personality

also built the analytical framework. This allowed the categories and the subcategories to be further refined.

Finally, a comparative analysis of the data from the five countries was carried out using this framework. Before coding the complete data-set, a sample of 30 interviews was coded independently by two people. Cronbach's alpha measured inter-coder reliability: for all categories and subcategories alphas were greater than 0.80.

Results

The results of the study are presented in response to the main research questions. The 'perceived effects' of the programme are reported first. Perceived *direct* effects are those in line with the original aims and purposes of this programme; perceived *indirect* effects are those that fall outside these aims and purposes. Later in this article, we present the findings concerning 'How and why the programme works'. Mothers' statements are specified by their individual code number and by country (Turkey-tur, Belgium-bel, Switzerland-sw, Saudi Arabia-sar, Bahrain-bah).

Mothers clearly stated that they attended the programme mainly for two reasons: either they wanted to have better parenting skills and be knowledgeable in parenting or they were not happy with how they had been reared.

> I thought I might have shortcomings. I realized that thinking 'what I know is enough for me' was wrong. I participated to see my mistakes. to be a better mother and wanted to see what more I could do for my child. (16.sw)

> We were raised up in quite different conditions than our kids. However, I want to be a better mother and an understanding mother; I always want to be by their side. Let's help them learn and develop, we have not improved ourselves, we have deficiencies. (1. sar)

Perceived direct effects

Mothers reported that as a result of their participation in MOCEP, they experienced many changes in their children, themselves and the mother–child relationship.

Perceived effects on children

The mothers' statements indicated that they had noticed changes in the social, physical and cognitive development of their child and that he or she had acquired basic cognitive skills that are necessary preparation for starting school. Mothers attributed changes in their child's cognitive functioning, (especially the learning of new concepts and improvements in concentration), to carrying out the CEP activities every day.

> Below, above, same, different, he tells the differences himself. He says, 'We are boys, you are girls'. When having dinner, if there is a different glass on the table, he talks about it. These attracted my attention. (5. bah)

The mothers also referred to changes in the social development of the child. They reported that the socio-emotional activities in CEP and the story books improved their child's understanding of other people's emotions and ideas. They reported that their children were more social, had greater self-confidence, and were better organised in their daily lives.

Before the program, when we went somewhere he didn't know, he would cling to me, he would get bored and cry from boredom. Now it is different. When we go somewhere, he sits and talks comfortably, his relationship with his friends is better. He wants to play with his friends. When we go to the park, he asks others to be friends with him. (9.tur)

He learned how to tidy up his toys and sometimes he makes his bed himself. He started to look for a similar responsibility from his sister after realizing his own. (4.sw)

Mothers' statements clearly indicate that the children also underwent some physical changes. For example, by using pencil and scissors in CEP activities, the children developed better control over to their small muscles.

She wouldn't completely color inside the shapes, she learned that. Her eye-hand coordination, so it is called, improved. Drawing properly over the dots and drawing and matching got better. (12. bel)

When all the positive effects on the child were compared across the five countries, Saudi Arabian mothers generated the highest percentage (33.5%), while those in Belgium (9%) had the lowest percentage (see Table 3). Taking the whole sample into account, the positive effects mentioned most frequently were the subcategories 'learned new concepts' (36%) and 'better small muscle use' (23.5%).

It is evident that mothers felt that they played a vital role in the changes the children experienced. They stated that they paid particular attention to taking the child out, or creating environments where the child could spend time with peers in order to enhance his or her social development and understanding of social rules. Mothers said that as a result of the programme, they read more books to their children, bought more educational games and toys, and gave more importance to activities like theatres and cinemas. Their statements also revealed that they tried to spend more time with their children. They also mentioned being more tolerant of their child's play both inside the home and outside. They believed that the changes they reported in their own behaviour towards their children had an important role in attaining the perceived effects on children.

I used to read him books and ask questions about the book. I asked him questions to understand whether he was listening to me or whether he got the story. I made him think. (8.sar)

We empty the dishwasher together. I believe that he learns while doing that because he separates the forks and the spoons. and tries to figure out how many plates. spoons or napkins he should put. (11.tur)

Perceived effects on mother's self-perception

The most significant change mothers reported related to their perception of motherhood. They considered that they developed greater conscious awareness of the child-rearing practices they implemented with their children after the programme. They reported feeling more valued and more self-confident as women because they were able to contribute to their child's development. These changes were reflected in their future plans, such as the desire to continue their education and to start working.

I now know what to do. I can now make a decision when I am stuck instead of asking for my mother's advice about what to do with my child. (18.tur)

I was very nervous and didn't have any self-confidence. My self-confidence increased. I remembered that I'm also an individual. that I'm me. I can say that I am present. I have learned to value myself. (1.bel)

For example, I wouldn't dare to go to the doctor's at first, fearing about what I would do if something happened, but now I'm more courageous in that matter. (17.sw)

As indicated in Table 3, the category 'Felt more conscious' as a mother of child-rearing practises was mentioned most frequently (36.2%) across the sample. Comparing the five countries, positive effects on the mothers themselves were identified most frequently by mothers in Belgium (23.5%) and Turkey (23%).

Perceived effects on mother–child relationship

Mothers also reported changes in the way they behaved towards their children. They felt that these changes mostly came about as a result of being more knowledgeable about child development after the programme. In particular, mothers mentioned that their use of negative discipline had decreased and said that they had adopted more tolerant and understanding behaviours. Their statements also indicated that they spent more time and had better communication with their children. Mothers stated that these changes in their own behaviour and attitudes created a more harmonious, close and peaceful mother–child relationship.

I am aware that I don't beat them anymore as I used to. My behaviour has changed somewhat. I am still nervous, but not as much as before. I used to beat a lot, but now I talk to them. Before the program, I would beat without asking them anything. (11.bah)

I learned that things could be solved through talking, not through getting angry. I learned the 'I language'. There were disputes with the children. Now we settle things talking and in agreement so he doesn't get angry. I don't get angry. There is no fatigue. The most valuable thing is that your way of speaking changes; you don't resort to violence or punishment anymore. This, in turn, has quite an influence on kids. (11.tur)

I listen so they come and tell me about anything, their sorrow and happiness. We have stronger communication. I guess he was telling me but I wasn't listening. I wasn't paying attention. Now I know about his problems, about who he likes or dislikes. (4.bel)

'Being more tolerant and understanding' and having 'better communication' were mentioned most frequently (25% and 25%, respectively) across the five countries. Saudi Arabia generated the highest percentage of positive perceived effects on the mother–child relationship with 28% (see Table 3).

Perceived indirect effects

The reported indirect effects of the programme reflect changes that mothers perceived in their behaviour towards their husbands, towards other children in the family and towards the people around them. Changes in their behaviour towards their husbands were reported as causing a difference in marital relationships. 'Better communication and fewer arguments with their husbands' had the most mention in the whole sample (60%).

Table 3. Frequencies and percentage of mothers' responses regarding the subcategories.

	Saudi Arabia		Bahrain		Belgium		Switzerland		Turkey		Total	
	n^a	%	n	%	n	%	n	%	n	%	n	%
The child												
Learned new concepts	13	8.7	7	4.7	9	6.0	14	9.4	10	6.7	53	35.6
Improved concentration	1	0.7	3	2.0	1	0.7	4	2.7	1	0.7	10	6.7
More social	7	4.7	4	2.7	0	0.0	0	0.0	2	1.3	13	8.7
Higher self-confidence	7	4.7	6	4.0	1	0.7	5	3.4	7	4.7	26	17.5
Better organised	6	4.0	1	0.7	1	0.7	1	0.7	3	2.0	12	8.0
Better small muscle use	16	10.7	2	1.3	2	1.3	8	5.4	7	4.7	35	23.5
Total	50	33.5	23	15.4	14	9.4	32	21.6	30	20.1	149	100
Mother's self-perception												
Perception of motherhood changed	7	3.3	4	1.9	9	4.2	7	3.3	8	3.8	35	16.4
Felt more conscious	15	7.0	15	7.0	20	9.4	17	8.0	10	4.7	77	36.2
Felt more valuable	11	5.2	9	4.2	8	3.8	1	0.5	13	6.1	42	19.7
Had more self-confidence	6	2.8	6	2.8	12	5.6	6	2.8	15	7.0	45	21.1
Felt beneficial	0	0.0	0	0.0	1	0.5	10	4.7	3	1.4	14	6.6
Total	39	18.3	34	15.9	50	23.5	41	19.3	49	23	213	100
Mother–child relationship												
More knowledgeable about child development	10	3.9	5	2	9	3.5	10	3.9	4	1.6	38	15.0
Decreased use of negative discipline methods	13	5.1	12	4.7	8	3.1	7	2.8	8	3.1	48	18.9
More tolerant and understanding	20	7.9	13	5.1	5	2.0	14	5.5	12	4.7	64	25.2
Spent more time	11	4.3	7	2.8	6	2.4	12	4.7	5	2.0	41	16.1
Better communication	18	7.1	8	3.1	12	4.7	11	4.3	14	5.5	63	24.8
Total	72	28.3	45	17.7	40	15.7	54	21.2	43	16.9	254	100
Father–child relationship												
Acted with more awareness	7	9.2	4	5.3	4	5.3	7	9.2	8	10.5	30	39.5
Spent more time and had closer relationship with the target child	11	14.5	9	11.8	7	9.2	7	9.2	8	10.5	42	55.3
Had closer relationship with other children	1	1.3	0	0.0	1	1.3	0	0.0	2	2.6	4	5.2
Total	19	25	13	17.1	12	15.8	14	18.4	18	23.6	76	100
Group process												
Felt a sense of belonging	17	7.9	14	6.5	13	6.0	5	2.3	10	4.6	59	27.3

Table 3 (Continued)

	Saudi Arabia		Bahrain		Belgium		Switzerland		Turkey		Total	
	n^a	%	n	%	n	%	n	%	n	%	n	%
Felt relief and psychological support	7	3.2	7	3.2	8	3.7	7	3.2	6	2.8	35	16.2
Learned from other people's experiences	18	8.3	18	8.3	18	8.3	17	7.9	14	6.5	85	39.3
Felt that she was not the only one	8	3.7	5	2.3	5	2.3	6	2.8	5	2.3	29	13.5
Felt valuable as she was listened to	1	0.5	0	0.0	3	1.4	1	0.5	3	1.4	8	3.7
Total	51	23.6	44	20.3	47	21.7	36	16.7	38	17.6	216	100
Cognitive education programme												
Contributed to the child's development	9	5.7	5	3.2	7	4.4	9	5.7	13	8.2	43	27.2
Helped the child to be more responsible	3	1.9	2	1.3	3	1.9	5	3.2	8	5.1	21	13.3
Better mother–child relationship	18	11.4	16	10.1	17	10.8	15	9.5	7	4.4	73	46.2
Mother felt proud of herself	14	8.8	0	0.0	7	4.4	0	0.0	0	0.0	21	13.3
Total	44	27.8	23	14.6	34	21.5	29	18.4	28	17.7	158	100
Teacher												
Her mastery in implementing the content	19	13.1	17	11.7	19	13.1	2	1.4	7	4.8	64	44.1
Her personality	20	13.8	17	11.7	19	13.1	16	11.0	9	6.2	81	55.9
Total	39	26.9	34	23.4	38	26.2	18	12.4	16	.0	145	100

[a]As 20 mothers in each country were interviewed, 'n' equals the number of times a particular subcategory was mentioned in the interviews rather than the number of mothers, as some mothers mentioned more than one subcategory in any one main category. Thus, column totals for each country represent the number of times a category was mentioned, summed across its subcategories. Row totals represent the number of times each subcategory was mentioned, summed across countries. Overall column percentages were calculated by dividing the total number of mentions per category by each country by the total number of mentions category summed across all countries. Row percentages were calculated by dividing the total number of mentions for each subcategory, summed across countries, by the total number of mentions per category.

> I used to hesitate to talk, to express myself. But now I feel comfortable telling what I like and what I don't like. It is like a routine. You could be working, but I am tired, as well. I have my own responsibilities as much as you. So, I tell him that he is responsible for that. (15.sar)

> I have become more patient as a spouse. For example, I would quarrel a lot with my husband because of the children's stress, we used to dispute all the time. He was nervous, I was nervous, but it has changed. For example, I am more relaxed toward him. (12.tur)

> I am sure that love and respect between me and my husband increased. The more you explain things to the other person, the more he respects you. (9.sw)

Mothers also indicated that their behaviour towards relatives and friends had changed and they had become more tolerant and more understanding. They were able to express themselves better and to state their demands and ideas. In addition, mothers said that they discussed what they had learned in the programme with the people around them and made photocopies of the handouts and distributed them to friends, neighbours and relatives. Sometimes they found solutions to their friends' problems by applying what they had learned in the programme.

> I am talking about patience; your attitude toward people changes, it can be your child, your spouse or others around. (12.sw)

> When my friends wanted to come over and when my child had to study, I couldn't tell them that I wasn't available, thinking that they might be hurt. Now, I tell them that my child has an exam or has to study so I am not available that day. (9.sar)

In addition, mothers also perceived changes in the fathers' behaviour and attitudes that brought about changes in family relationships. Fathers were reported to have closer relationships both with the target child and with other children in the family.

> He didn't use to share much with the kids. When he came from work, he used to watch television, a football match or a program he liked and didn't spend much time with the children. But now he can turn off the television when necessary and take care of them. (2.sar)

> He has started showing more of what he has done to his father, the pictures or his writings. He has been sharing more with his father. Now he can show whatever he has done easily to his father, talk to him about his problems. The program has a part in that. (4.sw)

Having a better relationship with the target child had higher mention (55%) than a better relationship with other children (5%) in the category, 'Perceived positive effects on the father–child relationship'. Across the five countries, the percentage of positive perceived effects on fathers was highest in Turkey (24%) and Saudi Arabia (25%) (see Table 3).

In their interviews, mothers revealed that a change in the fathers was possible when they shared and applied what they had learned with their husbands. Specifically, they mentioned that sharing handouts distributed during the programme with their husbands made a major contribution to change in fathers.

> I kept talking to my husband in the 'I' language. I kept talking and telling him about what we did at the meetings. He also read the handouts and was influenced by them. (13.tur)

Mothers' views on what makes the programme work

A major question for this study was 'What are the mothers' perspectives on what makes the programme work?' in other words, what did they attribute as causing positive changes to their children and themselves? Accordingly, the interview data were analysed further to identify what brought about the reported changes.

Mothers mentioned components of MOCEP, the MSP group process, the CEP and the teacher as the main factors contributing to positive change. The content of the information given and the successful implementation of the programme were also perceived to have a positive influence.

Group process

The mothers reported that during the group process they felt a sense of belonging to the group, felt relief and psychological support through sharing, and that they learned from other people's experiences.

> We used to talk about children, everything about ourselves as women, even sexuality. We started talking about things that we couldn't with others because there was no shame here. You can't go and tell a psychologist you don't know about everything; they wouldn't understand because they are foreigners. This program has been such a relief for me. (18.bel)

> During the meetings, everyone had experiences, they coped with stubborn children, and that affected me. I heard and benefited from their comments and points of view. I tried to practice what I had learned. We were sitting and talking about our problems. Solutions came up; everyone implemented those and commented on them. We benefited; it had a positive effect on us. (10.bah)

The mother's statement below revealed that when she listened to other mothers in the group meetings, she felt that she was not alone and realised that she was not the only one experiencing these problems.

> You see that it's not only between you and your child; you are not alone in that. There are others and they try out different methods to solve this problem. As I said before, you find a new way for the things you can do about education and so you return home more satisfied. This becomes a new reason to attend the program. (8.sw)

In addition, mothers also indicated that they felt valued as all the other mothers listened to them and that equal importance was given to each participant in the group. Their statements clearly indicated that this helped them enjoy the group process.

> Our teacher was letting all of us talk, we were all telling our opinions and you feel that you are valued there. (4.bel)

> If we hadn't had that environment, if it had been like a seminar where the teacher did all the talking, it wouldn't have meant anything for me. When I talk and share about a topic, I can internalize it. That's how I believe, I should talk, I should think as well. Just talking and letting people go without thinking is not useful. (15.sar)

When the contribution of the group process to the perceived effects was examined across the whole sample, 'Learned from other people's experiences' was the most pronounced (39%) subcategory. Saudi Arabia (24%) and Belgium (22%) mentioned the contribution of the group process to the perceived positive effects to a greater extent than other countries.

CEP

Although the activities of the CEP focused directly on the child's development, mothers' statements indicated that working on the CEP together with their child contributed to personal change. The CEP was perceived as a context that not only allows the mother to work with her child, but also to follow her child and find out what she/he knows or needs to know.

> I had great pleasure while studying the CEPs with him because I was teaching him something. I did it myself; we did it together with my husband. There was a lot of effort and the more the effort, the more the love. (8.sar)

It was clear from their statements that the implementation of these activities taught mothers new methods to use with their children. This had given them more confidence in themselves as the CEP activities also provided guidance about how to help their children in the future.

> After attending the program, I learned about what was given and what could be taught to the child and how they were taught actually, so that I should teach it the same way. (13.sar)

The mothers reported that they felt proud, as they had contributed to their child's development through the CEP activities. They also commented that their children now perceived them differently and had more confidence in their mother as they realised that she was more knowledgeable and could also teach them.

> She has more confidence in me, her perspective has changed. She thinks, 'My mom can do it'. It has been so gratifying, we have come closer. (14.tur)

Considering the contribution of subcategories in the CEP category, 'CEP affected the mother–child relationship positively' received the most mention (46%) across the five countries. As Table 3 illustrates, between the five countries, the perceived benefits of the CEP was highest in Saudi Arabia (28%) and Belgium (21.5%), and lowest in Bahrain (15%).

Teacher

Mothers reported that interaction and communication with their MSP teacher was an important change factor.

> She did not act like a teacher; she was more like a sincere, true friend. She created confidence in herself at first because she gave examples of herself and she criticized herself. She listened to you and tried to find a solution accordingly. You felt that she wanted the best for you and that you could trust her. (17.sw)

Mothers reported that their teacher's competency and mastery of the content and delivery of the programme, her personal characteristics, her communication style and being a good role model led to an effective group process and motivated them to use their new knowledge.

> She described things well; her explanations were clear. I could really understand her explanations. There is one thing I am certain, she was very knowledgeable. She was sincere. (14.sar)

> Her patience and punctuality affected me considerably. She was my role model. (1.bah)

In this category, the majority of mothers mentioned the two subcategories, 'teacher's personality and her communication style' (56%) and 'the teacher's mastery in implementing the content' (44%) as one of the most important contributions of the programme (see Table 3).

Finally, both before the programme and during its implementation, mothers said that they had received both positive and negative feedbacks from their spouses and other acquaintances. When asked about how much they were influenced by other people's negative reactions, mothers indicated that these had not had a negative effect. Their own decisions were more important to them than other people's reactions, as they believed that what they were doing would be beneficial for their child.

> I did not take them seriously; my decision was important. I didn't care about what they thought. I was thinking. 'I will continue going there no matter what they think'. (3.bel)

> Negative reactions did not affect me much because I knew that MOCEP would be good for my children. I continued despite negative reactions. (20.sw)

Mothers clearly indicated that the instrumental and emotional support they received from their spouse and other people around was important for the success of the programme. There were, however, mothers who reported that they had not received any sort of support during the programme either from their spouse or their friends. Nevertheless, these mothers stated that they had continued the programme.

Discussion

The findings reported above describe how mothers perceived the effects of the programme on their children's social, cognitive and physical development. The mothers we interviewed believe that they have brought about a substantial change in their child's development by creating a developmentally supportive environment. The perceived changes they observed in their children's development as a result of the programme were similar to those identified in evaluations of other intervention programmes (Blok et al. 2005; Campbell et al. 2002; Reynolds and Ou 2004; Schweinhart et al. 2005). The study's findings offer additional confirmation of the contribution made by mother's involvement in intervention programmes to the development of their children (Bohon, Macpherson, and Atiles 2005; Senechal 2006; St Clair and Jackson 2006).

The changes the mothers mentioned concerning their self-perceptions were also similar to those obtained by other researchers (Asscher, Hermanns, and Deković 2008; Conners, Edwards, and Grant 2007). Such changes deserve more attention than they get currently as they indicate how a change in the immediate context of a child can play a crucial role in his/her development. Concerning why mothers were motivated to enter the programme, our findings indicated that they entered because they wanted to raise their children differently and become better equipped for parenting. Their self-reports indicated that despite receiving negative reactions and feedback from others both before and during their participation in the programme, they continued to attend and remained motivated.

Our analysis also indicated that there were perceived indirect effects on both mothers and fathers. The mothers stated that they had better communication and fewer arguments with their husbands after attending the programme. This was reported as a mutual change. Fathers were also reported to have closer relationships especially with the target child as well as other children in the family. We identified these as indirect effects because the programme did not aim to change the relationship between mothers and fathers or between fathers and children. The mother seemed to play a key role in promoting these indirect changes. A reasonable explanation of these indirect effects might be that the changes taking place in the mother led her to influence the father to change.

Mothers considered the group context to be the most influential factor in promoting the changes they perceived in themselves. They stated that the group process allowed them to appreciate that they had a lot in common with other mothers in the group, and that they were not alone in experiencing certain problems. The group process allowed mothers to experience collective decision-making and solution generation through group discussion. They experienced being treated as equals as well as being listened to and deemed valuable. They were able to share stories about their lives and make friends. For these mothers, the group process was perceived as becoming a part of a social milieu. These various experiences led to a sense of belonging and a sense of being valued that lessened the mothers' feelings of being alone. Finally, the group process was perceived as providing relief and psychological support.

Mothers reported that their experiences with the teacher in the group were a critical factor for the effectiveness of the group process. The way the teacher implemented the programme, her personality and the role model she provided meant that mothers regarded her as playing a pivotal role in how they used the information they received, and in promoting the changes they perceived.

The implementation of the CEP allowed the mother to work and spend time with her child. Teaching him/her certain skills led her to experience a sense of responsibility and a feeling of being useful to the child. Parents reported that this experience helped them to get to know their child better and allowed them to use new, more effective learning methods with their child. The positive changes mothers observed in their child during this process, and his/her regard of the mother as a 'teacher' were also reported as important for increasing her confidence and in creating a feeling of 'I can teach'.

The findings reported above have implications for further implementations of MOCEP and for other parenting programmes as they demonstrate that such programmes need to include components both for the child and for the parents. Our results show that it is vitally important that parents should share certain activities and spend time with their children within the context of the programme. Similarly, mothers regard the group process that allows the sharing of knowledge and personal experience as centrally important for promoting the changes they perceived in themselves, underlining the necessity of including group process in such programmes. This study also revealed the importance of the teacher's skills and personality characteristics for the programme to achieve its aim and meet parents' needs. It is the teacher who makes the group process a nurturing experience for the participants.

There was a considerable similarity between the five countries regarding the subcategories of perceived direct and indirect effects that were mentioned most frequently. There were, however, some differences. For example, mothers in Saudi

Arabia were most likely to mention effects identified as important (i.e. subcategories with the highest percentages). The differences obtained across countries could be due to mothers' educational level, existing opportunities for children's education and development of children in the immediate locality, and the amount of contact the mothers have with the outside world. Our findings indicate that mothers with less education, such as those in Saudi Arabia, less contact with the outside world and fewer local opportunities for their children's development were most likely to identify perceived changes in the subcategories with the highest percentages.

The majority of the mothers in Bahrain and Belgium said that they lived with extended families and therefore had difficulties in practising the programme. Nevertheless, the group meetings were a means of social support for the mothers in Belgium as they had a strenuous home life, and for those in Bahrain the meetings helped them alleviate stress.

In all five countries, all the mothers we interviewed mentioned perceived changes related to their child's development. However, for other categories (mother's self-perception, mother–child relationship, father–child relationship, group process, teacher, CEP) one or two mothers reported no change although we did not observe any particular trends in the 'no change' responses.

Compared to mothers in other countries, those in Switzerland and Belgium raised different issues: they said that CEP implementations helped to change prejudiced feelings directed towards their children at school as the exercises supported children cognitively. Moreover, the activities were perceived to be helpful in supporting the child's mother tongue, Turkish. Mothers in Europe also mentioned that the programme helped them to understand and adopt the child-rearing practices of the country where they lived and also helped their own adaptation.

The target populations in Belgium, Saudi Arabia and Switzerland were similar to the original target population of the programme: they were all Turkish people even though they lived in different cultural contexts (Europe and Saudi Arabia). In Bahrain although there were some similarities, the mothers were native to the country and spoke Arabic.

Programme transfer can take different forms: adoption, adaptation or assembly (van de Vijver and Poortinga 2005). In most countries, transfer takes the form of 'adoption' where the programme, remains close to its original or 'adaptation' where there is a direct transfer of some programme elements with others being changed or replaced. In a very few countries, new development of major parts is undertaken resulting in 'assembly'. The form of transfer has been identified as an important element for programme success and sustainability. If transfer takes the form of assembly and the implementation is long term, (as happened with MOCEP programmes in Belgium-Gent and Bahrain), the institution which transfers and implements the programme in a country is as important as the form for a successful transfer. This institution is likely to plan and actualise the best transfer since they know the transfer culture best. The partnership between the institutions of original and transfer culture need to be close, however, in order to ensure that the programme is applied effectively.

When policy impact was considered, MOCEP has been transformational in two complementary ways in Turkey; expanding the narrow definition of formal, centre-based preschool education model to include home-based models. Parallel to this, in 2009, the Ministry of National Education initiated the development of a National Family Education Program, based largely on the methodology and approach of MOCEP, hence institutialising MOCEP as a national policy. As such MOCEP stands as one of the most successful examples of sustainable collaboration between a non-governmental organisation and the Turkish state, whereas in Saudi Arabia, the implementation of MOCEP with native people played an important role in introducing a new model of early childhood education in the country.

There are certain limitations to this study, which need to be mentioned. First, as interview and field notes were the only research methods, triangulation was not possible. Additional methods would have allowed us to cross-check the information and gain a more complete picture. It would have been ideal to select the sample from a larger population than the one used in the study. Finally, as the sample size and data-set was large, a standard qualitative software program would have assisted the analysis.

The findings reported here are in line with results obtained previously for quantitative evaluations of MOCEP. The present study provided important new qualitative information particularly about how the programme works for mothers, their motivations for taking part, and how they perceived the changes in themselves, their children and their environment that could be attributed to the programme. The results support the argument that intervention programmes based on an ecological approach play a key role in children's development by strengthening the immediate environment of the child and reducing potential risk factors.

Acknowledgement

This research is funded by Mother-Child Education Foundation (ACEV).

References

Asscher, J. J., J. M. A. Hermanns, and M. Deković. 2008. "Effectiveness of the Home-start Parenting Support Program: Behavioral Outcomes for Parents and Children." *Infant Mental Health Journal* 29 (2): 95–113. doi:10.1002/imhj.20171.

Bekman, S. 1998. *A Fair Start: An Evaluation of the Mother-Child Education Program*. Istanbul: AÇEV Publications.

Bekman, S. 2007. "Family Literacy Programme: Beispiele aus der Türkei [FamilyLiteracy Programs: Examples from Turkey]." In *Gemeinsam in Der Spache Baden: Family literacy [Together in the language bathing: Family literacy]*, edited by M. Elfert and G. Rabkin, 105–116. Germany: Ernst Klett Sprachen.

Benasich, A. A., J. Brooks-Gunn, and B. Chu Clewell. 1992. "How do Mothers Benefit from Early Intervention Programs?" *Journal of Applied Developmental Psychology* 13 (3): 311–362. doi:10.1016/0193-3973(92)90035-G.

Blok, H., R. Fukkink, E. Gebhardt, and P. Leseman. 2005. "The Relevance of Delivery Mode and other Programme Characteristics for the Effectiveness of Early Childhood Intervention." *International Journal of Behavioral Development* 29 (1): 35–47. doi:10.1080/016502504 44000315.

Bohon, S. A., H. Macpherson, and J. H. Atiles. 2005. "Educational Barriers for New Latinos in Georgia." *Journal of Latinos and Education* 4 (1): 43–58. doi:10.1207/s1532771xjle0401_4.

Bradley, R. H., L. Whiteside, D. J. Mundfrom, P. H. Casey, K. J. Kelleher, S. K. Pope. 1994. "Early Indications of Resilience and Their Relation to Experiences in the Home Environments of Low Birthweight, Premature Children Living in Poverty." *Child Development* 65 (2): 346–360. doi:10.2307/1131388.

Bronfenbrenner, U. 1979. *The Ecology of Human Development*. Cambridge: Harvard University Press.

Campbell, F. A., and C. T. Ramey. 1994. "Effects of Early Intervention on Intellectual and Academic Achievement: A Follow-Up study of Children from Low-income Families." *Child Development* 65 (2): 684–698. doi:10.2307/1131410.

Campbell, F. A., C. T. Ramey, E. Pungello, J. Sparling, and S. Miller-Johnson. 2002. "Early Childhood Education: Young Adult Outcomes from the Abecedarian Project." *Applied Developmental Science* 6 (1): 42–57. doi:10.1207/S1532480XADS0601_05.

Chang, M., P. Park, K. Singh, and Y. Y. Sung. 2009. "Parental Involvement, Parenting Behaviors, and Children's Cognitive Development in Low-income and Minority Families." *Journal of Research in Childhood Education* 23 (3): 309–324. doi:10.1080/02568540909594663.

Coleman, J. 1990. *The Foundations of Social Theory: 1014*. Cambridge, MA: Harvard University Press.

Conners, N. A., Edwards, M. C., and A. S. A. Grant. 2007. "An Evaluation of a Parenting Class Curriculum for Parents of Young Children: Parenting the Strong-willed Child." *Journal of Child and Family Studies* 16 (3): 321–330. doi:10.1007/s10826-006-9088-z.

Engle, P. L., and M. M. Black. 2008. "The Effect of Poverty on Child Development and Educational Outcomes." *Annals of the New York Academy of Sciences* 1136 (1): 243–256. doi:10.1196/annals.1425.023.

Evans, G. W. 2004. "The Environment of Childhood Poverty." *American Psychologist* 59 (2):77–92. doi:10.1037/0003-066X.59.2.77.

Gonzalez-DeHass, A. R., P. P. Willems, and M. F. Doan Holbein. 2005. "Examining the Relationship Between Parental Involvement and Student Motivation." *Educational Psychology Review* 17 (2): 99–123. doi:10.1007/s10648-005-3949-7.

Hart, B., and T. R. Risley. 1995. *Meaningful Differences in the Everyday Experience of Young American Children*. New York: Brookes Pub.

Harvard Family Research Project. 2006. *Family Involvement in Early Childhood Education:Family Involvement Makes a Difference*. No. 1. Cambridge, MA: Harvard Graduate School of Education.

Kagitcibasi, C., D. Sunar, and S. Bekman. 2001. "Long-term Effects of Early Intervention: Turkish Low-income Mothers and Children." *Journal of Applied Developmental Psychology* 22 (4): 333–361. doi:10.1016/S0193-3973(01)00071-5.

Kagitcibasi, C., D. Sunar, S. Bekman, N. Baydar, and Z. Cemalcilar. 2009. "Continuing Effects of Early Enrichment in Adult Life: The Turkish Early Enrichment Project 22 years later." *Journal of Applied Developmental Psychology* 30 (6): 764–779. doi:10.1016/j.appdev.2009.05.003.

Lamb, V. L., K. C. Land, S. O. Meadows, and F. Traylor. 2005. "Trends in African American Child Well-being, 1985–2001." In *African American family life*, edited by V. C. McLoyd, N. E. Hill, and K. A. Dodge, 45–47. New York, NY: Guilford Press.

McCormick, M. C., J. Brooks-Gunn, S. L. Buka, J. Goldman, J. Yu, M. Salganik, and P. H. Casey. 2006. "Early Intervention in Low Birth Weight Premature Infants: Results at 18 years of Age for the Infant Health and Development Program." *Pediatrics* 117: 771–780. doi:10.1542/peds.2005-1316.

Murnane, R. J. 2007. "Improving the Education of Children Living in Poverty." *The Future of Children* 17 (2): 161–182. doi:10.1353/foc.2007.0019.

Pehrson, K. L., and C. C. Robinson. 1990. "Parent Education: Does it Make a Difference?" *Child Study Journal* 20 (4): 221–236.

Pfannenstiel, J. C., V. Seitz, and E. Zigler. 2003. "Promoting School Readiness: The Role of the Parents as Teachers Program." *NHSA Dialog: A Research-to-Practice Journal for the Early Intervention Field* 6 (1): 71–86. doi:10.1207/s19309325nhsa0601_6.

Reutzal, D. R., P. C. Fawson, and J. A. Smith. 2006. "Words to Go! Evaluating a First-grade Parent Involvement Program for 'making' Words at Home." *Reading Research and Instruction* 45 (2): 119–159. doi:10.1080/19388070609558445.

Reynolds, A. J. 1999. "Educational Success in High-risk Settings: Contributions of the Chicago Longitudinal Study." *Journal of School Psychology* 37 (4): 345–354. doi:10.1016/S0022-4405(99)00025-4.

Reynolds, A. J., and S. R Ou. 2004. "Alterable Predictions of Child Wellbeing in the Chicago Longitudinal Study." *Children and Youth Services Review* 26 (1): 1–14. doi:10.1016/j.childyouth.2003.11.005.

Sameroff, A. 1975. "Early Influences on Development: Fact or Fancy." *Merrill-Palmer Quarterly* 21: 267–294.

Schweinhart, L. J., J. Montie, Z. Xiang, W. S. Barnett, C. R. Belfield, and M. Nores. 2005. *Lifetime Effects: The High/Scope Perry Preschool Study through Age 40* (Monographs of the High/Scope Educational Research Foundation, 14). Ypsilanti, MI: High/Scope Press.

Senechal, M. 2006. "Testing the Home Literacy Model: Parent Involvement in Kindergarten is Differentially Related to Grade 4 Reading Comprehension, Fluency, Spelling, and Reading for Pleasure." *Scientific Studies of Reading* 10 (1): 59–87. doi:10.1207/s1532799xssr1001_4.

St. Clair, L., and B. Jackson. 2006. "Effect of Family Involvement Training on the Language Skills of Young Elementary School Children from Migrant Families." *The School Community Journal* 16 (1): 31–41.

Van de Vijver, F. J. R., and Y. H. Poortinga. 2005. "Conceptual and Methodological Issues in Adapting Tests." In *Adapting Educational and Psychological Tests for Cross-cultural Assessment*, edited by R. K. Hambleton, P. F. Merenda and C. D. Spielberger, 39–63. Mahwah, NJ: Erlbaum.

Early childhood policy and practice in England: twenty years of change

Dorothy Faulkner[a] and Elizabeth A. Coates[b]

[a]Child and Youth Studies Research Group, Centre for Research in Education and Educational Technology, Faculty of Education and Language Studies, The Open University, Milton Keynes, UK; [b]Warwick Institute of Education, University of Warwick, Coventry, UK

This article offers a chronological account and critical appraisal of changes to early childhood education and care (ECEC) services in England over the past 20 years. It describes the policy initiatives, educational interventions and research programmes introduced by successive governments that have effected significant changes to ECEC since 1990. The article covers four key areas: policies designed to reduce social inequality; the professionalisation of the children's workforce and changing status of adults employed in preschool education and care settings; changes to early years pedagogy and the early years curriculum and finally how major research programmes such as the Effective Provision of Preschool Education project and the Millennium Cohort Study have informed our understanding of the effects of social disadvantage and the characteristics of 'high-quality' preschool provision that can alleviate this. There is now persuasive evidence that investment in state-maintained early education is highly cost effective, particularly for disadvantaged children. The current government, however, is shifting the burden of funding for professional training and high-quality integrated services for children and families from the state to the private and voluntary sectors. Time will tell if this is a backward step or movement in the right direction.

Over the past 20 years, young children and families in the UK have experienced a series of significant changes in the organisation and quality of the Early Childhood Education and Care (ECEC) services offered to them. During this period, successive governments have initiated a string of strategic initiatives and policy developments that have improved the accessibility and quality of these services, particularly for parents and children living in areas of social deprivation. In this article, we offer a critical review of some of these initiatives and identify the major, government-funded reports and research programmes that have informed them. Our review will be necessarily selective and will focus on ECEC in England, as space does not permit comprehensive examination of related policies (such as those concerning health care and child protection) or those introduced elsewhere in the UK.[1] In addition, we draw on the views of a panel of prominent early years specialists convened to offer a critical evaluation of past and current changes to early years policy and practice in England. The panel, Carol Aubrey, Pat Broadhead,

Tony Bertram, Debbie Castle, Jane Murray, Chris Pascal and Mary Wild, were invited to participate in an expert seminar held at the Warwick Institute of Education in October 2012 that informed the content and direction of this paper. Panel members and the postgraduate and early years practitioner audience discussed the impact of 20 years of policy change on:

- The levels of social inequality experienced by children and families in areas of social deprivation;
- The quality of the children's workforce; the experience and qualifications of adults employed in preschool education and care settings;
- Early years pedagogy and the content of the early years curriculum;
- Our understanding of the influence of high quality education and care during the preschool period on developmental outcomes for children.

The seminar's purpose was to collect a body of informed and reflective opinion on these and other issues that would allow us to identify underlying issues relating to ECEC that remain unresolved. All panel members gave their permission for the views expressed at the seminar to be represented in this paper where appropriate and have read and approved the seminar transcript (WIES 2012). Panel members' views on the issues above were analysed to identify cross-cutting themes or lessons, which might emerge from their comments and reflections. In this paper, these issues will be discussed in turn.

Levels of social inequality

During the twentieth century, it became increasingly apparent that even in relatively affluent countries, differences in children's individual and family circumstances have long-lasting effects on their health, well-being and educational attainment. The introduction of welfare reform and other measures to reduce social inequality has been a priority for all political parties in the UK in recent years, particularly during the period 1997–2010, when the Labour Government was in office as Aubrey explains:

> Tony Blair [the Prime Minister] said that it was his mission to eradicate poverty within a generation [and this led] within a year to a comprehensive spending review and a tranche of anti-poverty initiatives. Because central to the National Childcare Strategy (part of the Green Paper *Childcare Meeting the Challenge*, 1998) was [a focus] on increasing income for poor households and reducing the number of children growing up in families with no-one in work, so eliminating transmission of deprivation from childhood to adulthood. [New Labour] attempted to establish high-quality affordable childcare in every community to support parents into work or training. (WIES 2012, 15–16)

Nevertheless, the Organisation for Economic Cooperation and Development working paper, *Social Disadvantage and Educational Experiences* (Machin 2006) reported that the adverse impact of poor socioeconomic circumstances on young people's attainment was more marked in the UK than in any of the other 52 countries surveyed. Detailed analysis of the reasons for this lies beyond the scope of this paper. As Pascal points out, however, research evidence consistently demonstrates that children from low-income families are subject to deep-seated structural, systemic inequalities that are socially disadvantageous, restrict growth and development and act as a break to social mobility

(Bertram and Pascal 2000). Pascal made this point most forcibly during the WIES expert seminar:

> Inequality, the lack of social mobility remains a defining feature of English society, it has always been, it is, we are one of the most if not the most unequal societies in Europe, maybe in the developed world, we have the lowest levels of social mobility of any other country in the world. (WIES 2012, 18)

Of these systemic inequalities, Waldfogel and Washbrook (2010) argue that low income and adverse material circumstances are among the most significant. Using data from the UK, Millennium Cohort Survey of 12,644 British children born in 2000–2001, they established robust, statistical associations between poverty and key aspects of cognitive development. Their analysis established that by 2005, over one quarter of children in the Millennium Cohort lived in families with incomes below the average poverty threshold (after-tax income) of £16,500. By the time they were four to five years old, children in the lowest income band were on average 11 months behind children in the middle-income band in terms of expressive vocabulary, and five to six months behind on standardised, non-verbal tests of spatial ability and reasoning. High-level multivariate analyses allowed Waldfogel and Washbrook to establish eleven key factors in four domains contributing to what they term the 'low- to middle-income gap' in children's cognitive performance. These factors lie in the domains: parenting and the home environment, family material circumstances, maternal and child health conditions and maternal employment and childcare. A much clearer understanding of the relative contributions of these factors and domains to the long-term outcomes for children's growth and development has emerged from this research. Evidence such as this, together with that of earlier longitudinal cohort studies from the US, suggests that some interventions, such as effective parenting programmes, are more likely than others to make a real contribution to reducing social inequality.

Although analysis of the Millennium Cohort Survey data is beginning to identify some of the key factors contributing to social disadvantage, British research into the effects of poverty and social deprivation on children's long-term development is a relatively recent enterprise. Successive governments, therefore, have drawn on evaluations of long-term, early intervention programmes, such as the US High/Scope Perry Preschool Program that has followed the lives of 123 children over 40 years from 1962 (Schweinhart et al. 2005, and the Chicago Child–Parent Centre Program initiated in 1967 (Reynolds 1998). These evaluations have established that social and educational intervention for children and families during the preschool period is highly cost effective in the long term. The major goal of early childhood programmes in the US has been to develop socially competent children who, in the long term, would be able to meet family, school and individual responsibilities. Drawing on meta-analyses of the extensive, US research literature, Reynolds (1998) identified eight essential principles of effective early intervention programmes directly associated with both short- and long-term social competence and school success for economically disadvantaged children and families:

(1) Target children and families at highest risk of educational underachievement;
(2) Begin participation early during the preschool period and continue into the school period;
(3) Provide comprehensive child-development services;
(4) Encourage active parental involvement in educational and care provision;

(5) Adopt a child-centred, structured approach to the pre- and primary school curriculum;
(6) Ensure small class sizes and teacher/child ratios;
(7) Offer regular staff development and in-service training for qualified teachers;
(8) Undertake systematic evaluation and monitoring.

The US experience demonstrated that high-quality, preschool education in combination with the parental education could provide a solid foundation that allows children to succeed in life, to gain and retain employment, to enjoy stable relationships and to refrain from engaging in crime (Sylva 1994). In the early 1990s, these findings inevitably aroused the interest of the UK, Conservative Government. Their goals, however, were more economic than social, as they realised that not only was a well-educated child likely to become a successful adult, but in the long run, effective preschool education for four- to five-year-olds, coupled with good quality childcare for younger children would save the country money. As it was also apparent that parental employment and child poverty trends were closely related, particularly for lone-parent families, a further benefit of preschool education was that it allowed mothers to work, at least part-time. This, together with the desire of many women to return to work while their children were still very young, offered another potential boost to the economy.

At the time, as a report on ECEC in the UK by Bertram and Pascal (2000) revealed, preschool provision and childcare was extremely patchy. Some (but by no means all) local education authorities offered preschool provision for three to five year-olds in state-funded nurseries or nursery classes in primary schools. In other areas, parents had to rely on childcare offered by child-minders, relatives or the private and voluntary sector. There was little regulation of the quality of services provided. Many women complained that they could not afford to return to work as private childcare provision was expensive and the few state nurseries were difficult to access. Against this background, the Conservative Government began to look closely at the systems in place for preschool education. In 1993, John Patten, Secretary of State for Education, made one of its most controversial proposals. Denigrating working with children aged three to seven years to the level of unskilled childcare, he suggested the launch of a one-year course aimed at training mature non-graduates to teach nursery and infant classes using their experience as mothers, as an excuse to forgo the usual degree requirement. Dubbed 'Mum's Army' by the media (Abrams 1993), the idea was castigated by the teaching unions who had fought hard to keep the graduate status of the teaching profession. Faced by such opposition, Patten was forced to abandon his plan.

Reforms introduced by the Conservative Government: 1990–1997

In 1989, the Minster of State for Education, Angela Rumbold, was asked to initiate an inquiry into the quality of educational experiences offered to three- and four-year-olds. Her instructions were to focus on the continuity of education in order to ensure a smooth transition to the 1997 National Curriculum. Her final report, *Starting with Quality* (DES) was published in 1990. The inclusion of early years academics on the working party ensured that its recommendations reflected the particular requirements of the under-fives, although they also stressed that the formality of the National Curriculum created difficulties for the move to compulsory schooling. A subsequent report by Her Majesty's Inspectorate, *Aspects of Primary Education: The Education of Children Under Five* (DES 1989), provided examples of existing good practice. In the same year, the *United Nations*

Convention on the Rights of the Child (UNCRC; UNICEF 1989*)* was ratified, followed shortly in England by the 1989, *Children Act.* Although these various initiatives addressed wider issues such as social inclusion and inequality, the primary focus was education rather than health and welfare. Nevertheless, they were indicative of a growing awareness that tackling social inequality would require a more systematic approach to the care and welfare of young children. As the central ideology of the Conservative Government under John Major was free-market enterprise, at the time it was envisaged that any expansion of nursery education would be via the voluntary and private sectors in competition with the state-maintained sector.

In their final year of office, the Conservative Government introduced a voucher scheme that entitled all four-year-olds to a free nursery place. This proved controversial: a fall in the birth rate meant that many schools had spare capacity in their reception class (the first year of compulsory schooling) and encouraged parents to use their vouchers to send their four-year-olds to school. An unintended consequence (contrary to the spirit of free-market enterprise) was that this scheme had a devastating effect on the Preschool Playgroup Association (PPA). Since 1962, local community, PPA playgroups acted as a key alternative to state-funded provision. Although provision was locally based, the PPA was a national body made up of volunteers (usually parents) supported by paid staff at all levels. Playgroups provided an opportunity for children to mix socially on a part-time basis and at small cost. To keep costs down, parents using the service were expected to volunteer help at least once a week. This system was popular as it offered affordable childcare as well as a social outlet for many mothers. The voucher scheme's offer of free part-time education, however, proved too tempting to parents and the numbers of children in playgroups fell dramatically.

At the same time, the government published *The Desirable Outcomes for Children's Learning* (SCAA 1996). This offered curriculum guidance and a set of outcomes or learning goals that, given adequate provision, would ensure that young children were prepared for entry into compulsory schooling. Parents could only use the vouchers in approved institutions validated by inspectors charged with judging:

> The extent to which the quality of provision [was] appropriate to the desirable outcomes in each area of learning, rather than on the achievement of the outcomes themselves by individual children. (SCAA 1996, 1)

In 1997, just as the voucher scheme was about to be launched, the Conservative government lost the general election and the Labour Government assumed office. One of its first actions was to cancel the voucher launch. Nevertheless, by the end of the Conservative Government's term of office, two of the eight key principles of successful early intervention programmes (Reynolds 1998) were beginning to take shape; early participation in preschool education and a structured, child-centred approach to the preschool curriculum.

Reforms introduced by the Labour Government: 1997–2010

During the Labour administration, parents of young children, early years practitioners and other health and social care professionals (the 'Children's Work Force') have witnessed the launch of over 20 aspirational initiatives and interventions (Nutbrown, Clough, and Selbie 2008). As noted above, on assuming office, Prime Minister Tony Blair, delivered a landmark speech pledging that the central purpose of the newly elected Labour

Government would be to tackle social division and reduce inequality. Two years later, his government announced a series of ambitious targets to eradicate child poverty by 2020–2021, with interim child poverty targets for 2004–2005 and 2010–2011 (Brewer et al. 2010).

Cognisant of the popularity of the abandoned voucher scheme, in 1998, the Government introduced free early years education provision for all four-year-olds in England. The entitlement consisted of five weekly sessions of two-and-a-half hours for 33 weeks per year. The offer of a free place was extended to all three-year-olds from 2004. In 2006, the free entitlement was extended to 15 hours a week for 38 weeks of the year for all three- and four-year-olds. This enabled five, three-hour sessions to be offered, but recently a more flexible system has been introduced. Children can now attend nursery for blocks of two full days if required in order to allow women to be free for part-time employment. In 2010, towards the end of its period of office, the Government proposed to extend free education to include two-year-olds from deprived areas with the aim ultimately of providing this service to 130,000 children.

In 1998, as well as introducing free education to all four-year-olds, nurseries identified as particularly high quality were designated as Early Excellence Centres and were charged with acting as exemplars for other settings. A year later in 1999, the ambitious *Sure Start Local Programme* was piloted. Conceived as an early intervention programme, its stated aims matched several of the eight essential principles outlined by Reynolds (1998). *Sure Start* targeted families and children at highest risk for under-achievement; encouraged early participation and active parental involvement; offered a set of comprehensive services and a child-centred, structured approach to children's learning and development through the *Desirable Learning Outcomes*. The programme was aimed at families with children of four years or younger in the most disadvantaged areas in the country. *Sure Start* centres were set up as 'one-stop shops' under a designated manager. The team, coordinated by a manager, represented members from the major services, with the intention of enabling parents to access all the services they needed in one place. Such multi-agency working was recommended in the 1989 *Children Act*; this was the first serious attempt to make it work.

In 2003, Sure Start was extended as part of the strategy outlined in the Green Paper, *Every Child Matters* (ECM; HM Treasury 2003).[2] The actions recommended in ECM, demonstrated the Government's commitment to children's rights, as outlined in the UNCRC. ECM identified five outcomes that all early years and children's service providers should work to enable children to achieve:

- Being healthy – enjoying good physical and mental health and living a healthy lifestyle;
- Staying safe – being protected from harm and neglect and growing up able to look after themselves;
- Enjoying and achieving – getting the most out of life and developing broad skills for adulthood;
- Making a positive contribution – to the community and to society and not engaging in anti-social or offending behaviour;
- Economic well-being – not being prevented by economic disadvantage from achieving their full potential in life.

The Green paper recommended that by 2010, there should be 3500 *Sure Start* Children's Centres, so that all families with young children would have access. Many of these took over from existing Early Excellence Centres or other provision such as *Sure Start* local programmes, state-maintained nursery schools and the neighbourhood nurseries set up in 2001 to provide full-time affordable childcare in the poorest areas in England.

In addition, in 2003, the Department for Education and Skills (DfES) published the *National Standards for Under 8s Daycare and Childminding* guidance: a set of 14 national standards that established a baseline of quality that all day care and childminding providers were expected to meet. These were intended to drive continuous improvement in quality in all care settings for children under eight. The standards identified criteria on the suitability of carers and the qualifications/experience needed; the quality of the premises, equipment and facilities; the security of the children; their health and dietary requirements and provision for children with special educational needs or disabilities (DfES 2003). Finally, following the 2006, *Childcare Act*, the Department for Children Schools and Families (DCSF) introduced the *Early Years Foundation Stage Framework* (EYFS). The EYFS built on and replaced earlier frameworks and set the standards, 'for the learning, development and care young children should experience when they are attending a setting outside their family home, ensuring that every child makes progress and that no child gets left behind' and ensured 'That every child is included and not disadvantaged because of ethnicity, culture or religion, home language, family background, learning difficulties or disabilities, gender or ability' (DCSF 2008b, 7).

By the end of its term of office in 2010, the measures introduced to tackle social inequality by the Labour Government fulfilled at least four of Reynolds' (1998) characteristics of effective intervention programmes. These measures targeted children and families at high risk for educational underachievement; encouraged early participation during the preschool period; offered comprehensive child-development services and encouraged active parental involvement in educational and care provision. As Aubrey points out, however:

> The first national evaluation of the *Sure Start* local programmes, published in 2005 [...], sadly showed only limited across-the-board impact on the lives of young vulnerable children and families.[3] [...] Ten years on, we have got 3.6 million (27%) of people in poverty: One in four, concentrated in the poorest 100 wards [...] in those areas where there are *Sure Start* children's centres. Whilst there was evidence at one point, between 1998-9 and 2010-11 of one million families lifted out of poverty (through at least one parent working), there is a projected rise from 2012-13 in poverty with 300,000 more by 2015-16 and 4.2 million by 2020.[4] (WIES 2012, 16)

Although the Labour Government's target to halve the number of children in poverty by 2010 has not been met, the reasons for this are extremely complex and do not mean that measures recommended in ECM or the EYFS were ineffective. Other factors affecting parental employment and earnings, such as the generalised slow down in earnings since 2004–2005 that resulted from the global economic recession, have had a significant, adverse impact on attempts to reduce poverty and inequality of opportunity (Brewer et al. 2010).

The quality of the children's workforce

Another area that has seen significant change over the past 20 years has been the gradual professionalisation of the early years workforce. It is now widely recognised that the value of investing in well-qualified people to care for and educate children is an important plank of strategies designed to establish the foundations of health and education during the early years (e.g. Belsky, Bares, and Melhuish 2007; Schweinhart et al. 2005). When discussing the issue of qualifications, both Aubrey and Wild referred to the findings of the US, National Institute for Early Education Research policy brief (Barnett 2003) and the British, *Effective Provision for Preschool Education* (EPPE) study (Sylva et al. 2003, 2010). These studies offer strong evidence that the education level of early years staff predicted the quality of interactions between staff and children. The EPPE study (see below) also offers robust evidence that the quality of leadership in early childhood settings is of critical importance in terms of securing a high-quality experience for children and their parents.

Also, as discussed above, the changing nature of service provision exemplified by the *Sure Start* local centres identified a need for more effective interagency collaboration. This is particularly important when considering child protection issues, where there have been some notable failures in recent years as it indicates that early years professionals require new skills for the twenty-first century. For example, the 2004 *Children Act* made interagency working a legal requirement and there is now increased pressure on all services to work together, particularly at a local level. This has led to significant re-examination and redefinition of the roles and status of early years professionals as well as of the qualifications framework that underpins the profession (e.g. Aubrey, Godfrey, and Harris 2013). For example, the *National Professional Qualification in Integrated Centre Leadership*, a Master's level qualification equivalent to that for Head Teachers of State Nursery Schools was developed in 2004 for those people who were to lead the work of children's centres.

In the next section, we briefly outline the 1997–2010 Labour Government's response to the need for a new generation of highly qualified early years professionals, before going on to discuss changes to the qualification framework that have taken place over the past 20 years.

The children and young people's workforce strategy

In 2008, the Labour Government published the *2020 Children and Young People's Workforce Strategy* (DCSF 2008a). Ed Balls, then Secretary of State for Children, Schools and Families, outlined the thinking behind this strategy as follows:

> The core of our approach is to make sure that everyone who works with children and young people – whatever their role – has the skills, knowledge and motivation to do the best job they possibly can. They must be able to ensure that children and young people are safe and can develop and succeed across all of the outcomes, which underpin Every Child Matters. (DCSF 2008a, 2)

Referring back to Blair's 1997 commitment to 'tackle social division and reduce inequality', 10 years after coming to power, the Labour Government made the strong claim that:

> A world-class workforce was the single most important factor in achieving our ambitions for children and young people. Excellent practice by committed and passionate workers changes young lives. (DCSF 2008a, 2)

This is a far cry from Conservative Government's 1993 proposal that for non-graduates, a one-year course and experience as a mother was sufficient training for early years teachers. A recent study by Oberhuemer, Schreyer, and Neuman (2010) has identified Europe wide agreement that the education for three- to six-year-olds should be provided by people with graduate qualifications. However, this study also revealed a significant gap across Europe in the training and qualifications of professionals responsible for the care and education of birth to three-year-olds outside the home. In the next section, we look at how the nature and content of the English, early years qualifications framework has evolved since the early 1990s.

The development of qualifications 1993–2013

In addition to well established, educational qualifications for graduate teachers such as the Bachelor of Education, the Bachelor of Arts with Qualified Teacher Status (QTS) and the Postgraduate Certificate of Education, the development of new degrees in Early Childhood Studies in the mid-1990s was a natural outcome of a heightened awareness of the needs of young children. Rather than focusing solely on education, however, these degrees included the study of psychology, sociology, health and law. In the first instance, many were designed to provide nursery nurses with the opportunity to gain a further qualification and later the possibility of training as a teacher. As the new Early Childhood Studies degrees became established and the range of work widened, many younger students were attracted, gaining employment as teachers, social workers, play workers and family support workers.

Most of the qualifications achieved by people working in nursery education, however, were vocational. National Vocational Qualifications (NVQ) were available at two levels. Level-2 NVQ was equivalent to General Certificate of Secondary Education Ordinary level qualifications (GCSEs) usually taken at 16, and Level 3, the equivalent of GCSE Advanced level ('A' level) qualifications taken at 18. Other qualifications, such as the Cache Diploma, a full-time taught course with placements, enabled people to become nursery nurses. In 2001, Foundation degrees were introduced awarding a qualification equal to the first 2 years of a University Honours degree. For the early years sector, this meant a *Sector Endorsed Early Years Foundation Degree*, the content of which was laid down by the Government and included the study of child development, curriculum areas and child protection, mainly from a work-based perspective. Students on this part-time course were usually working as nursery nurses or teaching assistants in reception or Key Stage One classes for five- to seven-year-olds in primary schools. Gaining this level of qualification enabled many to achieve promotion to Higher Level Teaching Assistant posts. This was important, as career prospects for most early years workers were limited. Further opportunities were offered to those achieving this Foundation degree since they were eligible to 'top-up' to a Pass or Honours degree by studying for one or two years part-time, respectively.

In 2007, *The Children's Plan* (DCSF) introduced the requirement for every full day care centre to have a graduate on its staff. Originally, this was intended to be a teacher, but the introduction of the *Early Years Professional Status (EYPS)* looked set to supersede this idea (DCSF 2008b). Although training for this status was aimed at students, who had or were about to achieve a pass degree, it was not generally delivered by universities but by private consortia working in tandem with Higher Education Institutions. The length of training depended on the amount of experience the student had of working with children from birth to five years. Once achieved, EYPS graduates were regarded as qualified to lead delivery of the early years curriculum in full time, early years settings or children's centres. When introduced, the EYPS was marketed as being equivalent to qualified teachers status, but as is frequently the case this was not matched by equivalent pay and the qualification was not widely recognised, particularly by parents. As Wild pointed out:

> Even amongst fellow professionals sometimes, they [EYPS qualified staff] were still seen as not quite as good as the teacher, as the reception class teacher. (WIES 2012, 12)

During the Labour Government's term of office, although the qualification levels of early years professionals clearly improved, there was still a lack of consistency across the sector (e.g. Hadfield et al. 2012). In 2012, therefore, the Coalition Government commissioned Professor Cathy Nutbrown to undertake a review of early years qualifications. This revealed a confusing picture with over 400 early years qualifications covering different standards. Consequently, although very few of her recommendations were accepted outright, Nutbrown recommended a more streamlined qualifications framework; all childcare qualifications should cover the same set of standards and should be at a level equivalent to the traditional GCSE, 'A' levels. Also, she recommended that everyone aspiring to work with young children should have attained at least level 3 in English and mathematics. Castle, a highly experienced Nursery Manager was in complete agreement with this recommendation when the issue of qualifications was discussed at the WIES seminar:

> As a manager who interviews staff, candidates for posts, one of the things that I find really difficult is having applicants that can't fill in application forms, can't string sentences together on paper, let alone in an interview, and I wonder [...] how we can expect these people to provide excellent quality childcare [...] If they can't write about themselves how can they then transfer their skills into caring for other people's children. The expectations of parents, particularly in a setting like ours, is very high, our parents are very well informed about child development, early years education, and so we have to be able to match their expectations all the time. (WIES 2012, 7)

In January 2013, *More Great Childcare: Raising Quality and Giving Parents More Choice* (DfE 2013), a discussion paper by Elizabeth Truss, the Children's Minister, was published partly in response to the *Nutbrown Review*. Describing the current nursery provision as 'chaotic', this plan identified four key areas that the current Coalition government intends to address: Raising the status and quality of the workforce; freeing high-quality providers to offer more places; improving the regulatory regime and giving more choice to parents. This plan has proved controversial and has received a mixed reception from early years professional organisations, early years experts and parents' groups. For example, Truss recommended changes to the adult–child ratio in settings, standardisation of the nursery nurse qualification and a new *Early Years Teacher Status* (EYTS; to replace the EYPS). There was a robust, cross-sector challenge to the proposed ratio changes causing the government to abandon this part of the plan, however, changes to qualifications are taking place. To address the need for better-qualified staff for babies and very young children, the new EYTS training is intended as a qualification for teachers of zero- to five-year-olds. As this includes the reception class in school, critics of the scheme argue that as the EYTS only requires a pass degree, teachers qualified under this scheme will eventually replace the current early years teachers with Honours degrees and QTS who are more expensive. This is a retrograde step, perhaps not quite a return to a 'Mum's Army', but an undermining of the hard fought battle to keep parity of status for all areas of the teaching profession.

Also, although there is a clear commitment to raising the status and quality of the children's workforce through better quality training and a simplified qualifications framework, the plan also outlines a commitment to return to a free market economy in terms of the provision of this training:

> We will remove constraints on childcare training; for example, the obligation to use only local-authority-approved first aid training. This will ensure that there is competition in the market for high quality training and professional development. (DfE 2013, 29)

In order to ensure the quality of provision and the effectiveness of the new qualifications framework, new regulatory powers are proposed for the Office for Standards in Education, Children's Services and Skills, and providers are to be encouraged to develop their own national standards so that, 'Providers that can demonstrate a strong commitment to quality will be the ones that flourish, as parents become ever more demanding consumers of their services' (DfE 2013, 40). As Castle pointed out, however, even if there is a more consistent qualifications framework that will make it easier for early years settings to recruit staff, for the private and voluntary sector, for leaders and managers of early years settings, funding the cost of continuing professional development for those staff is problematic and may drive up costs:

> The continual professional development of my team, [...] is always very challenging, and also at times very expensive and when you're in the PVI sector, the profit line or the breaking even as it is in our case is an important part of my role, CPD can become a very expensive option for us. (WIES 2012, 13)

Thus, although 'More Great Childcare' recognises the importance of regular staff development, in-service training for qualified teachers and systematic evaluation and monitoring, it remains to be seen how this will play out in a consumer-oriented, market-driven environment.

Curriculum reform

The Desirable Outcomes for Children's Learning (DfEE 1996) was one of the first publications to offer non-statutory curriculum guidance for ECEC. In 2000, a Government Select Committee on Education and Employment conducted an inquiry into Early Years Education (House of Commons 2000). Its focus was education, but other relevant issues were taken into account including parenting, assessment, curriculum, play and the outdoors. Initially its intention was to look at the age range from three to seven years, but after taking advice from early years experts, its remit was broadened to cover birth to eight. An outcome of this was the development of the *Birth to Three Matters* framework (DfES 2002), which provided guidance for those working with the youngest children. This framework, and *The Curriculum Guidance for The Foundation Stage* (Qualifications and Curriculum Authority [QCA]; DfES 2000), which replaced *Desirable Outcomes*, aimed to provide a smooth path from birth into compulsory schooling. The *Curriculum Guidance* offered a play-based curriculum and considerably more detail than *Desirable Outcomes* although the areas of learning it identified as important were similar, the main difference being slight changes to the headings. Thus, Personal and Social Development became Personal, Social and Emotional Development; Language and Literacy became Communication, Language and Literacy and Mathematics became Mathematical

Development. The other areas: Knowledge and Understanding of the World; Physical Development and Creative Development remained the same. These curriculum frameworks were intended not just for those working in nurseries or children's centres; childminders were also required to follow them.

Finally, as discussed earlier, the 2006 *Childcare Act*, the first Act exclusively concerned with early years and childcare, paved the way for a further revision to the early years curriculum, *The Early Years Foundation Stage Framework* (EYFS; DfES 2007; DCSF 2008b). This focused on four themes: A Unique Child; Positive Relationships; Enabling Environment; and Learning and Development. In curriculum terms, however, the areas of learning differed little from the previous two frameworks although Mathematical Development became Problem Solving, Reasoning and Numeracy.

The new EYFS curriculum was extended to include school reception classes with the intention that these classes should offer a play-led curriculum rather than the more formal Key Stage One of the National Curriculum. This meant that the transition problems between the early years curriculum and the National Curriculum (which had previously occurred between nursery and school) now occurred when children moved from the reception class into the first year of Key Stage One. To counter these problems, the inspectorate recommended that there should be a gradual move away from a play led to a more formal approach to teaching and learning. Broadhead, however, is highly critical of simplistic notions that all early years pedagogy should be play-based or play-led (Broadhead, Howard, and Wood 2010). In her view:

> We're still confused about what play is. I'd like to put to you finally an idea that children in fact do not learn through play, that this is too unsophisticated a notion. […] If we keep harnessing play for a learning process [subject] to adult direction […] what we do is diminish its power and diminish its pleasure for children. We need to think about how the environment looks and […] about how playful learning and playful pedagogies are embedded in those environments and bring those ideas into our curriculum documents in the future. (WIES 2012, 3)

The pressure for schools to demonstrate that their pupils were performing well in national Standardised Assessment Tests at age 7 was so great, however, that in many instances teaching and learning in reception class has had to become relatively formal in order that children might adjust more easily (Aubrey 2004).

It was not only the UK government affecting the nursery curriculum, however, initiatives from abroad were also causing interest (Soler and Miller 2003). Three in particular were influential in shaping thinking about the early years curriculum. The first of these, the New Zealand *Te Whariki* (Ministry of Education 1996), emphasised developing reciprocal partnerships between families, early years professionals and the wider community, and informed the structure of *Birth to Three Matters* (2002) and the *Curriculum Guidance for the Foundation Stage* (2000). The second was Reggio Emilia in Italy that emphasised following the interests of the child (Edwards, Gandini, and Forman 1998). This had a widespread influence on the early years curriculum nationally (e.g. *Teaching and Learning Scotland* 2006). Reggio's employment of an artist in every early years setting, exhibitions and videos of the projects undertaken by the children, as well as the week long seminars offered to English teachers, saw a rise in the number of artists in residence working alongside nursery staff. The final influence on the curriculum came from the Scandinavian emphasis on outdoor education and Forest Schools (Maynard 2007). Many English nurseries and schools partitioned off an area as a 'forest school' although in reality many were little more than wild life areas as the available space was small. Teachers and nursery practitioners attended training courses to enable them to work effectively with children in these areas.

This interest in the outdoors was particularly important since there were concerns across all age groups children were spending too much time indoors, partly because of child protection issues but also because of the rise in the use of technology. The increasing use of computers and play stations means that many children lead a largely sedentary life. This is exacerbated by parents' concern for children's safety, which restricted freedom to play outdoors. This is a serious social concern that has led Bertram and others to call for a re-evaluation of how we assess risk in early childhood settings:

> I believe in child protection issues and I think you should have rightfully systems in place, but I think we can go too far. [...] We've lost our way in terms of risk [...] this is seriously impacting on the way that young children explore the world. We need to get this into context, of course there needs to be protection systems in place, but not so much that it interferes with actually development of children and that sense of adventure and exploration which I think is essential. (WIES 2012, 14–15)

In the next section, we offer a brief outline of key British research-based educational intervention and evaluation studies years that have had a significant impact on early years pedagogy, the nature of the curriculum and our understanding of the impact of high-quality, early years provision on later developmental outcomes.

Research on the impact of high-quality provision on later development

National evaluations of *Sure Start* established that active parental involvement in children's education and a strong home environment together with a child-centred, structured approach to the curriculum are important determinants of quality (NESS 2005; Siraj-Blatchford and Woodhead 2009). Two notable intervention projects initiated in the late 1990s had a significant influence on the *Sure Start* programme. These were *Raising Early Achievement in Literacy* (REAL; Nutbrown, Hannon, and Morgan 2005) and the *Peers Early Education Partnership* (PEEP, Evangelou and Sylva 2003). REAL, funded in part by the local education authority, has involved over 300 families, 50 schools, 100 teachers, nursery nurses and other professionals in Sheffield. The initial PEEP project involved 156 families in Oxford and further 86 families from Oxfordshire who acted as a matched control group and was part-funded by the DfES. Both projects involved parents and children in areas of social deprivation.

REAL was the largest preschool intervention study in the UK to focus on raising standards of attainment in literacy for three- to four-year-olds. It was an inclusive programme that offered both parents and children the opportunity to develop their literacy and learning. Its second phase included a randomised control trial involving 176 families, half of who served as controls. Children's literacy skills were tested before and after the programme. This trial established that the programme was particularly advantageous for children whose mothers had few educational qualifications.

PEEP had a broader remit and targeted improvement in literacy and numeracy as well as in prosocial behaviour and self-esteem. The three-year-old children participating in PEEP or its control group were tested on a range of standardised tests at the start of the programme and again aged four and five. Evangelou and Sylva (2003) reported that after two years of parental participation, children in the PEEP group were ahead of their matched (non-PEEP) peers in the following areas: Language and Literacy (Verbal

Comprehension, Vocabulary and Concepts about print); Numeracy (Early Number Concepts) and Self-esteem (Cognitive and Physical Competence).

These programmes were similar in that each provided a structured preschool curriculum alongside a parental education programme based on the *Opportunities, Recognition, Interaction and Modeling* framework (Hannon 1995). This framework encourages parents to participate in, recognise and value their children's opportunities for learning and their achievements. Parents are offered tutoring so that in informal learning contexts with their children, they can model appropriate literacy and numeracy behaviours. They are also provided with books and other support materials. Specially trained early years educators provide this tutoring at home and at children's centres, nursery schools or other settings for participating parents. Both programmes had, and continue to have, a significant impact on local authority preschool provision for children and families. They have also influenced government thinking about the Foundation Stage, the nature of the early years curriculum and the importance of planned, parental involvement in this curriculum.

In 1997, the DfES commissioned a substantial six-year research project focusing upon three-year-old children, their progress through preschool (the Foundation stage) and the first three years of formal schooling (Key Stage 1, five- to seven-year-olds). *The* EPPE research project, the largest of its kind in Europe, was designed to investigate how the individual characteristics of children are shaped by the environments in which they develop (Sylva et al. 2010). It compared the educational outcomes of 2800 children drawn from randomly selected preschool settings in six local authorities with those of 200 children who did not attend any form of early education. In addition to collecting information about these children, it also collected information about their families, their preschool setting and their neighbourhood environment. It was later extended: EPPE 3–11 ran from 2003 to 2008, and *The Effective Preschool, Primary and Secondary Education* (EPPSE) project has now followed children from the 1997 sample through to age 16. The EPPE and EPPSE projects have resulted in over 30 technical reports and research summaries.[5] The EPPE research team's account of children's progress over the preschool period identified the following key characteristics and effects:

- Age of entry is important; an earlier start is related to better intellectual development and improved independence, concentration and sociability; full-time attendance does not lead to better gains for children compared with part-time provision.
- Disadvantaged children in particular can benefit significantly from good quality preschool experiences, especially if they attend centres that cater for a mixture of children from different social backgrounds.
- The quality of preschool centres is directly related to better intellectual/cognitive and social/behavioural development. Children tend to make better intellectual progress in fully integrated centres and nursery schools.
- Quality was higher overall in integrated settings, nursery schools and nursery classes. Settings with good proportion of trained teachers on the staff, show higher quality and their children make more progress. This is also true of settings that view educational and social development as complementary and equal in importance.
- Effective pedagogy includes interaction traditionally associated with the term 'teaching', the provision of instructive learning environments and 'sustained shared thinking' to extend children's learning.

- Although parent's social class and levels of education were related to child outcomes, the quality of the home learning environment was more important. (Adapted from EPPE Team 2003, 2)

The EPPE studies have informed and shaped government policy during a time of significant change to the curriculum and the nature of provision (Sylva et al. 2003, 2010), and the EPPSE study continues to enrich our understanding of the nature and long-term effects of high quality preschool education.

Recent changes and developments to early years provision

After the 2010 election, the Conservative and Liberal parties formed a new Coalition Government. Also in 2010, *The Child Poverty Act* came into force (DfE 2010). This commits current and future governments to reducing the rate of child poverty in the UK to 10% by 2020. In December 2010, the *Field Report* published recommendations designed to lift families out of poverty. A year later, the *Allen Report* (2011a, 2011b) on early intervention appeared. Focusing on disadvantaged children in need of support, in line with the EPPE findings, it recommended identification and intervention as early as possible during the Foundation Stage to rectify potential problems before children started primary school. There were overlaps and similarities between these two reports recommendations that served to strengthen their impact. A further report, the *Munro Review* (2011), examined issues relating to child protection. It made recommendations for the way social services, ECEC settings and schools should safeguard children in their care.

Finally, in 2010, Clare Tickell was commissioned to review the latest evidence on children's development and what is needed to give them the best start at school; developmental assessment; the minimum standards required to keep children safe and support healthy development and whether there should be one single framework for all Early Years providers. Her review, *The Early Years: Foundations for Life, Health and Learning*, was published in 2011. It was informed by a comprehensive account of research on young children's development and learning that included the REAL, PEEP and EPPE findings (Evangelou et al. 2009). Tickell's recommendations were sent out for consultation in 2011. The revised EYFS framework that finally emerged from the consultation in 2012 (DfE 2012), while incorporating many elements of the original 2008 framework, simplified the curriculum so that teachers and practitioners now focus on 17 rather than 69 learning goals with fewer assessment points. The overriding aim of the revised EYFS, however, is to prepare children for school. It offers guidance on child protection issues, children's development during the Foundation stage developmental stages and the early years curriculum and a new developmental check for two-year-old children aimed at detecting possible problems and putting support in place to help overcome them. Needless to say, some of the changes, Tickell recommended have proved highly controversial, particularly those relating to the areas of learning and how these should be assessed.

These various reviews and reports have informed the Coalition Government's plan, *Supporting Families in the Foundation Years* (DfE/DoH 2012). This describes its vision for services for young children and their families and has 'early intervention at its heart' (2012, 5). Among other measures, it states that the national network of *Sure Start* Children's Centres is to be retained and free nursery education is to be extended to the most disadvantaged two-year-olds. Recently, however, changes in the funding environment for local authorities appear to have resulted in the closure of many Sure Start Centres, and the government has signalled that the £1.5bn allocated to councils to spend on early years projects is to be diverted to fund education for two-year-olds (Butler 2013).

Conclusion

Although reducing social inequality and educational disadvantage remain key drivers of government policy, there is increasing concern that the EYFS emphasis on preparing children for school and the proposal to extend education to two-year-olds, may constrain other aspects of their development, and is leading to increasing 'schoolification' of early childhood (OECD 2006). Without exception, members of our expert panel expressed concern about possible limitations to children's autonomy, their freedom of expression and their opportunities to play out of doors as Murray commented:

> In the past two decades I think we've seen English children becoming [...] ever increasingly subject to adult agendas, very often to the exclusion of their own. [...] Schoolification is evident in the pressing down [...] of literacy and numeracy on children's lives in early childhood education and care settings. Adultification is evident in commercialisation, lack of opportunities for children to play, and [...] this focus on school readiness, this focus once they're in primary school of having to meet their targets all the time. (WIES 2012, 17)

There is also concern that in spite of much progress, the proposals set out in *More Great Childcare* (DfE 2013) may not, as the government intends, raise quality, offer more choice and improve the quality of young children's learning experiences. The debate and discussion at WIES 2012 highlighted the following overarching concerns. Firstly, the political, social and economic constructs of early childhood and the purpose of education held by politicians of different parties, appear to have more influence on service provision than the views of children and families who use the services. Secondly, the need for statutory frameworks and stringent, child protection regulations curtail young children's access to spaces and places for play and limit their developmental opportunities. Finally, although we now have good knowledge and understanding of how to address this, as Pascal points out, social inequality is once more on the rise:

> Lack of social mobility remains a defining feature of English society [...] There is nothing more political than early childhood and early childhood education [...] It's about where possibilities are planted in people, it's where future lives are shaped and generated and it's where doors are opened, or by the way slammed shut [...] Early education can make a difference and the recent evidence that we've been looking at estimates that it can redress all those income inequalities by about 50%.[6] Now that's a lot, that's worth fighting for, 50% difference to a life, 50% of children being shifted, 50% of life chances opening up, I think is worth fighting for. (WIES 2012, 19)

Acknowledgements

We gratefully acknowledge the contributions to this paper of Carol Aubrey, Emeritus Professor, University of Warwick; Tony Bertram, Professor/ Director, Centre for Research in Early Childhood, Birmingham; Pat Broadhead, Emeritus Professor, Leeds Metropolitan University; Debbie Castle, Manager, Warwick University Nursery; Jane Murray, Senior Lecturer, University of Northampton; Chris Pascal, Professor/Director, Centre for Research in Early Childhood, Birmingham; Mary Wild, Senior Lecturer, Oxford Brookes University.

Notes

1. See Appendix for a chronology of key strategies, policies and reports.
2. In the UK, a Green Paper is a Government publication that identifies possible courses of action in terms of policy and legislation. Green Papers are commissioned from a relevant government department when new legislation is required, is in need of modification. Green Papers offer recommendations; they do not commit the government to action.
3. See for example the account of this evaluation in Belsky, Bares, and Melhuish (2007)
4. 'Child poverty facts and figures', Child Poverty Action Group, 2012 available from http://www. cpag.org.uk/child-poverty-facts-and-figures.
5. These reports area available for download from http://www.ioe.ac.uk/research/153.html.
6. Pascal et al. (2013).

References

Abrams, F. 1993. "Mum's Army' Idea for Non-Graduates Likely to be Dropped or Watered Down." *The Independent*, August 11. http://www.independent.co.uk/news/uk/mums-army-idea-for-nongradu ates-likely-to-be-dropped-or-watered-down-ministers-to-back-down-over-infant-teacher-plan-1460370.html.

Allen, G. 2011a. "Early Intervention: Smart Investment, Massive Savings." *The Allen Report*. London: The Cabinet Office.

Allen, G. 2011b. "Early Intervention: The Next Steps." *The Allen Report*. London: The Cabinet Office.

Aubrey, C. 2004. "Implementing the Foundation Stage in Reception Classes." *British Educational Research Journal* 30 (5): 633–656. doi:10.1080/0141192042000234629.

Aubrey, C., R. Godfrey, and A. Harris, 2013. "How Do They Manage? An Investigation of Early Childhood Leadership." *Educational Management Administration and Leadership* 41 (1): 5–29. doi:10.1177/1741143212462702.

Barnett, W. S. 2003. "Better Teachers, Better Preschools: Student Achievement Linked to Teacher Qualifications." *Preschool Policy Matters 2*. New Brunswick, NJ: National Institute for Early Education Research.

Belsky, J., J. Bares, and E. Melhuish, eds. 2007. *The National Evaluation of Sure Start: Does Area-Based Early Intervention Work*. Bristol: Policy Press.

Bertram, T., and C. Pascal. 2000. *The OECD Thematic Review of Early Childhood Education and Care: Background Report for the United Kingdom*. http://www.oecd.org/unitedkingdom/ 2479205.pdf.

Brewer, M., J. Browne, R. Joyce, and L. Sibieta. 2010. "Child Poverty in the UK Since 1998–99: Lessons From the Past Decade." *IFS Working Paper 10/23*. London: Institute of Fiscal Studies.

Broadhead, P., J. Howard, and E. Wood, eds. 2010. *Play and Learning in the Early Years*. London: Sage.

Butler, P. 2013. "Hundreds of Sure Start Centres Have Closed Since Election, Says Labour." *The Guardian*, January 28. http://www.theguardian.com/society/2011/nov/14/sure-start-centre-closures-coalition.

DCSF (Department for Children Schools and Families). 2007. *The Children's Plan: Building Brighter Futures*. Norwich: The Stationary Office.

DCSF (Department for Children Schools and Families). 2008a. *2020 Children and Young People's Workforce Strategy*. Nottingham: DCSF.

DCSF (Department for Children Schools and Families). 2008b. *Practice Guidance for the Early Years Foundation Stage*. Nottingham: DCSF.

DES (Department for Education and Science). 1989. *Aspects of Primary Education: The Education of Children Under Five*. London: HMSO.

DES (Department for Education and Science). 1990. "Starting With Quality: Report of the Committee of Inquiry into the Quality of Educational Experiences offered to 3- and 4-Year Olds." *The Rumbold Report*. London: HMSO.

DfE (Department for Education). 2010. *The Child Poverty Act*. http://www.legislation.gov.uk/ ukpga/2010/9/contents.

DfE (Department for Education). 2012. *Statutory Framework for the Early Years Foundation Stage.* http://www.education.gov.uk/aboutdfe/statutory/g00213120/eyfs-statutory-framework.

DfE (Department for Education). 2013. *More Great Childcare – Raising Quality and Giving Parents More Choice.* https://www.gov.uk/government/publications/more-great-childcare-raising-quality-and-giving-parents-more-choice.

DfE/DoH (Department for Education/Department of Health). 2012. *Supporting Families in the Foundation Years.* http://www.education.gov.uk/childrenandyoungpeople/earlylearningand childcare/early/a00192398/supporting-families-in-the-foundation-years.

DfEE (Department for Education and Employment). 1996. *Nursery Education Desirable Outcomes for Children's Learning on Entering Compulsory Schooling.* London: Schools Curriculum and Assessment Authority/DfEE.

DfES (Department for Educations and Skills). 2000. *Curriculum Guidance for the Foundation Stage.* Qualifications and Curriculum Authority Publications. http://webarchive.nationalarchives.gov.uk/20040117082828/dfes.gov.uk/foundationstage/.

DfES (Department for Education and Skills). 2002. *Birth to Three Matters.* London: DfES.

DfES (Department for Education and Skills). 2003. *National Standards for the under 8s: Day Care and Childminding.* Nottingham: DfES.

DfES (Department for Education and Skills). 2007. *Practice Guidance for the Early Years Foundation Stage.* Nottingham: DfES.

Edwards, C., L. Gandini, and G. Forman, eds. 1998. *The Hundred Languages of Children.* 2nd ed. New York: Ablex.

EPPE Team. 2003. 'The Effective Provision of Pre-school Education (EPPE) Project: A Longitudinal Study Funded by the DfES." Symposium presented at the annual meeting of the *British Educational Research Association Conference*, Edinburgh, September 11–13. http://www.bera.ac.uk/events/conference-archive/annual-conference-2003.

Evangelou, M., and K. Sylva. 2003. "The Effects of the Peers Early Education Partnership on Children's Developmental Progress." *DfES Research Report RR489.* Nottingham: DfES.

Evangelou, M., K. Sylva, M. Wild, D. Glenny, and M. Kyriacou. 2009. *Early Years Learning and Development: Literature Review.* Nottingham: DCSF.

Field, F. 2010. "The Foundation Years: Preventing Poor Children Becoming Poor Adults." *The Field Report.* London: The Cabinet Office.

Hadfield, M., M. Jopling, M. Needham, T. Waller, L. Coleyshaw, M. Emira, and K. Royle. 2012. "Early Years Professional Status: An Exploration of Progress, Leadership and Impact – Final Report." *Department for Education Research Report DFE – RR239c.* http://www.cedare-reports.co.uk/eyps/index.php.

Hannon, P. 1995. *Literacy, Home and School: Research and Practice in Teaching Literacy with Parents.* London: The Falmer Press.

HM Treasury. 2003. *Every Child Matters* (Cm 5860). London: The Stationary Office. http://webarchive.nationalarchives.gov.uk/20130401151715/https://www.education.gov.uk/publications/eOrderingDownload/CM5860.pdf.

House of Commons. 2000. *Select Committee on Education and Employment: First Report on Early Years.* http://www.publications.parliament.uk/pa/cm200001/cmselect/cmeduemp/33/3302.htm.

Machin, S. 2006. "Social Disadvantage and Education Experiences." *OECD Social, Employment and Migration Working Papers, No. 32.* Paris: OECD.

Maynard, T. 2007. "Forest Schools in Great Britain: An Initial Exploration." *Contemporary Issues in Early Childhood* 8 (4): 320–331. doi:10.2304/ciec.2007.8.4.320.

Ministry of Education. 1996. *Te Whariki: Early Childhood Curriculum.* Wellington, NZ: Learning Media.

Munro, E. 2011. *The Munro Review of Child Protection: Final Report – A Child-Centred System.* Norwich: The Stationery Office.https://www.gov.uk/government/publications/munro-review-of-child-protection-final-report-a-child-centred-system.

NESS (National Evaluation of Sure Start). 2005. "National Evaluation Report: Implementing Sure Start Local Programmes, An Integrated Approach." *Sure Start Report 10.* Nottingham: DFES.

Nutbrown, C. 2012. "Foundations for Quality." *The Nutbrown Review.* Cheshire: Department for Education. http://www.education.gov.uk/nutbrownreview.

Nutbrown, C., P. Clough, and P. Selbie. 2008. *Early Childhood Education: History, Philosophy and Experience.* London: Sage.

Nutbrown, C., P. Hannon, and A. Morgan. 2005. *Early Literacy Work with Families: Policy, Practice and Research*. London: Sage.

Oberhuemer, P., I. Schreyer, and M. J. Neuman. 2010. *Professionals in Early Childhood Education and Care Systems: European Profiles and Perspectives*. Opladen & Farmington Hills, MI: Barbara Budrich.

OECD (Organisation for Economic Co-operation and Development). 2006. *Starting Strong II: Early Childhood Education and Care*. OECD. http://www.oecd.org/edu/school/startingstrongiiearly childhoodeducationandcare.htm.

Pascal, C., T. Bertram, S. Delaney, and C. Nelson. 2013. *A Comparison of International Childcare Systems: Research Report*. Sheffield: Department for Education, John Simes. https://www.gov. uk/government/uploads/system/uploads/attachment_data/file/212564/DFE-RR269.pdf.

Reynolds, A. J. 1998. "Developing Early Childhood Programs for Children and Families at Risk: Research-Based Principles to Promote Long-Term Effectiveness." *Children and Youth Services Review* 20 (6): 503–523. doi:10.1016/S0190-7409(98)00021-8.

SCAA (School Curriculum Assessment Authority). 1996. *Desirable Outcomes for Children's Learning*. London: SCAA and Department for Education and Employment.

Schweinhart, L. J., J. Montie, Z. Xiang, W. S. Barnett, C. R. Belfield, and M. Nores. 2005. "Lifetime Effects: The High/Scope Perry Preschool Study Through Age 40." *Monographs of the High/Scope Educational Research Foundation, 14*. Ypsilanti, MI: High/Scope Press.

Siraj-Blatchford, I., and M. Woodhead, eds. 2009. *Effective Early Childhood Programmes. Early Childhood in Focus*. Milton Keynes: Open University.

Soler, J., and L. Miller. 2003. "The Struggle for Early Childhood Curricula: A Comparison of the English Foundation Stage Curriculum, Te Whariki and Reggio Emilia." *International Journal of Early Years Education* 11 (1): 57–68. doi:10.1080/0966976032000066091.

Sylva, K. 1994. "The Impact of Early Learning on Children's Later Development" In *Start Right: The Importance of Early Learning*, edited by C. Ball. London: RSA.

Sylva, K., E. Melhuish, P. Sammons, I. Siraj-Blatchford, and B. Taggart. 2003. "The Effective Provision of Preschool Education Project: Findings from the Preschool Period." *Research Brief RBX15-03*. London: Institute of Education. http://www.ioe.ac.uk/RB_summary_findings_from_ pre-school(1).pdf.

Sylva, K., E. Melhuish, P. Sammons, I. Siraj-Blatchford, and B. Taggart, eds. 2010. *Early Childhood Matters: Evidence from the Effective Pre-school and Primary Education Project*. London: Routledge.

Teaching and Learning Scotland. 2006. *The Reggio Emilia Approach to Early Years Education*. Glasgow: Teaching and Learning Scotland.

Tickell, C. 2011. "The Early Years: Foundations for Life, Health and Learning." *The Tickell Review*. http://www.education.gov.uk/tickellreview.

UNICEF. 1989. *UN Convention on the Rights of the Child*. UNICEF UK. http://www.unicef.org.uk/ UNICEFs-Work/Our-mission/UN-Convention/.

UNICEF. 2007. "Child Poverty in Perspective: An Overview of Child Well-being in Rich Countries." *Innocenti Report Card 7*. Florence: UNICEF Innocenti Research Centre. http:// www.unicef-irc.org/publications/pdf/rc7_eng.pdf.

Waldfogel, J., and E. Washbrook. 2010. Low Income and Early Cognitive Development in the UK: A Report for the Sutton Trust. http://www.suttontrust.com/public/documents/1Sutton_Trust_- Cognitive_Report.pdf.

WIES (Warwick Institute of Education Seminar). 2012. *"The Changing Face of Early Childhood Policy and Practice in England over the Past Twenty Years: An Expert Seminar."* Transcript of seminar proceedings, Warwick, November 23. http://oro.open.ac.uk/view/person/dmf5.html.

Appendix. An outline of the education acts, reviews, reports and other significant events concerning early years education referred to in the text

1989	The Education of Children Under Five (HMI Report).
1989	United Nations Convention on the Rights of the Child.
1989	Children Act.
1990	Starting With Quality (The Rumbold Report).
1992	Education (Schools) Act for Children's Learning.
1992	Ofsted inspections introduced.
1993	Mum's Army proposed.
1996	Nursery Voucher Scheme (Nursery Education: The Next Steps).
1996	The Desirable Outcomes for Children's Learning framework.
1996	Counting to Five: Education of Children Under Five (Audit Commission).
1997	Change of Government from Conservative to Labour.
1997	Nursery Voucher Scheme abandoned.
1997	Early Excellence Centres introduced.
1997	Effective Provision of Preschool Education research project Commissioned.
1998	Baseline Assessment introduced.
1999	Sure Start Local Programmes opened.
2000	Curriculum Guidance for the Foundation Stage framework.
2000	Select Committee on Education and Employment report on Early Years Education.
2001	Neighbourhood Nurseries set up.
2001	Introduction of Foundation Degrees.
2002	Birth to Three Matters framework.
2003	Every Child Matters – green paper.
2003	National Standards for the Under 8s: Childcare and Childminding.
2004	Children Act.
2004	National Professional Qualification in Integrated Centres Leadership (NPQICL) introduced.
2006	Childcare Act.
2007	UNICEF: Child Poverty in Perspective: An Overview of Child Well-being in Rich Countries (Innocenti Card 7).
2007	The Children's Plan.
2007	Early Years Professional Status programme began.
2008	Early Years Foundation Stage framework introduced.
2008	2020 Children and Young People's Workforce Strategy.
2010	Change of Government from Labour to Conservative.
2010	The Foundation Years: Preventing Poor Children Becoming Poor Adults (The Field Report).
2011	Early Intervention: The Next Steps (The Allen Report: 1st Part).
2011	Early Intervention: Smart Investment, Massive Savings (The Allen Report: 2nd Part).
2011	The Early Years: Foundations for Life, Health and Learning (The Tickell Review).
2011	The Munro Review of Child Protection (The Munro Review).
2012	Revised Early Years Foundation Stage framework introduced.
2012	Foundations for Quality (The Nutbrown Review).
2012	Supporting Families in the Foundation Years (Discussion paper).
2013	More Great Childcare (Discussion paper).
2013	Early Years Teacher Status introduced.

Appendix: An outline of the education acts, reviews, reports and other significant events concerning early years education referred to in the text

Index

Note: Page numbers in *italics* represent tables
Page numbers followed by 'n' refer to notes